THE POWER OF
COLLECTIVE PURSE STRINGS

THE POWER OF COLLECTIVE PURSE STRINGS

The Effects of Bank Hegemony
on Corporations and the State

DAVITA SILFEN GLASBERG

UNIVERSITY OF CALIFORNIA PRESS
BERKELEY   LOS ANGELES   LONDON

University of California Press
Berkeley and Los Angeles, California

University of California Press, Ltd.
London, England

© 1989 by
The Regents of the University of California

Library of Congress Cataloging-in-Publication Data

Glasberg, Davita Silfen.
  The power of collective purse strings.

  Includes index.
  1. Banks and banking. 2. Commercial loans.
3. Corporations—Finance. 4. Debts, Public. I. Title.
HG1573.G57 1989   332.1   88-27861
ISBN 0-520-06489-5

        1 2 3 4 5 6 7 8 9

Contents

Acknowledgments   ix

1. The Importance of Financial Institutions in the
   Political Economy   1

   The Role of Financial Institutions in the Corporate
   Community   3
      Lending Relations   6
      Institutional Stockholding   8
      Interlocking Directorates   11
   Financial Institutions and the State   13
   The Role of Finance Capital in the State   16
   Finance Capital and the Social Construction of Crisis   17
      Corporate Crisis   19
      State Crisis   21
   The Process of Bank Hegemony   21
   Organization of the Book   24

2. W. T. Grant: The Social Construction of Bankruptcy   25

   Managerial Decisions and Financial Difficulties   26
   W. T. Grant's Lending Relations with Banks   34
   Chapter XI and Beyond: The Struggle Continues   45
   Conclusion   56

3. Chrysler Corporation: Bailing Out the Banks   60

   Setting the Stage: Managerial Decision Making,
   the Economy, and the Banks   61
   The Loan Agreement   69

Conditions of the Loan Agreement: The Struggle   70
    The Banks   70
    The United Auto Workers   80
    State and Local Governments, Dealers, and Suppliers 88
Aftermath   89
Assessing the Losses   95
    The Banks   95
    Labor   96
Conclusion   97

4. Leasco Corporation Versus Chemical Bank:
    The Political Crisis   102

    The Struggle   105
    Conclusion   116

5. The Default of Cleveland: Constructing Municipal
    Reality   119

    The Storm Clouds Build   120
    The Banks, CEI, and MUNY   127
    The Struggle Continues   135
    Conclusion   138

6. Mexico's Foreign Debt Crisis: Bank Hegemony, Crisis,
    and the State   144

    Setting the Stage   150
    Riding the Debt Spiral   154
    The Struggle Intensifies   161
    The Scorecard   162
    Disciplining the International Banking Community   164
    Bailing Out the Banks   166
    Outcome   172
    Class and Intraclass Conflict   176
        The State Versus Labor and the Poor   177
        Banks Versus Labor and the Poor   177
    Conclusion   178

7. The Social Construction of Economic and
    Political Reality   181

    Bank Hegemony   182
    The Social Construction of Economic Crisis   184
    Interlocking Directorates: Sources of Power or Traces of
    Power?   187

The Social Construction of Political Reality and the Relative
Autonomy of the State   188
Conclusion   191

Appendix 1. Using Government and Legal Documents   195
Appendix 2. Sample Outline of Court Documents for
            W. T. Grant Company   201
Appendix 3. Sample Interview Questionnaire for
            W. T. Grant Company   205

References   211

Index   231

Acknowledgments

Many people have given generously of their time, experience, and expertise to help me finish this book. Some of them suffered through the earliest kernels of ideas and suggested more fruitful avenues of analysis. Others were remarkable in their willingness to read repeated reformulations and to continue to offer support and guidance. I owe each of them my gratitude and respect. Thanks to Mitchel Y. Abolafia, Michael Ames, Diane Barthel, James Bearden, Charles Bonjean, Christine Bose, Richard Braungart, Laura Cates, Steven Cole, Donna DiDonato, Paul DiMaggio, G. William Domhoff, Mark S. Granovetter, Linda Grant, Paul Hirsch, Christine Huskey, Randy Hodson, David Jacobs, Eugene Lebovics, Donald Luck, Harry Makler, Patrick McGuire, Beth Mintz, Mark S. Mizruchi, Donald Palmer, Dana Powers-Courtin, Richard Ratcliff, Ed Royce, Dmitri Shalin, Linda Brewster Stearns, SUNY-MACNET, SUNY-Stony Brook Sociology Workshop, Sociology Faculty Seminar at SIU-C, Michael Useem, the late Eugene Weinstein, J. Allen Whitt, Maurice Zeitlin, Lynn Zucker, Sharon Zukin, several business analysts, and the various lawyers of W. T. Grant Company's estate.

I owe particular thanks and gratitude to Michael Schwartz and Kathryn Ward for their friendship and support and for their honesty in challenging me to write clearly, provide evidence for my analysis, and refrain from using "gloppy jargon." Their efforts and encouragement taught me much about writing, research, and tenacity. Thanks for being there and for believing. I also owe a great deal to Marshall and Shelley Goldberg Silfen, the "angels" of the book. Without them, this book would have taken at least twice as long to write.

This book could not have been finished were it not for the support and enthusiasm of my editor, Naomi Schneider. She has been a joy to work with. Thanks, Naomi. Many thanks, too, to Mary Lamprech and Amy Klatzkin for wonderful copy editing.

I dedicate this book to Clifford Leon Glasberg and Gillian Silfen Glasberg. Gillian taught me perspective and the value of unconditional love. As my dearest and closest friend, Cliff has been wonderful in his unwavering tolerance, forbearance, aid, and comfort. He believed when I didn't, understood my distracted moments, made room for my frustrations, and "high-fived" my successes. You are both the best.

Chapter One

The Importance of
Financial Institutions
in the Political Economy

[Banks are] . . . in a position where they can exert significant influence . . . on corporate decisions and policies. . . . [L]argely unknown is the extent to which these institutions actually use the power . . . to influence corporate decisions.

—Julius W. Allen,
Library of Congress

The international financial system is not separable from our domestic banking and credit system. . . . A shock to one would be a shock to the other. In that very real sense we are not considering esoteric matters of international finance. . . . We are talking about dealing with a threat to the recovery, the jobs, and the prosperity of our own country.

—Paul A. Volcker, Chairman of the
Federal Reserve

Observers have long recognized the power of individual banks to advance or deny loans to industrial corporations (Hobson 1905; Hilferding 1910; Lenin 1917; Menshikov 1969; Fitch and Oppenheimer 1970; Kotz 1978). Yet the processes and effects of banks' collective control of capital flows remain murky. What happens when an industrial corporation faces an organized financial community? National and local governments throughout the world imitate corporations by borrowing to finance various projects. What happens when the state confronts an internationally organized banking community? What is the effect on the state's relative autonomy? Do state capital flow relations look like those in the corporate community? Many observers and theorists have offered intriguing speculations about these issues, but no one has systematically substantiated them. This book explores what happens to corporations and governments when the banking community pulls the collective purse strings. It uses comparative case studies that together provide a broader perspective than would each alone. Although all the cases presented here are well known, they have not previously been drawn together to form a coherent picture of capital flow relations and their consequences.

I argue that the collective control of finance capital flows empowers banks to define crisis and noncrisis situations. When banks define the economic situation as noncrisis, they may support a firm by providing loans and buying stocks with pension and trust funds. Access to cash enables firms to invest in a variety of pursuits, such as research and development, expansion, mergers (or defense against hostile takeover attempts), relocation, and so forth. Similarly, loans enable governments to pay for social welfare and development programs.

But when banks define the situation as a crisis, for economic or political reasons, they may decide to deny loans or sell large blocks of a firm's stock. The banking community may also demand repayment or deny loans to the state (again for both economic and political reasons). In such instances, the process of defining a situation as a crisis sets into motion all the consequences of that definition and can create an actual crisis even where none existed before.

Organization strengthens the banking community's ability to define crisis situations. This organization results from the banks' common presence in lending consortia, similar investment patterns on behalf of the pension and trust funds they administer, and interlocking directorates. The structural unification of banks gives them access to substantial proportions of finance capital resources and large and lucrative corporate, state, and municipal business. Moreover, unification eliminates competition between individual banks, forcing customers to struggle with the organized banks collectively. The power of these collective purse strings is the focus of this book.

In the remainder of Chapter 1 I examine the theoretical debates at stake here by outlining the role of financial institutions in the corporate community and the state, and by specifying the notion of bank hegemony as the process by which collective purse strings evolve. Finally, I describe the role bank hegemony plays in socially constructing crisis.

The Role of Financial Institutions in the Corporate Community

Most research on the power structure of business places financial institutions at the center of intercorporate relations. This central position offers a great potential for bank control and power, as Julius W. Allen testified to the Metcalf Committee in the statement cited above. What remains to be specified are the circumstances under which banks realize that potential and the processes by which banks formulate and exercise that power. We must therefore analyze the effects of lending relations, institutional stock-holding, and interlocking boards of directors on the exercise of bank power.

For the purposes of this study I distinguish finance capital from industrial capital and money capital. Industrial capital includes raw materials, labor, land, and the other tangible resources necessary for production and commerce. Finance capital includes relations involving stocks, bonds, loans, and pension funds, that is, the resources needed to purchase all other resources of production, commerce, and the management of the state. Money capital is cash.

The earliest analyses of financial institutions examined the role banks played in the economy at large (Hobson 1905; Hilferding 1910; Lenin 1917). In particular, they focused on the transformation from industrial capitalism (characterized by the domination of capital in general) to finance capitalism (characterized by the domination of money capital specifically). Capital was increasingly concentrated in a diminishing number of financial institutions. This consolidation fundamentally altered the role of banks from simple intermediary to an increasingly "powerful monopoly which controls a major proportion of the available wealth of society" (Mintz 1978, 50). Simultaneously, the industrial sector needed more and more capital to continue to expand and grow. This increasing need changed the structural relation between the industrial and financial sectors. Less and less capital belonged to the industrialists, who ultimately used it in production. Financial institutions became industrial capitalists. Banks had to invest in industry for that money to remain productive capital (and therefore profit producing). Finance capital became a fusion of industrial and money capital (Lenin 1917), placing banks in an increasingly central position in the political economy. As the process of increasing concentration of capital continues, those who control this capital (the "financial oligarchy") progressively gain power. Their pivotal position enables them to know the precise financial position of industrial capitalists and to "control them, to influence them by restricting or enlarging, facilitating or hindering credits and finally to entirely determine their income, deprive them of capital, or permit them to increase their capital rapidly and to enormous dimensions, etc." (Lenin 1917, 37).

Whereas Lenin defined finance capital as a fusion of industrial and money capital, Hilferding (1910) saw it as the separation of those capitals. For Hilferding, finance capital was money controlled by banks but used by industrial capitalists for production. Lenin criticized Hilferding for omitting the process of increasing concentration of both production and capital, a process Lenin argued leads to monopoly. I argue here that money has remained separate from production in that industrial and commercial capitalists must use it; but the accessibility of money remains under the control of financial institutions. Although commercial banks clearly exert control over money flows, they are by no means the only institutions to do so. Insurance companies, investment companies, and savings and loan associations also control money flows.

Lenin argued that increasing concentration leads to the development of capitalist monopolies. But although we have witnessed a pattern of increasing concentration, we cannot say it has led to capitalist monopolies. The financial community includes thousands of banks, insurance companies, and investment firms (referred to collectively as "banks" in this study). Although structural arrangements frequently bind these firms in their relations to borrowers, they hardly constitute a monopoly. Nor can we say banks and industries have become fused into monopolies. True, many major U.S. banks grew out of industrial empires and still retain some of those ties or influences. But those ties are neither immutable nor discreet (see Mintz and Schwartz 1985; Mizruchi 1982). As we shall see later, serious rifts often separate those who control money from those who use it in production, commerce, and the management of the state. This separation does not necessarily mean that banks are wholly independent of industrial capital or the state. Financial institutions depend on both corporations and the state for their most lucrative business, because money must be invested in the production of wealth to increase profits. (Although the state does not produce wealth, it absorbs some of that wealth in taxes, which it passes on to banks as interest on state loans.)

Thousands of individual financial institutions participate in various ways in the process of absorbing surplus money and redistributing it throughout the political economy. Of great importance is their ability to organize to collectively influence the fate of the users of that surplus. Many observers consider banks more powerful than nonfinancial corporations because of the banks' control over finance capital. In particular, observers look at control over loan capital (Lenin 1917; Menshikov 1969; Fitch and Oppenheimer 1970), control over trust and pension funds (Rifkin and Barber 1978), stock ownership (Perlo 1957; Knowles 1972; Menshikov 1969; Kotz 1978), and interlocking corporate boards of directors (Rochester 1936; Baum and Stiles 1965; Chevalier 1969; Pelton 1970; Levine 1972; Scott 1978, 1979; Mintz 1978; Mintz and Schwartz 1981a, 1981b, 1983, 1985; Mizruchi 1982). The relative importance of these sources of financial institutions' power is the subject of continuing debate. But what is the effect on financial relations when banks organize to collectively provide capital?

In sum, financial institutions are important to the business community because of their structural positions as controllers of lending capital, institutional stockholders, and central figures in networks of interlocking directorates. Further, they dominate the process of defining crisis. Debate continues over the theoretical implications of finance capital in the relations and structures of the state and over the role of banks in intercorporate relations and the political economy. We have yet to document the precise processes and significance of capital relations, the role of bank hegemony and the unified control of capital flows, and the relative significance of the various sources of bank power.

Lending Relations

Lending empowers banks in their relations with nonfinancial firms in several ways. First, the ability to advance or deny loans and credit to nonfinancial firms enables banks to elicit major stock options and representation on recipients' boards of directors (Hilferding 1910; Lenin 1917; Menshikov 1969; Fitch and Oppenheimer 1970). More specifically, lending relations in and of themselves represent potential bank power. For example, bonds can be a source of bank power because financial institutions are the major holders and administrators. Bonds differ from stocks in that bonds are typically longer-term loans (over ten or fifteen years). As such, bondholding by banks produces long-standing capital relations between banks and nonfinancial firms. The significance of these relations is that "even large corporations which sell bonds sign agreements stipulating their dependence upon the creditors" (Menshikov 1969, 173). Furthermore, banks usually hold bonds, whereas individuals usually own stocks (Rochester 1936). Unlike stocks, bonds carry no voting rights and therefore do not entitle their holders to participate directly in decisions affecting the internal affairs of the firm. But they still represent a source of power, particularly during periods of corporate crisis. For example, when a firm goes bankrupt, bondholders' claims take precedence over stockholders' claims.

The short-term loan, which matures faster than bonds, is also a source of bank power. Most nonfinancial firms (including the largest corporations) depend on external sources of investment capital to meet their immediate needs. These large borrowing needs require lending consortia composed of several commercial banks and insurance companies, because banking laws restrict a single bank's exposure to one client to 10 percent of the bank's assets. By spreading the risks of large loans over many banks, lending consortia also minimize the competition between individual banks (Menshikov 1969, 175–176).

The popular belief in competition between creditors is greatly exaggerated. Financial institutions acknowledge and respect one another's role as main organizing or lead bank for a particular corporation or group of corporations. For example, "a banker will not begin to negotiate a loan with an industrial corporation if it is known to be the client of another banker without the latter's consent. Attempts to break this rule lead to joint disciplinary measures against the transgressor" (Menshikov 1969, 180). The development of long-standing relations between investment banks and specific firms is a key element in bank power. These relations "magnif[y] the influence that investment banks can exert" (Kotz 1978, 21). Furthermore, common participation in lending consortia reduces the number of nonparticipating competitors and fuses the interests of the participants.

The manager clause, often included as a term-loan stipulation (or condition of the loan), positions banks at the heart of a business. This clause stipulates banks' rights "to demand either the appointment of executives at their discretion or the placing of the firm's controlling block of stock under bank trusteeship" (Menshikov 1969, 176). Thus banks reserve the right to intrude into executive and personnel decisions should the current management displease them.

These lending arrangements produce structural bases of bank power in capital flow relations. Banks have held this powerful structural position for more than fifty years because of nonfinancial corporations' reliance on external sources of financing for investment capital (Lintner 1966; Sweezy and Magdoff 1975; Gogel 1977). Moreover, the largest firms are often the most dependent on outside sources of investment capital, for several reasons. Participation in mergers, acquisitions, and new ventures is increasingly expensive. So are high dividend payout rates, defensive strategies against hostile takeover attempts, and responses to economic and accounting constraints. For example, a reliance on loans contributes to the illusion of huge corporate profits:

In trying to maintain a false image of prosperity, U.S. corporations are literally throwing away money that they sorely need not only to pay current bills but also to bankroll future investment. As a result, they are forced to lean more heavily on external sources of funds. (*Business Week*, 19 Mar. 1979, 108)

Inflation also stimulates corporate borrowing because borrowers will eventually pay off the debt in depreciated dollars. Further, "many managers contend that debt can be . . . a cheaper source of capital than equity, because of depressed stock prices" (*Business Week,* 9 Apr. 1979, 108). Similarly, recession forces corporations to rely more on external capital. Cash flows are difficult to maintain during economic downturns because corporate profits decline (*Business Week,* 31 Dec. 1979, 153–155). But even the bull market of 1987 did not reduce corporations' need for loans because it was fueled partly by "merger mania." This reliance on external investment capital places banks at the center of the business community.

Some observers regard lending as a mutually beneficial and reciprocal relation between banks and nonfinancial corporations. They argue that the constraining influence of banks is counterbalanced by the power of nonfinancials, which have large deposits in the banks (Herman 1973, 1981; Stearns 1982). If banks interfere in the operations of their borrowers, the alienated nonfinancials might withdraw their deposits. The nonfinancials might also refuse to deal with the offending banks in the future. But such an analysis overlooks the way large organized lending consortia tip the balance of power in favor of the banks. When the major lenders take a concerted, aggressive position against a corporate borrower, they severely restrict the target firm's sources of loans. Furthermore, that banks recognize and respect each other's lead bank status prevents nonfinancials from exploiting competition between banks.

Institutional Stockholding

Institutional stockholding as a source of bank power results from a historical transformation of capital sources. The post–World War II boom in pension plans and the resultant growth of bank trust departments created a new source of capital. Pensions rivaled traditional capital-supplier relations as the major source of financial control. Furthermore, the share of outstanding stock held by personal trust funds has grown steadily. This concentration of personal trust funds has increased the power of large trustee banks.

Just nine New York City banks handled four-fifths of the city's personal trust business in 1954, and hence perhaps two-fifths of the national total.

These New York banks appear again and again among the 20 largest stockholders of record in the country's largest corporations in the prewar TNEC [Temporary National Economic Committee] tabulations. (Perlo 1958, 346)

In the last several decades banking institutions have increased their acquisition of stocks and currently represent almost 50 percent of the value of all shares for public sale (that is, in circulation). According to Menshikov (1969, 161), "This percentage is high enough to ensure complete control over industry by the combined capital of the country" (see also Kotz 1978; Rifkin and Barber 1978; Villarejo 1961).

The increasing concentration of stockholdings in pension funds contributes much to the growth of institutional stockholding, because these funds are controlled not by their beneficiaries but by financial institutions, primarily commercial banks. In 1965 pension funds held only 6.7 percent of total outstanding stock, but they increased their portfolio holdings more than any other type of investor (Chevalier 1969). Moreover, these funds were concentrated in a few major banks, notably, Mellon National Bank, Morgan Guaranty, First National City Bank (Citibank), and Bankers' Trust Company (Chevalier 1969). By 1974, 56.7 percent of the assets of private uninsured pension funds were invested in stocks (Kotz 1978, 68). By 1978 pension funds held at least one-fourth of the shares of firms on the New York and American Stock Exchanges. According to Rifkin and Barber (1978, 114), "the 100 largest banks already control[led] over $145 billion in pension assets, with the top 10 banks controlling nearly $80 billion between them. The banks invest a majority of these funds in the equity and debt financing of America's largest companies."

Pension funds in the 1980s have amounted to approximately $600 billion. At a growth rate of 10–11 percent annually, they could quickly top $1 trillion (Born 1980). Because pension funds have become the major shareholders of corporate stocks, whoever manages and administers them holds the purse strings of the business community. Indeed, institutions buying large blocks of stock in the name of pension and trust funds spurred the 1987 bull market, which collapsed under the computer programs of these same institutions.

The control of pension funds represents substantial clout in the business community. As Rifkin and Barber (1978, 91) note, these funds are "increasingly being relied on to prop up an economic system that has all but run out of steam." Lane Kirkland, president of the AFL-CIO, acknowledged the power of pension funds when he ridiculed the presence of United Auto Workers' President Douglas Fraser on Chrysler's board of directors: "A far more effective tool for labor unions" in the struggle against corporations, he said, would be for labor to control its own deferred wages (*New York Times,* 16 Nov. 1981, A1).

Though most people presume that banks invest pension funds prudently, evidence indicates otherwise. Between 1961 and 1971 the return on pension fund investments was 33 percent below the average annual return rate for the 500 index stocks of Standard and Poor's (Rifkin and Barber 1978), and they continue to perform well below the Standard and Poor's averages (*Business Week,* 13 Aug. 1984, 93). Why would funds managed by "prudent investors" consistently perform so poorly?

Banks often maintain holdings of a customer firm in their pension fund portfolios despite the risk of substantial losses or the opportunity to make more profitable investments elsewhere (Herman 1975). Several cases suggest that this practice is standard. "In each case, the bank either continued to hold on to the securities even after the stock plummeted or only sold them well after they should have" (Rifkin and Barber 1978, 119). The difference between the stocks a bank holds in its own portfolio and the stocks it administers for pension funds is significant. Pension funds represent the deferred wages of workers, that is, other people's money. Their investment therefore does not pose any financial risk for the administering bank. The consistently poor performance of pension funds and the evidence of investment criteria other than prudence underline the notion that "banks are not the instrument serving the fund. Rather, the fund is the instrument serving the banks" (Rifkin and Barber 1978, 117).

Banks use pension funds to control corporations in two ways. First, banks control the voting rights attached to the securities purchased with pension funds, and second, they can dispose of stocks held in the name of pension funds. Indeed, "the easiest way for a bank to make a recalcitrant company toe the line is to sell its stock" (Menshikov 1969, 215). Compounding the impact of institutional stockholding are the strong similarities of pension fund and trust fund portfolio profiles. Large-scale sales of a given firm's stock typically cause panic "dumping" by other institutions and money managers. This "herd effect" forces the stock value to plunge, and the precipitous drop shatters the firm's credit standing, further obstructing its attempts to eliminate financial problems. The business press widely accepts the power of financial firms as institutional stockholders and administrators of pension and trust funds. Wall Street analysts now assume that sudden sharp declines in stock values are caused by institutional dumping (*New York Times*, 17 Dec. 1976, D2).

Although we know much about the stock ownership of nonfinancial firms, we know relatively little about that of banks, particularly the largest banks. What we do know is based primarily on the Patman Committee's 1963 findings and the findings of a few researchers (see, e.g., Menshikov 1969). The data indicate that "in most cases the leading shareholders of the biggest U.S. banks are commercial and savings banks, insurance and investment companies. A considerable part of the shares of banks are held in their own trust departments or trust departments of other banks" (Menshikov 1969, 151). We have no evidence to indicate that this trend has declined at all, particularly in the light of continued increases in pension fund assets administered by the banks' trust departments.

This finding suggests two important points. First, the concentration of banks' stocks in trust fund departments reinforces a structural basis of unification among financial institutions. Second, institutional stockholding is not symmetrical within the business community. Although banks maintain and administer large holdings of nonfinancial firms in their trust departments, nonfinancials do not maintain similar holdings of banks' stocks. Hence banks exert greater influence over nonfinancial firms than vice versa.

Interlocking Directorates

Financial institutions in general, and banks in particular, occupy highly central positions in networks of interlocking corporate boards of directors.[1] Observers disagree over whether banks use

1. Bearden et al. 1975; Bunting 1976–1977; Bunting and Barbour 1971; Chevalier 1970; Dooley 1969; Gogel 1977; Gogel and Koenig 1981; Koenig 1979; Koenig, Gogel, and Sonquist 1979; Levine 1972; Mariolis 1975, 1978; Mintz 1978; Mintz and Schwartz 1981a, 1981b, 1983, 1985; Mizruchi 1982;

interlocks to exercise power. They also disagree over whether control over capital flows is a more important source of power than a seat on a financial company's board.

For example, many observers argue that corporate board interlocks represent functional, mutually beneficial relations between specific firms with shared goals (Pfeffer and Salancik 1978; Perrucci and Pilisuk 1970; Herman 1973). This analysis suggests that banks are no more powerful than nonfinancial institutions. Therefore banks' representation on corporate boards of directors is not a mechanism of bank power.

Other observers challenge this symbiotic viewpoint (see Palmer 1983; Stearns and Mizruchi 1986), arguing that the vast potential power of banks serves as a mechanism of cohesion and cooperation within the business community. Those banks that control critical resources "develop key positions" in networks of interlocking directorates, becoming the "'pillars of the establishment,' the first among equals" (Koenig, Gogel, and Sonquist 1979, 25).

Patterns of interlocking directorates support the analysis of banks as agents of social control that can steer corporate decision making. Financial institutions, particularly large commercial banks, form the hubs of these interlocking directorates, with insurance companies linking the hubs and their satellites (Mintz 1978; Mintz and Schwartz 1978a, 1978b, 1985). Mintz and Schwartz interpret this configuration as indicative of bank hegemony. Joint investment ventures may produce a common interest overriding competitive tendencies. Strong similarities of investment portfolios and of the ebb and flow patterns of such investments further consolidate mutual interests. Finally, from their position at the hubs of these corporate board interlocks, banks can "mediate intra-class conflict" (Mintz and Schwartz 1981b, 93).

To examine the implications of interlocking directorates and of the power banks derive from them for capital flow relations, we need to trace relations between banks and nonfinancial firms by examining specific cases. And since members of the business community also actively participate in civic and government agencies, they produce another pattern of interlocking similar to that within the corporate community (Domhoff 1978, 1983; Useem 1979,

---

Mokken and Stokman 1978; Pennings 1980; Sonquist and Koenig 1975; U.S. Congress, House 1968.

1984). Futhermore, governments rely a great deal on loans from banks. In the next section we will examine whether the state's capital flow relations are similar to those in the corporate community.

Financial Institutions and the State

The role of the state in capitalist society has increasingly become the focus of debate. Weber (1947) argued that the increasing complexity of the capitalist economy required the development of rational, unbiased bureaucracies to manage society's needs. Therefore he viewed the state as a politically neutral entity that mediated competing interests and demands, producing compromises in the common good. Although he recognized potential problems in state bureaucracies, he attributed them to individual leaders and their styles. He did not consider the dynamics of structural and social contradictions that are the context of bureaucratic processes. And because he also did not include a class analysis of the interests of those individuals who fill leadership positions within the state bureaucracy, he did not address how leaders' class interests and allegiances might affect the neutrality of the state in balancing competing interests.

Pluralists share Weber's premise that the state is a neutral arbiter that enforces politically unbiased laws and rules (see Dahl 1961; Lipset 1960; Rose 1967). According to this argument, the state is able to function as referee for several reasons. First, there is a balance of power within the state between competing agencies and branches. The natural give and take among these groups produces compromise and negotiation, which constrains each group's ability to dominate (Latham 1976; Neustadt 1976). Second, competing branches and agencies offer the various interest groups a variety of state agencies to which they can appeal, thereby ensuring multiple avenues of access to the state (Truman 1951). Third, competition between parties limits domination by any one party (Aron 1950; Presthus 1964), reinforcing the process of negotiation and compromise in the common good.

The pluralist analysis of the state as neutral mediator assumes equal strength and equal resources among all competing interest groups, parties, and government agencies—an assumption that bears examination rather than assertion as fact. Furthermore, pluralists ignore the allegiances and interests of state leaders, arguing that in the long run competition between the political parties assures that neither party will dominate. This analysis presumes fundamental differences between the interests represented by each party. And it assumes that, once in office, state leaders will eschew their prior allegiances and legislate in the interest of the common good. The definition of "the common good" remains unspecified. Various observers have taken issue with the pluralists' conception of the state as neutral arbiter of competing and equal interests. The key participants in the ensuing debate over the role of the state in capitalist society have been instrumentalists, structuralists, and class dialectic theorists. Instrumentalists (Domhoff 1983, 1984; Kolko 1976; Miliband 1969; Useem 1984; Weinstein 1968) and structuralists (Poulantzas 1973, 1975, 1978; Mandel 1978; Jessop 1982) assume a separation between the economic and political sectors, although they disagree about which sector dominates the other. Class dialectic theorists (e.g., Skocpol 1985; Whitt 1979, 1980, 1982) see some overlap between the two sectors, but they also disagree about which sector dominates.

Instrumentalists argue that the economic sector dominates the state. Capitalists capture key positions within the political structure to attain their goals and further their interests. Mills (1956) specified these relations in his analysis of the circulation of the power elite among the commanding positions of military, corporate, and government institutions.

Both Domhoff (1967, 1978, 1984) and Miliband (1969) present a variant of the instrumental viewpoint. Capitalists need their representatives to capture the state only to maintain the state rule in the interests of capital accumulation. Moreover, capitalists may generate the continuing state support of their interests because they can bring economic power to bear on the state. But this type of analysis (with the notable exception of O'Donnell 1973) does not clearly differentiate between industrial and commercial capitalists, on one hand, and finance capitalists on the other. Therefore it does not weigh the relative significance of the resources each can bring to bear on the state. The case studies of state crises analyzed in this book—Cleveland's 1978 default and Mexico's 1982 foreign debt crisis—help unravel the problem by tracing the various resources the participants used in each case.

Structuralists (Poulantzas 1973, 1975, 1978; Mandel 1978; Jessop 1982) reject the instrumentalists' "capture theory" of the state. Instead, they argue that the political sector is relatively autonomous from the economic sector. For example, Poulantzas (1973, 1975) argues that the state mediates class struggles. In his view the state's relative autonomy from control by individual capitalists derives from the presumed competition between capitalists. But Poulantzas never specifies the mechanisms by which the state acts as mediator or policy maker in the interest of the capitalist class without being run by that class. Like the instrumentalists, he does not differentiate between industrial and commercial capitalists and finance capitalists. The failure to make this distinction obscures the varying resources, pressures, and tactics each may apply to the state.

Class dialectic theorists view the state as the arbiter of class antagonisms. They argue that the state has more autonomy than instrumentalists or structuralists presume. It is possible, for example, for the state to implement policies that benefit the poor and working class while still preserving the long-run interests of the capitalist class. For example, although unemployment insurance, food stamps, and Aid to Families with Dependent Children are social welfare programs targeted at the poor, these same programs protect capitalist interests by ensuring a minimum level of consumerability in the broader economy. Unlike pluralism, the class dialectic perspective acknowledges power differentials between various interest groups and classes.

Whereas instrumentalists, structuralists, and class dialectic theorists presume the separation of economic and political sectors, critical theorists assert a fusion of these two spheres (see Offe 1972a, 1972b, 1974; O'Connor 1973; Habermas 1975). They argue that the state must regulate and take on the economic functions of the "free market" economy because of the deepening contradictions and crisis tendencies of capitalism. At the same time the state relies on the private corporate giants to provide jobs to the working class. The increasing economic crises produce a political crisis, or legitimacy crisis, for the incumbent administration. State expenditures, such as social welfare programs, may mediate class struggle by cooling off the working class (Piven and Cloward 1978). State regulation of the economy may temporarily postpone fiscal and economic crises. Yet these contradictory expenditures set the stage for deeper state fiscal crises in the long run, including burgeoning budget deficits (see Blain 1985). This critical analysis implies the possible role of finance capital in influencing the relative autonomy of the state (primarily by financing deficits), although critical theorists have never specified the influencing process. The critical viewpoint also emphasizes the state's ability to make decisions affecting the allocation of resources already at its disposal. But it does not specify how collective capital flows to the state affect the relative autonomy and discretionary powers of the state.

The Role of Finance Capital in the State

Although the state does not sell stocks as a corporation does, its behavior resembles corporate financial relations, particularly lending relations. The same structural contingencies that lead to lending consortia for corporate borrowing also operate in state borrowing. Most municipal and national governments require such huge capital infusions that no individual bank can (or wants to) provide the crucial loans. Moreover, even the wealthiest national governments provide for their capital needs with debt. For example, the U.S. federal government recently acknowledged its status as the largest debtor nation.

Although the state does not technically operate with a board of directors parallel to a corporate board, evidence suggests similar patterns of interlocks, primarily between the capitalist class and the agencies and organizations that influence state policy formation (Domhoff 1978, 1983, 1984; Ratcliff, Gallagher, and Ratcliff 1979; Useem 1979, 1984; Whitt 1979, 1982). For example, Domhoff (1978) identifies strong business community participation in such policy organizations as the Council on Foreign Relations, the Committee for Economic Development, the Conference Board, and the Business Council. Furthermore, businesspeople were the most politically active members of policy- and decision-making organizations (Useem 1979, 1984). Despite important parallels between interlocking corporate directorates and business community involvement in various agencies of the state, the presence of members of the business community does not necessarily mean they control the state. That remains an empirical question. Furthermore, we must specify the actual mechanisms and processes by which capitalist-class participation translates into control of the state. We need to evaluate the relative power of finance

capitalists in these processes. Finally, we must compare the significance of capitalist-class participation with that of capital flow relations. The case studies included in this book respond to these
issues by looking at the actual state crises of Cleveland and Mexico.

Finance Capital and the Social
Construction of Crisis

The concept of crisis has not been clearly developed sociologically.
Conventional usage assumes a medical model that understands crisis as a critical turning point in institutions (O'Connor 1981). Traditional Marxist theory borrows from this medical model, defining
economic crisis as "an interruption in the accumulation of capital"
(O'Connor 1981, 301; see also Fine 1975, 51). This model views
economic crises in capitalism as objective processes or turning
points within the structure of the political economy—the product
of the system's internal laws, independent of conscious human
creation or prevention (although human effort can postpone the
inevitable crisis).

O'Connor (1981, 1987) identified three kinds of crises in Marxist writings. Some observers (Haberler 1958; Sherman 1979;
Mandel 1978) identify crises as a recurring tendency in the normal
business cycle. Others believe they are structurally produced by
the long-term tendency for the rate of profit to decline (Mandel
1978; Sweezy 1970) or by the deterioration of one structure of
capital accumulation and its replacement with another (Hobsbawm
1976). Still other theorists identify crises as uneven development
caused by the tendency for capital to accumulate in some regions
or sectors at the expense of others (Bluestone and Harrison 1980).

These three Marxist analyses assume that the capitalist political
economy is inherently unstable, with a normal tendency toward
crisis. And all three share the premise that capitalism is "crisis-
dependent," in that "crises are the mechanisms whereby capitalism
regulates itself" (O'Connor 1981, 304). Because traditional Marxist thought conceives of economic crisis as a broad, objective, inherent feature of the capitalist political economy, it overlooks the
role humans play in defining, and thereby creating, crisis. Moreover, it fails to analyze crisis as a *political* economic process rather
than a purely objective economic force.

Neo-Marxist theorists (e.g., Habermas 1975) reject the notion of crisis as an objective economic dynamic and broaden the arena of crisis to include social, political, and cultural spheres. According to Habermas, crisis occurs "when the consensual foundations of normative structures are so much impaired that society becomes anomic. Crisis states assume the form of the disintegration of social institutions" (Habermas 1975, 3). This formulation introduces human experience and interpretation as an element in crises, though retains the traditional Marxist assumption of the inherent instability and crisis tendencies of capitalism. Neither model entertains the notion of crisis as a social construction.

O'Connor's notion of crisis combines the structural tendencies of the capitalist political economy with human experience (O'Connor 1987; 1981, 325). He does not define crisis as anomie and the deterioration of social structures, but rather as a dialectical process of struggle and "social reintegration." This conception allows for the understanding of crisis as a social construction, particularly in its argument that entrenched dominant classes or factions will struggle vehemently against perceived threats to those structures and relations that foster their position.[2] Thus for O'Connor the inherent contradictions and instabilities of capitalism make possible the social construction of "crises in established institutions and social and economic processes [that] are produced through reconstituted human intervention" (O'Connor 1981, 326). This analysis of crisis still focuses on the broader structural levels of economic, social, and political institutions, but its insights help us analyze corporate and state crises as social constructions manifested in struggles between banks, nonfinancial corporations, labor, local and federal governments, and nation-states.

Because the study of crisis has been confined largely to the discipline of economics, it usually assumes a purely economic definition of the concept. A sociological understanding of crisis improves our grasp of intercorporate and state behavior patterns and the pro-

2. Berger and Luckmann (1966) developed the term "social construction of reality" in their analysis of the ideological production of knowledge. I use the term here to indicate the sociopolitical processes of the production of economic and political reality. Their guiding question remains appropriate for the analysis of the power of collective purse strings to determine reality for corporations and governments: "How is it possible that subjective meanings BECOME objective facticities?" (Berger and Luckmann 1966, 18; emphasis in original). O'Connor's notion of crisis allows us to analyze the phenomenon as a social construction.

cesses of power they entail. Moreover, approaching crisis as a social and political process helps us articulate the processes of bank power and unification.

In arguing that corporate crises and state fiscal crises do not necessarily begin as objective economic situations, I will examine actual processes and relations to specify how the banks' definition of a situation affects the business community and the state.

Corporate Crisis

Observers typically define corporate crises in vague and narrow terms of managerial discretion (or indiscretion). For example, Ross and Kami (1973, 21) argue that corporations experience crises when managers violate the "Ten Commandments of Management" governing managerial behavior and the internal structure of the firm. This focus implicitly examines the firm in isolation and fails to acknowledge the external constraints on managerial discretion. For example, relations with financial institutions, networks of corporate board interlocks, and joint ventures between firms all serve as constraints, as does the general state of the economy. Economic definitions thus equate crisis with low or declining profitability, overlooking corporate crises that have nothing to do with low profitability. Furthermore, the restricted definition of crisis does not consider possible dynamic or interactive aspects of the phenomenon, treating it instead as a singular event or point in time (see James and Soref 1981).

One perspective that includes some notion of external constraint on managerial discretion is the theory of the "invisible hand" (Smith 1776). According to this view, widely accepted by business analysts, unseen forces of the market act as an external constraint on managerial discretion. But that constraint appears as a neutral mechanism free of conscious or subjective interference. In this sense the invisible hand defines managerial decisions as the cause of corporate difficulties and defines crisis, once again, as a situation of low or declining profitability.

I argue that a corporate crisis is not always a mechanical economic reaction of the invisible hand of the market brought on simply by low profitability. Rather, it is a reflexive definitional process, involving shifting levels of discretion and constraint, that can seriously damage a firm's long-term business trajectory. Because banks play a central role in capital flow relations, they often control this definitional process. And the structural organization of the banking community enables them to enforce their definition.

According to W. I. Thomas (1928, 572), "If men [*sic*] define situations as real, they are real in their consequences." Banks' collective definitional perception and self-fulfilling prophesy determine whether a given corporation's financial position will threaten its business trajectory (Merton 1968, 475–490). Once banks define the situation as a crisis, other persons and institutions will respond as if it is. Consequently, in a reflexive process these responses may actually produce the crisis presumed to exist. As a self-fulfilling prophesy, the crisis is then no longer a subjective political decision but a matter of economic fact. Indeed, sometimes the crisis may escape the control of those whose definition originally precipitated it.

Financial decline and corporate crisis are thus not synonymous. Declining financial health may result from poor managerial decisions, from decisions constrained by economic imperatives that are detrimental to the firm in the long run, or from a poor general national economy. But until a declining performance is defined as a crisis, no real crisis exists. I argue that the financial institutions can exercise this definitional power because of the banking community's collective control of capital flows.

The business press often refers to self-fulfilling prophesy as the "herd effect." Individuals and small institutions assume that large financial institutions act on "inside information." They therefore follow the large institutions' lead for fear of being the last investor to sell their holdings or to call in their loans from a crisis-ridden firm. The more institutions that divest in or deny loans to a given firm, the greater the chance that other investors will follow suit. The herd effect also operates when financial institutions determine that a firm is "healthy": "The more institutions that invest [in a firm], the greater the chance that the others will follow" (*Business Week*, 28 Jan. 1980, 87). Furthermore, the herd effect is often long-term or permanent. In contrast, singular responses by the banking community to individual instances of low profitability are not necessarily permanent or without alternatives. Other competing banks can define the situation differently. Ongoing and active intervention by the banking community into corporate affairs is unnecessary to perpetuate the banks' definition of the situation.

Some observers argue that banks would only invoke bankruptcy or stock dumping as a last resort to extreme situations. For example, Emerson (1981, 1) claims that "last-resort" sanctions are invoked only when "'normal remedies'. . . are specifically inappropriate or . . . have failed to contain the trouble." Although Emerson focuses on the use of last-resort sanctions in social control institutions (such as mental institutions, correctional institutions, and so on), his thesis suggests that extreme bank behavior such as stock dumping and provoking bankruptcy and default could also be interpreted as actions of the last resort. In the following chapters we will examine case studies to determine whether the banks' decisions to pull their collective purse strings were indeed remedies of the last resort after less extreme approaches had failed.

State Crisis

State crises are as poorly understood as corporate crises. Some observers portray state crises as the result of legitimacy crises produced by despotic, corrupt, or inept governments (Breckenfeld 1977). This is the political version of the invisible-hand theory of the marketplace. Other observers root state crises in economic cycles that inexorably bring the state to recessions, depressions, and budgetary slumps (O'Connor 1973; Habermas 1975). Still others attribute state fiscal crises to the failure of state leaders to keep expenditures in line with revenues (Mollenkopf 1977; Schultze et al. 1977). As with corporate crises, no one has analyzed state crises as definitional processes or examined them as social constructions caused by capital flow relations. And like corporate crises, state crises often reach public forums (such as congressional hearings) that uncover the processes of financial relations that may either avert or precipitate a crisis of the state. The disinvestment and redlining of St. Louis illustrate the social construction of urban decline (Ratcliff 1980a, 1980b, 1980c). In contrast, New York City in the early 1970s is an example of a crisis averted (Lichten 1986). The case study of Mexico's 1982 foreign debt crisis reveals the processes of international crisis formation.

The Process of Bank Hegemony

The theory of bank hegemony and finance capitalism offered here describes the structural bases of unification of the banking community. Hegemony occurs because of the dominant actors' privileged access to the major institutions of society. Such access enables these actors to promote values that support and legitimate their position and empowers them to squelch views considered detrimental to their position (Gramsci 1971; Sallach 1974; Williams 1960).

I have broadened the term *hegemony* here to include a structural component for the analysis of capital flow relations (see Patterson 1975). Cohesion within the business community develops from structural relations that suppress or obliterate conflicts and points of cleavage. These relations include lending consortia, common pension and trust fund investment patterns, and interlocking directorates. Organized capital flow relations condition and suppress friction (particularly between banks) by fusing their specific interests in the short run (Mintz and Schwartz 1985). The state's interest in maintaining a stable economy (at least during the tenure of existing administrations) fuses its interests with those of the business community. There may in fact be a long-term basis for a community of interests in maintaining a stable market economy.

Structural financial domination does not imply control of individual nonfinancial corporations or the state by individual banks. Rather, as a group banks may dominate all firms in the corporate community and the state. The legal and financial inability of individual banks to provide the loans sought by corporations and governments, and the consequent formation of large lending consortia, produces this general dominance. In addition, the similarities of trust and pension fund portfolios further homogenize the banks' interests, minimizing competition among banks (Mintz and Schwartz 1978b, 4; see also Mintz and Schwartz 1985).

Although all financial institutions absorb and reallocate surplus finance capital in general, they do not compete for the sources of that capital. "Commercial banks and property insurance companies mainly accumulate the free money available in the course of reproduction and circulation of capital. Life insurance companies, savings banks, savings and loan associations, and investment companies accumulate chiefly personal savings" (Menshikov 1969, 145). There are several points of cleavage and competition within that community, particularly between large and small banks, regional and money center banks, and commercial banks and savings and loans. One recent indicator of this competition was the flurry of takeovers of savings and loan associations by large commercial banks, made possible by banking deregulation. Furthermore, although the largest banks in New York may share the common interest of maintaining that city as the financial hub of the country, they are not necessarily united at all times on all issues. Several financial groups in New York have exhibited some competition between them, "sometimes sharp, sometimes muted" (Kotz 1978, 85). These include the Chase group (Chase Manhattan Bank, Chemical Bank, Metropolitan Life Insurance Co., and Equitable Life Assurance Society), the Morgan group (Morgan Guaranty Trust, Bankers Trust, Prudential Life Insurance Co., Morgan Stanley and Co., and Smith Barney and Co.), the Mellon group (Mellon National Bank and Trust and First Boston Corporation), and the Lehman–Goldman Sachs group.

But one must not overstate these indicators of competition within the banking community. Of particular importance here, in addition to the anticompetitive influence of lending consortia, is the process by which large commercial banks can discipline small regional savings and loan firms and investment banks during crises. "Structural hegemony" refers to all the processes that produce coalescence among banks and other financial institutions. I will develop this theme in detail in the case studies in Chapters 2–6.

I do not use the term *hegemony* to denote monolithic, absolute power. Indeed, as the case studies here will show, banks sometimes fail to attain their ultimate goals (for example, in Cleveland) or lose large sums of money (for example, in W. T. Grant's bankruptcy). Sometimes circumstances or the process of struggle may force banks to accept unwanted compromises (for example, in Chrysler's bailout process). In other instances banks face real threats to their investments, as in the recent informal evolution of a debtor's cartel in Latin America (*Business Week*, 28 Dec. 1987, 88–89). And there are times when the large banks break ranks and betray one another. (For example, when the Bank of Boston and Citibank performed write-downs of problematic loans to developing countries, they left the Bank of America overextended. The Bank of America faced the choice of either writing down its loans as well or taking the risk without the enhanced power or shared risk of a unified banking community.) But when the struggle is over, financial institutions tend to emerge with more of their goals met than any other participant, because they act collectively to control capital flows and wield more of the resources needed by both corporations and the state.

Even when clear-cut crises are precipitated by managerial decisions or economic constraints rather than by the actions of financial institutions (as in the case of Penn Central Corporation), banks' capital flow decisions are likely to alter the timing of the crises.

By examining the process of crisis formation, we can follow the alteration of business and state trajectories and trace bank hegemony formation and the development and dispatch of bank power. To elucidate this process, we will examine specific cases of each of the theoretical types of crisis formation. These include crises leading to bankruptcy (W. T. Grant Company), crises averted (Chrysler Corporation and Mexico 1982), and crises caused by political struggles between banks and nonfinancials or the state (Leasco Corp. and Cleveland 1978). Because crises and bailouts precipitate congressional investigations, hearings, and other legal proceedings, publicly accessible records and documents (including transcripts of proceedings, supportive documents, testimony, and so on) reveal the process of crisis formation, the related processes of bank power and bank hegemony formation, and the relative weight of the various postulated sources of bank power. The notion of the social construction of corporate and state crisis is critical to uncovering these processes of bank empowerment.

Organization of the Book

The remainder of this book develops a theory of crisis formation and bank hegemony through a detailed analysis of specific case studies of corporate and state crises and their resolution. Chapters 2–4 focus on three corporate crises: W. T. Grant Company's bankruptcy, Chrysler Corporation's bailout, and Leasco Corporation's struggle with Chemical Bank. Chapters 5 and 6 focus on municipal and international state crises: Cleveland's default in 1978 and Mexico's near default in 1982. Chapter 7 outlines the key evidence revealed in these case studies that supports the notion of bank hegemony. As examples of the techniques used in researching this book, appendixes describe the methodology used and give a sample document outline and interview questionnaire for the W. T. Grant Company case study.

Chapter Two

W. T. Grant: The Social Construction of Bankruptcy

The banking community . . . took a big pub-
lic company . . . and ran it into the ground.
—Marvin Jacob, regional head,
Securities and Exchange
Commission

A corporation facing a serious cash flow shortage—either because of a poor general economy or because of poor or shortsighted managerial decision making—does not inevitably go under or even sustain permanent damage. Under Chapter XI of the bankruptcy code, the troubled firm receives protection from its creditors while it reorganizes for recovery. Once the firm's creditors acknowledge a serious cash flow shortage, a decision-making process founded on capital flows determines the outcome. Financial institutions may decide to advance the necessary loans to postpone or head off a crisis, or they may decide to withhold such loans, precipitating the collapse of the ailing corporation. When W. T. Grant Company faced a massive cash flow shortage, the outcome of the decision-making process was not in its favor, and the huge department store chain went bankrupt.

W. T. Grant's notable bankruptcy was the largest retailing bankruptcy in U.S. history and second in size only to that of Penn Central Corporation (*New York Times*, 3 Oct. 1975). In the early 1970s the firm was the seventeenth largest retailer in the United States, with 1,200 stores producing profits of $38 million on $1.6 billion in sales (*Business Week*, 19 July 1976, 60). Yet within a few years this giant corporation lost $288 million before filing for protection under Chapter XI in October 1975 (*Business Week*, 19 July 1976, 60). By that time Grant had closed 1,073 stores and laid off 80,000 workers. Its banks had "written off approximately $234 million in bad loans and its suppliers $110 million in receivables" (*Business Week*, 19 July 1976, 60).

The recession of 1974–1975 brought rising interest rates that hurt the economy at large (*New York Times*, 1 Jan. 1975, 2; 23 Nov. 1984, 41; 20 Dec. 1975, 33). But giants such as W. T. Grant rarely fall victim of a shrinking economy, because the federal government usually bails out major corporations in crisis. Lockheed and Chrysler are only the more famous of over four hundred such federal bailouts (U.S. Congress, House 1979a; Bearden 1982). What happened to cause such a major corporation to collapse? What role did managerial decisions play, and what were the factors influencing those decisions? What were Grant's capital flow relations with the banking community, and what role did those relations play in the bankruptcy? Was managerial discretion unrestrained? If not, what were the forces of constraint on that discretion? What role did corporate board interlocks play? Finally, what was the locus of power in the struggle over the distribution of Grant's remaining assets after bankruptcy?

Managerial Decisions and Financial Difficulties

W. T. Grant became mired in finance capital markets partially because a long series of unrestrained managerial decisions produced severe cash shortages. These decisions included exceedingly rapid overexpansion, a poorly conceived and inadequately managed in-house credit system, an incomprehensible inventory system, and an ill-conceived and confusing attempt to shift its merchandising emphasis from soft goods to durable goods. The net result of these managerial decisions was that by 1974 Grant had suffered substantial cash losses, and it eventually filed a Chapter XI bankruptcy. A prolonged investigation, prompted by contentious litigation over the firm's liquidation, revealed the banking community's tacit approval and encouragement of management's decision making. Through their representation on the firm's board of directors, the banks were in a position to know of and to participate to an extent in these managerial decisions (*Morgan Guaranty Trust Company of New York v. Charles G. Rodman, as Trustee of the Estate of W. T. Grant Company*, 1975, hereafter cited as *Morgan v. Grant*).

An example of Grant's unrestrained and shortsighted managerial decisions was its store expansion program. The company's objective was to open stores in relatively small towns where rival major department stores had not yet gone. Outside director DeWitt Peterkin, Jr., vice chairman of the board of directors of Morgan Guaranty Trust, testified that this expansion program was "a management decision." (See Dramatis Personae 1 for the names and positions of actors in W. T. Grant's bankruptcy.) Yet no one on the board asked management to defend its selection of expansion sites or questioned why other major retailers weren't in these areas if the proposed locations were so good. No one even asked for an analysis of "who the Grant customer was" (Peterkin, in *Morgan v. Grant*, 366–367, 32, 34). The expansion program was so fast that between 1969 and 1973 Grant opened 369 stores. According to James G. Kendrick, a former chief executive officer, "The expansion program placed a great deal of strain on the physical and human capabilities of the company." Said another former executive: "Our training program could not keep up with the explosion of stores. . . . And it did not take long for the mediocrity to show" (*Business Week*, 19 July 1976, 60–61).

Another example of poor and unchecked managerial decisions was Grant's credit system. Credit was extremely easy to obtain from Grant, and repayment schedules were often as low as one dollar per month. The firm instituted this program to induce its customers to purchase expensive appliances and furniture. Managers, who are traditionally expected to maximize profits, were under constant pressure to increase credit sales. These same managers were responsible for giving the final approval on new credit accounts. A former finance executive stated that "the stores were told to push credit and had certain quotas to fill." One former manager grumbled, "We gave credit to every deadbeat who breathed" (*Business Week*, 19 July 1976, 61). Since each store was responsible for promoting credit, collecting payments, and maintaining credit information, Grant in effect had 1,200 credit offices. Indeed, custom-

Dramatis Personae 1. The Bankruptcy of W. T. Grant
(in order of appearance)

DeWitt Peterkin, Jr.   Director, vice chairman of the board, Morgan Guaranty Trust Co.; director, W. T. Grant; chairman, W. T. Grant audit committee

James G. Kendrick   Chief executive officer, president, and chairman of the board, W. T. Grant (1974–1975)

Richard W. Mayer   Chief executive officer, president, and chairman of the board, W. T. Grant; trustee, W. T. Grant Trust (1968–1974)

John G. Curtin   Financial vice president and treasurer, W. T. Grant (1967–1974); executive vice president of finance, W. T. Grant (1974)

Raymond H. Fogler   Director and former president, W. T. Grant

Louis C. Lustenberger   Director and former president, W. T. Grant

Charles G. Rodman   Court-appointed trustee of W. T. Grant

Edward Staley   Trustee, W. T. Grant Trust and Grant Foundation

John P. Schroeder   Executive vice president, Morgan Guaranty; director and vice chairman of the board, Morgan Guaranty and J. P. Morgan Co.

Harry Pierson   President, chief operating officer, and acting chief executive officer, W. T. Grant (June 1974–September 1974); executive vice president, W. T. Grant (September 1974)

Robert A. Luckett   Corporate services vice president, controller, and director, W. T. Grant

John Sundman   Director and financial vice president, W. T. Grant (1974)

Robert A. Anderson   Chief executive officer, president,
                                  and chairman of the board, W. T.
                                  Grant (1975)
Joseph W. Chinn, Jr.   Director, Wilmington Trust Co.;
                                  director, W. T. Grant; member,
                                  W. T. Grant audit committee
Judge John Galgay   Presiding judge, U.S. Southern
                                  District Court
Marvin Jacob   Securities and Exchange Com-
                                  mission regional director

ers could build up huge amounts of credit by opening separate accounts in different Grant stores.

Richard W. Mayer, Grant's chief executive officer, president,
and chairman of the board, testified that the store managers were
responsible for both sales and credit granting because of corporate
founder William T. Grant's philosophy that "the store manager
was . . . 'The King.' And he [sic] had control over all functions in
the store. There is no more reason why he [sic] should not have
control over his [sic] credit program" (Mayer, in *Morgan v. Grant*,
82–83). Mayer indicated that no one from Grant's accounting
firm (Ernst and Ernst) or Grant's board of directors ever questioned why the same store manager handled the conflicting functions of sales and credit.

The ill effects of the easy-credit lure instituted in 1969 appeared
as early as 1970. Yet the company did not become concerned
about the situation until after the fiscal report of 1971, which revealed the credit problems. According to John G. Curtin, financial
vice president and treasurer at Grant, there was a steady and significant "rise in write-offs of uncollectible credit accounts. Un-
collectibles rose from 2.1% in fiscal 1970 to 3.2% in fiscal 1972"
(*Women's Wear Daily*, 4 Feb. 1977, 24).

Peterkin told the court that the company's lax policy toward delinquent creditors was a product of the recession. Since so many of
Grant's customers seemed to be adversely affected by the recession,
management decided "not to go after delinquencies so hard as
they might have otherwise in the hopes that economic conditions
were going to improve and these customers were going to be able
to get back on current basis" (Peterkin, in *Morgan v. Grant*, 188).

Grant extended its customary grace period to accommodate its delinquent customers: "Until 1975 it allowed 36 months to pay, with a minimum payment of $1 per month" (*Business Week*, 19 July 1976, 61). Under this lax policy, Grant's delinquent accounts increased "appreciably" from 1972 to 1973. By 31 January 1973, Grant had approximately 56,000 delinquent accounts. The following year that number had increased to around 102,000 (Peterkin, in *Morgan v. Grant*, 321). This figure represented a loss of $602.6 million, compared with $556 million in 1973, "and up 86% over the $324 mllion in 1969" (*Business Week*, 19 July 1976, 61).

On top of this lax payment plan, Grant's managers consolidated delinquent accounts to "make them current." They "would take two different types of credit accounts of a Grant customer and consolidate them into one account. And where one or both of the accounts were delinquent, [they] would make the new account current" (Peterkin, in *Morgan v. Grant*, 329).

Furthermore, Grant had a policy of "refinancing" a delinquent account: "A new credit agreement would be arranged whereby payments would be spread out over a longer period of time and the . . . new account would thereby be characterized as current." Delinquent customers could make their accounts current by paying small amounts of money toward them (Peterkin, in *Morgan v. Grant*, 331–332). Again the easy credit was promoted in a short-term effort to increase sales during the recession, to the long-term detriment of accounts receivable.

Store managers were hardly in control of the situation. They disliked being pressured by Grant's reward-punishment manner of promoting increased credit sales and new accounts. For example, managers and clerks were "offered $1 bounties for each customer they signed up for a [credit] card" (*Forbes*, Apr. 1976, 110). Any store manager who failed to sign up his quota of new credit customers suffered the public humiliation of "eating beans instead of steak at the next promotion dinner . . . or having his tie cut off . . . or getting a pie in his face . . . or having to wear a diaper" (*Women's Wear Daily*, 4 Feb. 1977, 1).

They disliked even more the responsibility of final approval of new accounts, since it often conflicted with their responsibility to maximize credit sales. The situation deteriorated the retailer's finances so quickly that when the credit system was dismantled in 1974, it was really too late to undo the damage.

To gain some control over the alarming increase in delinquent accounts, Grant's management decided to "centralize the collection function away from the stores" (Peterkin, in *Morgan v. Grant,* 340). But centralization addressed only the collection of delinquent accounts, leaving the power of granting credit with store managers who were still responsible for sales. Furthermore, the situation was already so problematic that centralization did little to ease the crisis.

Few of Grant's managers and directors were concerned about Grant's credit promotions. Indeed, Peterkin could name only two who were: Raymond H. Fogler and Louis C. Lustenberger (both directors and former presidents of the firm), who had suggested that Grant might be "pushing too hard on credit." Peterkin suggested, however, that these two directors' concerns were ignored because, "of course, this [credit promotion] was an effort in order to increase sales and sales were the name of the game" (Peterkin, in *Morgan v. Grant,* 335). Defending the directors' silence on the firm's lax credit policies, one former senior Grant executive asked, "What could the board do?" (*Business Week,* 19 July 1976, 61). Such a question by one of the firm's own executives suggests that the board had little power to control the corporation.

Although the company's management did not seem fully aware of its actual inventories and accounts receivable, there were ample signs of declining health. Sales volume per square foot declined 33 percent from 1966 to 1975. Although sales increased from $1.2 billion in 1969 to $1.8 billion in 1974, "inventories more than doubled to $450 million" (*Business Week,* 19 July 1976, 60). The company's earnings per sales dollar also declined from 7 cents in 1969 to 2 cents in 1973. Lustenberger and Fogler tried in 1971 to "mobilize the outside board members to force a change because they were alarmed by the company's rapid expansion, inventories, and general lack of leadership" (*Business Week,* 19 July 1976, 60). They were ignored until September 1974, at which point the board appointed James G. Kendrick of Zeller's, Ltd. (Grant's Canadian subsidiary), to be president, chairman, and chief executive officer of Grant. "He immediately went public with the bad news, which had not been disclosed" (*Business Week*, 19 July 1976, 60). As a result, by the end of October Grant had to publish a restatement of its earnings for the entire year: $177 million in losses, $92 million of which was written off as bad debt.

Court-appointed trustee Charles G. Rodman opened an investigation after the firm went bankrupt. He suggested that several of Grant's policies (including insufficient inventory controls, insufficient credit controls, and rapid overexpansion) encouraged the exercise of managerial discretion with few constraints. This discretionary power appeared to be an important factor in the internal generation of the firm's cash flow problems. Ironically, instead of pursuing financially sound goals, the banking community (well represented on Grant's board) continued to extend credit and failed to constrain managerial decision making despite great evidence of mismanagement.

Since financial institutions and corporate board interlocks sometimes act as constraints on such discretionary power, Rodman was interested in ascertaining the precise role banks played in Grant's operations. He charged that to further their own interests the lead banks concealed the real financial state of the retailer. He carefully investigated the Grant Foundation, which he named as a defendant in his suit against the banks. This foundation was reputedly a charitable organization instituted by founder William T. Grant and Connecticut Bank and Trust Company, which was also the agent for a number of the founder's private trusts. Rodman alleged that funds from the foundation were used for "fraudulent stock purchase deals with the company" (*Women's Wear Daily*, 21 Dec. 1977, 11). The suit sought damages of $50 million from the Grant Foundation.

In 1969 the foundation, which held 1.3 million shares of Grant's stock, decided to sell "to diversify its holdings." To avoid depressing the price of Grant's stock, the retailer and the foundation agreed that Grant would gradually buy back its stock from the foundation "rather than have that amount of stock in effect unloaded on the market" (Lustenberger, in *Morgan v. Grant*, 392). Rodman testified that Morgan Guaranty's trust department "had a very substantial position in Grant stock," estimated to be greater than 10 percent of Grant's common shares. Morgan sold these holdings around 1973 (Rodman, in *Morgan v. Grant*, 45, 46).

Richard Mayer indicated that he knew of Morgan's substantial holdings and of its sale of Grant stock because he received quarterly reports of all large holdings. He testified that he never asked outside director Peterkin (from Morgan Guaranty) why Morgan decided to liquidate its entire position in Grant stock. Mayer claimed that the situation was of "very little concern" to him in 1973 (Mayer, in *Morgan v. Grant*, 55). The precise reason for the sale is still unclear: no crisis had yet been declared. Perhaps Morgan, which was clearly in a position to know of Grant's developing difficulties, sold the stock to escape the impending crisis. As an important managerial consequence of that sale, Morgan relinquished the operational constraint such holdings would have imposed on managerial decision making. Clearly, the banks were not concerned about this apparent loss of their proxy constraint on the firm through Morgan's holdings. The power of collective purse strings in their loan departments would serve them better.

Mayer was a trustee of the W. T. Grant Trust, which purchased Grant stock between 1970 and 1972. Several letters written during that time indicate that Edward "Staley, as trustee of both W. T. Grant Trust and Grant Foundation, determined when and how the stock was to be purchased" (Mayer, in *Morgan v. Grant*, pt. 9, 72). Staley admitted that he "had power of attorney" over Mr. Grant's affairs, indicating that it was Staley's "decision for the Grant Foundation and the Grant Trust to start liquidating stock in '68" (Staley, in *Morgan v. Grant*, 1005–1006). Staley's remark signals a careful program of purchases. Furthermore, a letter from the Connecticut Bank and Trust Company dated 6 November 1969 indicates that the bank sold 246,664 shares of Grant common stock to the retailer (Mayer, in *Morgan v. Grant*, pt. 9, 74). These letters and events suggest that the stock purchases were "attempt[s] to solidify control of the company" and thus to increase managerial autonomy (Mayer, in *Morgan v. Grant*, pt. 9, 74). In a letter that supports this analysis, Staley wrote that he and William T. Grant established a "program . . . in 1968 to over a period of time liquidate the Grant stock holdings in the Grant Foundation and the trusts established by Mr. Grant in a way so that large holdings of Grant's stock would not fall into unfriendly hands" (Mayer, in *Morgan v. Grant*, pt. 9, 85). Under the schedule of purchases, Grant acquired 800,000 shares of its stock from the foundation between 1969 and 1972 (although no stock was purchased in 1971 as Grant's finances began to get tight). When the agreement was terminated in 1973, Grant had purchased its own stock from the trust at a cost of $35 million (an average of $43 per share) and had spent another $15 million purchasing its stock from several trusts. These purchases represented a large portion of the retailer's cash flow.

Less than a year after Grant finished buying the stock, it was desperately in need of cash to pay its bills. Here, the constraints on managerial discretion posed by the banks' control of capital resources began to solidify. Since Grant had tied up its capital in stock purchases, it would have to rely on the banks for loans. "Ultimately, the stock became worthless as Grant's failed in an attempted Chapter XI reorganization and was liquidated" (*Daily News Record*, 12 Apr. 1978, 9).

Although many of Grant's difficulties clearly derived from a series of poor managerial decisions, some of those decisions were influenced by the presence of banks in its daily affairs. Between 1971 and 1973 Grant "was substantially in excess of the industry average in paying dividends as a percentage of earnings—eighteen percent or more in each of those years" (Staley, in *Morgan v. Grant*, 1008). Evidence of a significant positive correlation between dividend payout rates and a firm's interlocks with banks suggests that banks favor high dividends because such a policy "add[s] to the value of their stockholdings" (Gogel 1977, 174). High dividend payout rates also deepen the firm's dependence on external sources of investment capital, because substantial amounts of internally generated capital are diverted to stockholders. Consequently, high payout rates ordinarily make a stock attractive to banks. More important than attractive dividend rates to banks is the critical effect of these rates on Grant's cash flow position. This analysis suggests one role that banks may have played in producing the firm's cash flow problems.

W. T. Grant's Lending Relations with Banks

Before 1973 W. T. Grant conducted its business with only minimal participation by the financial community.

Grant generally satisfied its short term cash needs through the commercial paper market. The lines of credit at money center banks were utilized to cover Grant's short term interim cash needs that resulted from the delays inherent in placing and selling commercial paper through W. T. Grant Financial Corp. [which was organized for the business of making loans to Grant and borrowed funds for that purpose]. ("Order Fixing Time and Place for Hearing to Authorize and Approve Agreement of Compromise and Settlement with Bank Claimants," in *Morgan v. Grant,* 4; hereafter cited as "Order Fixing Time")

This conversion also solidified the long-term relations between Grant and the banking community and deepened the latter's role in Grant's affairs. Banks' presence on nonfinancial boards can thus facilitate access to capital, as many corporations acknowledge.

By the spring of 1974 Grant's management had converted some of its short-term debt of commercial paper into long-term debt. With the help of Peterkin, who sat on both Grant's and Morgan's boards, Morgan Guaranty organized a five-year unsecured term loan of $100 million for Grant and became the agent for eight other banks ("Order Fixing Time," 4).

The sequence of events leading to Grant's difficulties actually began before December 1973, when high dividend payout rates coupled with inefficient managerial discretion caused a 78 percent decline in earnings (*New York Times,* 26 July 1974, 64; see also "Order Fixing Time," 6). Both Moody's and Standard and Poor's downgraded Grant's commercial paper rating from prime 1 to prime 2 and also downgraded Grant's long-term securities. This downgrading, together with Grant's declining performance, forced the retailer to resort to its bank lines of credit, which stood at more than $200 million. "As a result, Grant's overall borrowing increased sharply—by approximately $167 million—during 1973." The retailer's performance continued to decline through January 1974, when "Moody's withdrew Grant's commercial paper rating and substantially downgraded Grant's long term securities" ("Order Fixing Time," 6, 7). Grant could therefore no longer cover its short-term cash requirements through the commercial paper market and was forced to rely once again on the banks for its equity-to-debt conversion.

By March 1974 "Grant had $284 million of commercial paper outstanding of which $32 million was maturing on March 5, and

more than $100 million scheduled to mature the following week"
("Order Fixing Time," 7). Grant asked Morgan and the banks to
reestablish the $100 million in credit lines that the banks withdrew
when they made the $100 million loan to the ailing retailer. The
banks agreed to reestablish this credit line, with Morgan Guaranty, Chase Manhattan, and First National City Bank (Citibank)
each increasing their loans to Grant by $79 million. The total
loans and credit lines the nine banks made were $415 million at
this point.

The banks were clearly aware of their power as organized controllers of loan capital to destroy or rescue the firm, to define crisis,
and to constrain managerial decision making. John P. Schroeder
(executive vice president of Morgan Guaranty, and director and
vice chairman of the board of both Morgan Guaranty and J. P.
Morgan) testified that the banks met to discuss "what other sources
besides the banks there would be for Grant. . . . [and] it was pretty
apparent that the options for Grant had been reduced to banks,
and banks alone" (Schroeder, in *Morgan v. Grant*, 18).

In June 1974 twelve of Grant's major banks met to discuss the
retailer's situation (Schroeder, in *Morgan v. Grant*, 35). Apparently the banks recognized that they had a common problem by
virtue of their involvement in Grant's lending consortium. That
such a meeting (and many similar meetings throughout this case)
took place attests that cooperation is standard practice among
banks. Lending consortia facilitate and often necessitate such communication, and the consequent development of bank unity, because the situation they create fuses the interests of consortia
members.

The new loans and credit lines did not stem the declining performance of the retailer. In July 1974 Grant was troubled by "severe
cash shortages, was in default on a number of its short term notes
and was running overdrafts at its lead banks." By August 1974
Morgan Guaranty, Chase Manhattan, and Citibank had each
given Grant $5 million more in secured loans. Each bank was now
exposed by $84 million to Grant. These loans were "secured by an
assignment of certain customer accounts receivable of Grant"
("Order Fixing Time," 7). Accounts receivable are running records
of customers' credits, payments, and balances due. Control of accounts receivable means control of the lifeblood of the firm, be-

cause these records provide invaluable information for corporate decisions. Furthermore, payments are made to whomever controls the accounts. Hence when the banks seized control of Grant's accounts, they were in a position to intercept any payments customers made on their bills. They were also able to control information regarding the firm's actual financial condition, thereby hindering management's ability to make defensible decisions. The banking community was able to gain control over this essential element of Grant because of their collective control of capital flows: they defined the situation as a crisis and demanded control of accounts receivable in exchange for the infusion of desperately needed capital. By extending loan capital when such an investment appeared imprudent and then seizing accounts receivable, the banks were able to delay bankruptcy to position themselves for their own maximum benefit.

The banks then escalated their constraining influence to control the hiring and firing of Grant's top personnel. In the spring of 1974 Grant's directors discussed "relieving Mr. Mayer of his duties" because of the firm's declining profitability. Peterkin testified to the banks' activism and intervention in Grant's decision-making processes, stating that he had personally discussed Mayer's ouster with several outside board members beyond the confines of formal board meetings (Peterkin, in *Morgan v. Grant*, 36, 38–39). As the pressure mounted, Mayer resigned as chief executive officer in June 1974. The banks then pressured Grant to name a permanent chief executive. Schroeder testified that Morgan Guaranty, Chase Manhattan, and Citibank "made it known as loudly and as vocally as possible that the absence of a new chief executive officer was impeding [their] efforts to line up the bank group." All "three major committee banks acting in concert . . . provided the communication" to Grant that their "disposition to proceed will be sharply influenced by" the selection of a permanent chief executive (Schroeder, in *Morgan v. Grant*, 50, 51–52).

In September 1974 James G. Kendrick was brought in from Zeller's, Ltd. (Grant's Canadian subsidiary) as president, chairman, and chief executive officer after the banks (represented by the outside directors who forced Grant's reorganization) strongly implied that Kendrick would cooperate with the banking community. Rodman suggested that Kendrick was named on a "request from

Citibank": The banks "hit the gong pretty hard with that request. Kendrick was named" (Rodman, in *Morgan v. Grant*, 77, 78). Indeed, one former senior executive noted that "the company joke was you got to be a director by how fast you could say yes. And the outside directors looked to Staley and . . . Peterkin for guidance" (*Business Week*, 19 July 1976, 61). Rodman asserted that the banks "wanted it [Kendrick's appointment] done before they went further on the accommodation of Grant with the extension of the credit" (Rodman, in *Morgan v. Grant*, 78). In fact the announcement of Kendrick's selection was speeded up because Citibank refused to go along with the loan agreement until Kendrick was named. Citibank knew Peterkin "was involved in the selection of the new chief executive officer and called him directly" (Schroeder, in *Morgan v. Grant*, 109–110). That Citibank could freely call Peterkin of Morgan Guaranty to press for a speedy announcement of Kendrick's appointment demonstrates the ease of interbank communication and, more important, the extent to which banks now controlled Grant's strategic decision making and operations.

When Kendrick took the top position at Grant, Peterkin sent him a letter to "encourage" his efforts and to let him know that "we [at Morgan were] going to do all we could to help him in his new work." "We at Morgan expect, in fact demand total credibility," Peterkin wrote, referring to the banks' anger at Grant management's previous secretiveness and lack of cooperation. Peterkin also hinted at the banks' power over the retailer, thanks to their loans to the firm and the substantial holdings of Grant stock in some of their trust funds: "At Morgan Guaranty failure is unacceptable. We are going to seek a way to get the job done. We, the banks, have a far greater investment in Grant than any other element of the Grant ownership" (Peterkin, in *Morgan v. Grant*, 3, 4, 6). Peterkin's letter was a veiled threat to Kendrick that failure to cooperate with the banks' demand for information and cooperation would lead to his downfall, as it had to Mayer's. Schroeder testified that the banks were "pleased" that Kendrick had taken over Mayer's job (Schroeder, in *Morgan v. Grant*, 52). This episode suggests the banks' ability to affect personnel decisions in the firm as well as their satisfaction that Kendrick would cooperate.

When Kendrick grasped the full extent of Grant's financial problems, he went public with the bad news. By September 1974

Grant, Grant Financial, and Morgan Guaranty (as agent for itself and 143 other banks) entered into a loan and guaranty agreement. Under this agreement the unsecured loans as well as the secured loans advanced to Grant Financial were extended to 2 June 1975. The agreement also increased the commitments for loans made to Grant Financial, raising total bank loans and advances to $700 million.

Of the 143 banks involved in loans to Grant at the time of its demise, 14 supplied over 83 percent of the $600 million in short-term loans and all of the $100 million in long-term loans (see Table 1). As collateral for the guaranty, the banks were granted security interests in Grant's accounts receivable and 6,399,300 common shares (51.3 percent) of Zeller's, Ltd. ("Order Fixing Time," 8–9).

Notably, when Grant's managers had earlier proposed to sell their receivables, the banks were opposed. Indeed, Schroeder testified that "the banks . . . require[d] bank approval of any such receivable sale." Although Schroeder insisted that Grant "never formally asked for approval," he agreed "it was understood that the banks' approval would be required before any such sale could take place." Grant's management understood that "there wouldn't be any loan agreement if such a sale went through" (Schroeder, in *Morgan v. Grant*, 70). That Grant deferred the sale of its receivables until after the loan agreement was made (whereupon the banks seized control of the accounts receivable) attests to the banks' constraining power to press management to delay decisions until the banks were in a more favorable position.

Rodman told the court that the banks' procurement of Grant's receivables "was prejudicial to the rights of other creditors" because "it set them [the banks] up with a claim to those assets. The accounts receivable were the single largest assets of Grant, with apparent priority over the other creditors." Rodman suggested that the banks procured these receivables "by virtue of their control and domination," since "it was up to Grant's best interest to cooperate . . . with the banks." Grant had to cooperate because the banks had the power to "force Grant into a very awkward situation" by calling in their demand notes (Rodman, in *Morgan v. Grant*, 75–76, 76–77, 76). Indeed, Grant executives Harry Pierson and Robert A. Luckett complained later that "the banks were running the company" (Schroeder, in *Morgan v. Grant*, 350).

TABLE I.   *Major Bank Lenders to W. T. Grant*

Bank	Amount of loans (in millions of dollars)
Morgan Guaranty Trust	96.973
Chase Manhattan Bank	96.973
First National City Bank (Citibank)	96.973
Bank of America	48.487
Continental Illinois Bank	48.487
Manufacturers Hanover Trust	48.487
Chemical Bank	40.508
Bankers Trust	32.529
Sanwa Bank	20.000
Marine Midland Bank	18.962
Irving Trust	18.962
Mellon Bank	18.962
Security Pacific National Bank	6.138
Bank of New York	6.138

Source: *Women's Wear Daily,* 17 Jan. 1975, 3.

The banks appear to have dominated Grant by virtue of their ability to advance or deny loans and thus to force the retailer to accept terms that were not in its interest. According to a Citibank document, "Bankers voiced the opinion that Grant died when [the banks] . . . took collateral and started a chain which made it [Grant] unrehabilitatable" (Schroeder, in *Morgan v. Grant,* 183). These struggles underscore a general pattern of bank intervention in Grant's decision making.

Not all the banks in Grant's consortium readily agreed with the lead banks' strategy of increasing Grant's lines of credit. Schroeder testified that he worked closely with John Sundman (director and financial vice president of Grant in 1974) between June and August 1974: "Our mission was to put together banks into a cohesive, committed operating group, and it was a very difficult mission" (Schroeder, in *Morgan v. Grant,* 30–31). One incident that illustrates the resistance of the small banks was the struggle with the Toms River Bank in central New Jersey.

To settle its account with Grant and discontinue involvement, Toms River Bank filed suit to recover its loans. Schroeder testified that "we [Morgan] had to have that suit dropped in order to proceed [with Toms River Bank's increased line of credit]. . . . The notion here was that no one of the banks was going to buy out any other bank." Bankers at Toms River hoped their suit would make them "difficult enough and provide a difficult enough scene so that we [Morgan Guaranty], in fact, would buy them out. But they didn't realize that our position was really quite adamant." Schroeder noted that if Toms River's suit was successful, the action would have forced Grant into bankruptcy (apparently before Morgan Guaranty was ready to precipitate Grant's bankruptcy). The lead banks began to apply pressure on Toms River: "The sound and furor within our sort of agent bank circles . . . about this Toms River Bank was very real. We sent a delegation down there to try to dissuade them. . . . We approached the management of that bank from a number of sources" (Schroeder, in *Morgan v. Grant*, 57, 58, 59).

One of those sources was the head of the Philadelphia Federal Reserve District, who "was . . . in touch with the management of the Toms River Bank, expressing . . . his great concern over" Toms River's suit. Schroeder acknowledged that such a communication from the Federal Reserve "would certainly be taken with greater seriousness by any bank manager." He told the court that at this request, the New York Federal Reserve District "authorized us [Morgan Guaranty] as the agent bank to mention the fact that we had a meeting with the Fed to the [recalcitrant] banks." A Continental Illinois Bank document indicated that "Morgan [Guaranty] was authorized . . . to report to Federal Reserve authorities such banks as refused to participate." Schroeder told the court that Morgan made telephone calls to Toms River to remind bankers there of Morgan's authorization to report recalcitrant banks to the Washington, D.C., Federal Reserve and to try to convince them to join the major banks in increasing Grant's credit line to $6 million (Schroeder, in *Morgan v. Grant*, 59, 60). The mounting pressure was apparently too great for the small New Jersey bank to resist. Toms River capitulated, withdrew its suit, and joined the other banks in a cohesive strategy toward Grant.

Schroeder testified that such communication between banks is a standard operating procedure (Schroeder, in *Morgan v. Grant,* 63). By facilitating the modification of dissident viewpoints among banks, it creates a coalescence of policy within the banking community as a whole and produces a unified force confronting non-financial corporations. The structure of the lending consortium was the key factor here in the achievement of bank unity. Grant would have been forced to default on its loans without bank support in restructuring its debts. Therefore, since the large banks insisted that all members of the consortium participate in that restructuring arrangement, the small banks were constrained to remain in the consortium to recover their money.[1]

The formation of coalitions was evident in both the structure of Grant's lending consortium and the establishment of an advisory committee. In November 1974 Grant's three lead banks formed the advisory committee (later called the steering committee) "to give [Grant's management] . . . a forum for discussing with [the banks] . . . ideas that would have . . . consequences [for], or . . . need input from the banking group" (Schroeder, in *Morgan v. Grant,* 185). Grant was clearly aware of the power of the banks and was trying to line up the banks' approval before making any policy decision that might anger them.

Further constraining influences were mobilized on 1 April 1975, when Grant, Grant Financial, and Morgan (as agent for all 143 banks in the consortium) entered into the loan extension agreement.

This agreement provided (1) for payment of outstanding loans made by 116 banks, in the aggregate principal amount of $56,509,610; and (2) for the extension of the maturity date to March 31, 1976, of outstanding loans made by the Bank Claimants in the aggregate principal amount of $540,916,978. ("Order Fixing Time," 9)

By extending lines of credit and loans totaling $700 million to Grant, and by entering into the loan extension agreement, the banks strengthened their constraining influence on Grant's poli-

---

1. At one point, Grant's management was told "not to contact the dissident banks" to try to persuade them to participate in the $6 million loan agreement: "We [Morgan Guaranty] didn't want anybody else muddying up the water. We wanted to end up this ballgame on our own in our own way" (Schroeder, in *Morgan v. Grant,* 118–119).

cies. Since Grant now depended heavily on the banking community for survival, its management was not free to make decisions
that might antagonize the banks. A covenant of the loan extension
agreement stipulated bank participation and intervention into
Grant's decision-making processes, including personnel and resource allocation. The agreement called for "bank approval of the
changes in . . . voting control of the stock" (Schroeder, in *Morgan
v. Grant*, 307). The banks also now demanded that Grant replace
Kendrick with someone with expertise in merchandising who
would be able to forcefully change, retain, and/or dismiss personnel and policies as necessary. Peterkin headed the search committee, which brought in Robert A. Anderson, a former vice president
of Sears Roebuck and Co. (Peterkin, in *Morgan v. Grant*, 27). The
process by which a search committee headed by a bank represen-
tative selected Anderson as Grant's chief executive illustrates how
Grant's management acted to satisfy the banks.

Although the banks selected Anderson, he quickly had "substantial and loud disagreements with respect to Grant's inability to
get merchandise." He threatened to resign, complaining that the
banks were not meeting Peterkin's promise of bank support. Chase
Manhattan Bank issued a memo on 16 June 1975 that stated, "I
believe our only hope is a very senior level meeting with Anderson
to try to convince him to stay within our ground rules." Schroeder
told the court that Anderson "was not cooperating with the banks
[and] . . . he was later told he was expected to. . . . He had 27 banks
that were working their heads off to help him and [I told him] that
he might just cooperate with them a little better" (Schroeder, in
Morgan v. Grant, 321, 325–326).

The struggles between the banks and Grant's management continued against the backdrop of power plays by the major banks
against the minor banks. On 2 June 1975 the major banks "convinced the 117 smaller banks to accept a 40% payment" of their
loans to Grant, thus reducing the number of banks involved in
Grant's indebtedness (Schroeder, in *Morgan v. Grant*, 312). This
action, under which the minor banks recouped only a small portion of their loans to Grant, also precluded them from gaining access to Grant's assets when the major banks later declared the firm
insolvent and forced it into bankruptcy.

The banks responded collectively to Anderson's "noncooperation" when he told them in September 1975 that Grant would need them to help put "more cash . . . into the company" (Kendrick, in *Morgan v. Grant,* 736). After exending so much support to the firm, the banks suddenly told Grant that they would not provide any more money to enable the retailer to reorganize. Instead, the banks entered into a subordination agreement in August 1975 to persuade vendors and suppliers to continue to ship goods to Grant. Under this agreement the banks "agreed to subordinate $300 million of Grant's indebtedness to them to certain trade obligations of Grant" ("Order Fixing Time," 10). But according to Anderson the subordination came too late to rescue Grant from bankruptcy, and Kendrick testified that both he and Anderson had requested the subordination as early as April or May 1975 (Kendrick, in *Morgan v. Grant,* 764–766).

Grant filed for Chapter XI bankruptcy on 2 October 1975. At that time the banks "set off approximately $94,523,110 of Grant's funds on deposit with them. . . . $90,300,000 of the set-off funds was subsequently advanced to Grant as a debtor-in-possession" ("Order Fixing Time," 10). By this action the banks essentially lent Grant its own money.

The banking community initially responded to Grant's cash flow shortage and deleterious patterns of managerial decision making by concurring that Grant's approach to business needed to be restructured and by agreeing that the firm should be allowed the opportunity to reorganize under Chapter XI bankruptcy proceedings. This approach is by and large reserved for firms that seem able to reemerge from reorganization as healthy, competitive businesses. The agreement by the banking community to allow Grant to file for reorganization protection indicated that at this point the banks did not define Grant's predicament as a crisis (that is, as permanently damaging to Grant's business trajectory). Rather, they defined it as a problematic situation that was expected to respond positively to reorganization efforts. A creditors' committee (composed of six banks and five trade creditors) was formed ostensibly to aid the firm in its reorganization attempts. Yet the question remains, Why did Grant's banks continue to extend increasing amounts of loans and lines of credit to a firm whose cash flow situation was clearly desperate?

Chapter XI and Beyond: The Struggle Continues

Although there is general agreement that poor managerial decisions led to W. T. Grant's financial difficulties, evidence suggests that Grant's bankers were aware of those difficulties as they developed. Rodman alleged that Grant's banks continually took "action to assist in the concealment and suppression of the true facts regarding the financial condition and business of Grant" (Rodman, in *Morgan v. Grant*, 85). Furthermore, Mayer testified that none of Grant's bankers "express[ed] any concern about the quality of Grant's receivables, . . . the quality of management information or information systems at the Grant company, . . . internal controls at the Grant company, [or] . . . any phase of its operating other than the fact that it wasn't earning as much profit as it had in the past" (Mayer, in *Morgan v. Grant*, pt. 8, 27).

Because Grant's banks were involved in the firm's day-to-day decision-making processes, they must have been aware of the retailer's growing problems and poor managerial decisions. Several bank representatives sat on Grant's board of directors, including Peterkin, of Morgan Guaranty (Grant's lead bank), and Joseph W. Chinn, Jr., of Wilmington Trust Co. (*Moody's Industrial Manual*, 1974, 1331). In addition, both Peterkin and Chinn were members of Grant's audit committee, and Peterkin chaired that committee from 1969 until Grant's demise. The audit committee, which met at least once a year, received "accountants' audited statements" and would review "the balance sheet and the income statement on a line by line basis." Peterkin admitted that he periodically called Mayer to ask about the poor performance of several of Grant's stores. He further conceded to the court that "there were a lot of stores that were not meeting the 'target'" of sales and profitability (Peterkin, in *Morgan v. Grant*, 244–249, 336).

In addition to bank participation on Grant's audit committee, the bank advisory committee (composed of representatives from Morgan, Chase Manhattan, and Citibank) was kept abreast of developments with progress reports on the retailer. Peterkin testified that John Sundman (Grant's financial vice president) told him as early as 1972 that "there would come a point in time when Grant would run out of money if it paid all of its bills" (Peterkin, in *Morgan v. Grant*, 60, 183). Schroeder also testified to having had periodic "routine" discussions with Peterkin concerning Grant: "We did have a line of credit. Mr. Peterkin in the ordinary course of his activities would be aware of that, and I in the ordinary course of my activities would review our lines with him" (Schroeder, in *Morgan v. Grant*, 6).

Peterkin's presence on Grant's board created a one-way information network. Throughout this case information concerning Grant flowed from Peterkin to the bank, but information did not flow from the bank to Grant. In fact Peterkin's one-way information flow continued beyond Morgan Guaranty to the rest of the banking community. This wider network came to light in a Chemical Bank document indicating that Peterkin had had conversations about Grant's problems "with at least one banker from Chemical" (Schroeder, in *Morgan v. Grant*, 107). The evidence indicates that even though the banks knew of the retailer's developing problems and often considered the company insolvent, they did not interfere with the firm's day-to-day operations. Despite top-level managerial changes, the store expansions, credit system, and merchandising practices continued.

In 1974 Grant's banks finally admitted that the firm had substantial problems. In a memorandum prepared in December 1974, Peterkin expressed his opinion "that Grant was at that time on the verge of bankruptcy." Peterkin clearly "knew Grant was insolvent in December of 1974," and yet he continued to make further obligations and loans to the retailer (Rodman, in *Morgan v. Grant*, 96). Schroeder testified that Grant became a "problem credit" as early as the spring of 1974. He suggested that Peterkin was also aware of Grant's problems because of the bankers' "routine" reviews of credit lines to the retailer. Schroeder told the court that the banks placed Grant on a "special review list" of problem credits in March 1974. This special review indicated to Morgan that "in early July, 1974 . . . it didn't seem prudent . . . to extend additional credit to Grant." At this time, the Irving Trust Company questioned Grant's ability "to survive the crisis." Later that summer several small banks, including the Toms River Bank, concluded that Grant was insolvent, despite denials from the large banks. When asked for his definition of *insolvent*, Schroeder told the court that "from a banker's point of view it . . . means . . . inability to pay . . . [the firm's] debts when due." But he denied that Grant was insolvent in 1974, even though the retailer was failing to pay its bank notes "as they matured" and had slowed down its payments to suppliers. According to Schroeder's testimony, he did not conclude that Grant was insolvent until September 1975 (Schroeder, in *Morgan v. Grant*, 6, 48, 66, 112, 121, 365). Peterkin did not admit Grant's insolvency until December 1974 (Peterkin, in *Morgan v. Grant*, 365; Rodman, in *ibid.*, 67). In fact, a Morgan Stanley document indicates that the bank had discussed taking large write-offs of Grant's credit operations back in "late August or early September" of 1974 (Schroeder, in *Morgan v. Grant*, 123–124).

Despite misgivings about the prudence of further bank involvement, the financial community continued to extend further credit to the company. Although the banks insisted they took this unusual step because they were convinced they could "turn this thing around," Schroeder testified that they acted to "save their own hides." By late summer 1974 "Morgan and the other banks were looking at the Grant credit from a point of view as to how to recoup the most amount of money as possible on the Grant loans." Schroeder further admitted that the reason the banks refrained from liquidating Grant at that point was "because the banks felt they could get more money by keeping it alive" (Schroeder, in *Morgan v. Grant*, 367, 125). This is a clear statement of the divergence of interests between the banks and the retailer.

A liquidation analysis performed by Citibank in the summer of 1974 indicated that "the banks would get 68 cents on the dollar." The same analysis demonstrated that "in liquidation it was estimated that the Grant liabilities exceeded its assets." In other words, the banks knew Grant would not be able to repay the full amount of their loans if they chose to liquidate the firm at that time. Schroeder told the court that the banks never intended a long-term solution: "We would not be thinking in anything more than a temporary rescue operation." Although according to Schroeder the banks theorized that a short-term rescue would "make cash flows begin," the terms of the loans were too short to allow the deeply troubled firm to repay successfully. Schroeder acknowledged that the banks understood "that it would at least be a number of years before repayment was made" (Schroeder, in *Morgan v. Grant*, 90, 132, 22, 25). If the banks were convinced (as they continually testified) that they could transform the retailer from a desperately ailing firm to a profitable one, why was Grant finally thrown into bankruptcy?

Grant's board was apparently aware of the banks' power to reduce Grant to insolvency and of the banks' sudden decision that no more money would be forthcoming. At a meeting on 23 September 1975 Grant's board weighed the prospect of reorganizing under a Chapter XI bankruptcy proceeding. Chapter XI would allow the company to "continue to operate and endeavor to cure its problems under the protection of the court" from its creditors; whereas in the alternative, "Chapter X, the court appointed a trustee, and for all practical purposes, the company management ceased to direct its affairs" (Kendrick, in *Morgan v. Grant*, 758).

Banks' collective constraining influence in managerial decisions (including the decision to reorganize or to liquidate) became evident once again. While Grant's board was considering Chapter XI, the banks were also conducting meetings to discuss Grant's bankruptcy. Schroeder testified that Morgan Guaranty disseminated a great deal of information about Grant to the other banks in the consortium. He told the court that the information was "rather complete . . . in order to do our job as the agent bank" and that it was communicated both "at meetings of the banks" and "in written form" (Schroeder, in *Morgan v. Grant*, 158–159). On 26 September 1975 Morgan Stanley bankers held one such meeting at Morgan headquarters, and after a period of discussion among themselves, they invited Kendrick to join them. Having already decided that a "Chapter XI was inevitable," they told Kendrick that they preferred Chapter XI to Chapter X because under the former Grant's management would continue to direct the firm as debtor-in-possession "and therefore would stand a better chance of securing shipments of merchandise." Under Chapter X, however, the firm would be run by a court-appointed trustee who "could at any time with the permission of the court liquidate the company" (Kendrick, in *Morgan v. Grant*, 769, 774, 789). Apparently, nervous vendors could be persuaded to ship goods to the retailer only by a guarantee that the banks would pay. Moreover, Schroeder testified that the banks equated Chapter X with liquidation (Schroeder, in

Morgan v. Grant, 187). Peterkin testified that the banks wanted no part of a bankruptcy liquidation (that is, Chapter X) at that time "because [they] wanted to maintain the control of the company" (Peterkin, in *Morgan v. Grant,* 77–78).

Resisting the banks' pressure for Chapter XI or bankruptcy, Grant's management wanted to recapitalize with more money from the banks. In the end management reluctantly gave in, however, and agreed that without recapitalization a Chapter XI proceeding was preferable to Chapter X: "A Chapter XI petition would be filed if the banks were willing to cooperate . . . [because] they would use their best efforts in keeping the company in Chapter XI when appearances were made before the Securities and Exchange Commission." At this point the banks agreed to cooperate "on the condition that Grant close approximately half its stores" (Kendrick, in *Morgan v. Grant,* 793, 795; see also Peterkin, in *ibid.,* 42–44).

The issue of store closings generated more conflict between Grant and its banks, underscoring their divergence of interests. Before September 1975 several bank representatives had told Anderson and Sundman that Grant had to close down more than five hundred stores to increase the retailer's cash flow. Kendrick complained that the banks were "relating it entirely to a cash flow situation." Apparently Grant's banks were primarily interested in augmenting the size of Grant's estate in bankruptcy rather than in reorganizing the firm into a viable retailer. A larger estate in bankruptcy would mean a larger proportion of recovery for the banks. If Grant actually reorganized under Chapter XI protection from its creditors, the banks would be unable to recover any of their money for a long time. According to Kendrick's testimony, Sundman presented the banks with figures indicating that Grant's cash flow "would and could be better than was being projected by the banks . . . [and that] on the basis of the way he saw the cash flow developing that it wouldn't require that many stores to be closed" (Kendrick, in *Morgan v. Grant,* 733, 734). He estimated that only three hundred to five hundred stores needed to be closed to effectively reorganize Grant into solvency. These events and testimony suggest that the banks were indeed attempting to increase the firm's immediate cash flow position, to the detriment of its future viability.

A Citibank memorandum noted the divergence of interests between Grant and the banks: as early as December 1974 the banks recognized that "it was in . . . [Grant's] best interest to file a petition in bankruptcy while at the same time it was recognized that it was not in the bank's best interest to do so." According to Schroeder, the banks acknowledged that "the company's problems with the trade would be solved to a large degree by the filing of a bankruptcy petition." The Citibank memo indicated, however, that "it was important [to the banks] to get into February [1975], since the banks' lien on receivables and Zeller's taken in September would not be perfected until early in that month." Schroeder conceded that "it was the banks' strategy to buy as much time as possible in order to avoid jeopardizing their collateral position." Moreover, a Morgan Guaranty liquidation analysis (found in several other banks' files as well) indicated the deliberateness of this strategy to buy time. To that end the banks secured an agreement from Grant that it would give the banks advance notice of the filing of a Chapter XI petition (Schroeder, in *Morgan v. Grant*, 221, 222, 254, 408). Grant's managers thus had to seek the banks' permission to go ahead with the very action even the banks acknowledged was in the retailer's best interest. Rodman's testimony indicated that the banks had delayed to position themselves more advantageously before pushing the retailer into bankruptcy.

In late September or early October 1975 Grant's management decided "to actively seek the support of the banks in the filing of the Chapter XI petition." Peterkin acknowledged that "if the banks did not support the filing of the Chapter XI petition . . . [the only alternative] was Chapter X" (Peterkin, in *Morgan v. Grant*, 87). The banks pressed for the substantial store closings as a condition for their cooperation in a Chapter XI reorganization (Kendrick, in *Morgan v. Grant*, 797; Peterkin, in *ibid.*, 42–44), thus increasing the firm's immediate cash flow position. But closing so many stores undermined Grant's future chances of effective reorganization. Although Sundman and Anderson maintained that Grant could reorganize with fewer store closings, the banks were adamant. Grant's management finally acquiesced to an action they clearly viewed as unnecessary and ill advised, and they verbally agreed to comply with the banks' demand.

Grant's managers eventually closed 714 of their 1,073 stores, leaving 359 stores to operate Grant's business. They fired almost fifty thousand employees and attempted to revamp their merchandising policies by focusing on seasonal merchandise and soft goods (primarily clothing and domestic items) and phasing out the furniture and major appliances that allegedly helped provoke their financial difficulties. The losses incurred by closing down so many stores and holding huge sales of heavily discounted inventory items amounted to approximately $177.3 million for the 1975–76 fiscal year. This discounted inventory loss equaled the total loss for the 1974–75 fiscal year. Grant's managers also replaced their in-house credit system with the use of national bank credit cards, at the suggestion of the banks (Schroeder, in *Morgan v. Grant*, 139). These changes in Grant's policies indicated a substantial loss of managerial discretion to the banks, which now seemed to run the company altogether. By early 1976 a committee of creditors (consisting of six banks and five trade creditors) formed to consider the future of Grant. John Ingraham, vice president of First National City Bank, chaired the committee.

Meanwhile, Grant went about its radical reorganization to restore the creditors' confidence (or, more accurately, to stave off bankruptcy). The consultants advised the creditors that Grant's survival could not be determined with certainty for another six to eight years. That conclusion prompted the banks to flex their muscles and exert their ultimate control over the future of Grant. The trade creditors, who were completely secured, still seemed willing to do business with the retailer. But the banks were strongly in favor of liquidation, and they were said to be "hungrily eyeing the $320 million in cash accumulated from store closings and liquidations" (*New York Times*, 14 Oct. 1976, 61). Ironically, only the banking community wanted liquidation of the firm. Despite opposition from the trade creditors and Grant's management, the process of bank-dominated decision making (based on their collective control of desperately needed loan capital) led to a resolution of the struggle in favor of the banks. On 10 February 1976 the committee of creditors decided that Grant should be declared bankrupt. That move touched off "the biggest liquidation in retailing history" (*Daily News Record*, 11 Feb. 1976, 1).

In March 1976 Federal Judge John Galgay signed the order that called for Grant's liquidation within sixty days. By now Grant had debts to the banks of $640 million and to trade creditors and debenture holders of more than $500 million. The committee of creditors' original vote was seven to four in favor of liquidation; by the time the committee presented its case to Judge Galgay, the decision was unanimous. The banks' collective power and their motivations were not lost on Judge Galgay, who pointedly asked the committee, "Was it more comfortable to pull the plug after Grant's had already built its cash up from $90 million to $320 million?" (*New York Times,* 13 Feb. 1976, 1).

Securities and Exchange Commission regional head Marvin Jacob pressed Anderson about whether or not he felt Grant could survive if he were allowed to use $150 million of Grant's $320 million in bank deposits. Anderson responded that he thought Grant's chances were "relatively good if we could just undo the results of the committee's decision" (*New York Times,* 13 Feb. 1976, 1). Here Anderson alluded to the fact that when the committee voted to "pull the plug," suppliers of merchandise refused to ship to Grant any longer, thereby exacerbating the firm's situation by depleting inventory. The action of the committee, led by the banks, illustrates the process of the social construction of corporate crisis. The decisions of the banking community to define Grant's cash flow problems as a crisis permanently altered Grant's business trajectory from slow but eventual recovery to liquidation. Moreover, only the financial institutions had the power, based on their collective control of critical loan capital, to enforce their definition over the opposing assessments of the situation by Grant's management.

At this point Grant's assets totaled $400–475 million, including $320 million cash, $43 million in inventory at cost, $75 million in accounts receivable, and $25 million in stock of Zeller's, Ltd. The creditors scrambled to secure recovery of a portion of these assets. *Business Week* reported:

First crack at the assets goes to holders of $24 million worth of senior debentures. Then, because of an unusual lien arrangement, come trade creditors, with $110 million owed. The banks, which subordinated to the trade $300 million of their $640 million loan to Grant's, come next and have an additional $90 million that gets preferred treatment; it was lent after the filing for reorganization. Then come junior debenture holders, with $94 million, and finally the unsecured debt, including $300 million in landlord claims and utility bills. . . . And Grant will owe approximately $15 million in severance pay to its 84,000 employees, although this is not a priority payment. An unresolved Internal Revenue Service claim of $60 million plus interest could possibly take precedence over unsecured creditors. But legal fees, which will run into the millions, are likely to assume a priority status. (*Business Week*, 1 Mar. 1976, 21)

Clearly there would be little or nothing left to cover the unsecured debt.

The banks did not have to step in and overtly seize control of Grant's executive positions to produce the managerial decisions they wanted. They merely relied on their collective control of capital flows to persuade Grant's management team to acquiesce, precluding consideration of decisions that would displease them. The same power could not have been exerted by single banks acting alone. The organized concerted control of capital flows engendered and enhanced the banking community's power over W. T. Grant.

Pointing to the links between Morgan Guaranty and Grant formed by Peterkin and Chinn, Rodman charged that this interlocking relation had existed "for an extended period of time prior to the commencement of bankruptcy proceedings by Grant." The interlocks helped the banks exercise control over Grant's board and management. Peterkin and Chinn's presence facilitated the dissemination of information about Grant to the banking community and served as a constant reminder to Grant's management that the banks could define the situation as a crisis at any time and withdraw their capital support. The presence of the bankers was a source of preemptive power, in that Grant's management took only those decisions that would please the banks (Rodman, in *Morgan v. Grant*, 63, 71–74).

By March 1977 Rodman had begun making assessments and proposing plans to Judge Galgay on how to meet Grant's obligations for severance and vacation pay owed to former employees. Since Grant originally filed under Chapter XI, claims made while the firm functioned under bankruptcy and those made during the four months prior to the filing would be recognized. Claims made after the filing of Chapter XI would be prorated from the bankrupt estate. Consequently, employees who quit before Grant filed under Chapter XI received all their benefits, whereas those who remained with the company to the bitter end received almost nothing.

Severance and vacation pay constituted only a part of the cost of Grant's bankruptcy that fell on the workers' shoulders. There was also the question of the account employees had with Grant for the purchase of securities in the firm. Judge Galgay informed the workers that the prospects of recovery of the account's funds looked "bleak"(*Wall Street Journal,* 11 Mar. 1977, 20). In the end workers had to pay the bill for Grant's (and the banks') excesses. Moreover, other workers outside the firm also shouldered some of that burden. A large proportion of the investors in Grant's sinking fund were the Illinois and Michigan teachers' pension funds.

In early 1978 Rodman reached an agreement with twenty-six of Grant's lender banks on a tentative settlement of their claims of $560 million against the company. This settlement provided for the orderly distribution of the assets of the now bankrupt retailing giant. As part of the compromise agreement, Rodman agreed to discontinue prosecuting the banks to recover $57 million. (That sum represents payments the company made to the banks in June 1975, before it declared bankruptcy.) The terms of the compromise settlement of Grant's estate were as follows:

1. The participating creditors (including secured suppliers, senior debenture holders, and holders of the outstanding sinking fund) were initially given 25 percent of their filed claims and then pro rata distributions of their claims ("Agreement of Compromise and Settlement Among Charles G. Rodman, as Trustee of the Estate of W.T. Grant Company, Bankrupt, and the Banks Listed on Exhibit 1 Hereto," in *Morgan v. Grant,* 24 Feb. 1978, 3; hereafter cited as "Agreement of Compromise"). The holders of the sinking fund were offered 100 cents on the dollar, but without interest, on their loans. Those creditors who benefited from the trade subordination agreement with the banks have gotten 70 percent of their claims ($90 million), and the unsecured creditors have gotten 39 percent of their claims.

2. The bank claimants agreed not to "enforce security interests and liens against the Bankrupt Estate" to avoid depleting the assets of the estate in litigation prompted by Rodman's suit. The banks' claims would "be allowed in at least an aggregate amount of $650,000,000" ("Agreement of Compromise," 4). Thereafter, prorated payments from the estate would be made to the banks at six-month intervals after settlements were made of the

other claims against the firm's estate. By July 1978 the banks had recovered more than 60 percent of their claims, with more to come. Indeed, these six-month payments may "ultimately result in the banks' recovering a higher percentage of their claims than those of the participating creditors," thanks to the compromise settlement provision specifying that "the participating creditors will receive no more than 50% of their claims or the percentage of their claims that the banks recover, whichever is less" (*New York Times*, 31 July 1978, D3).

The case is still not completely settled. Pro rata distributions of the estate are still being made to the banks, and the court is still considering contested distributions. Moreover, the pace of the settlement has slowed since the death of Rodman (who has been replaced by his assistant, Joseph Pardo) and of Judge Galgay (replaced by Judge Edward J. Ryan). Still, the compromise settlement between Rodman and the banks attests to the power the banks exercised over W. T. Grant. They have recovered much more of their investment than any other participants in the case. According to a telephone conversation with one of Grant's lawyers, the unsecured creditors have recovered approximately 39 percent and debenture holders 19 percent of their claims, whereas the banks have recovered more than 60 percent thus far. In fact, the banks are the only creditors who will continue to receive payments from the remaining $22 million of the estate. The estate's lawyers indicated that the banks will ultimately recover about 80 percent of their claims—that is, 97–98 percent of the remaining estate, with the other 2–3 percent of the estate devoted to administrative costs.

Clearly the banks did not enjoy absolute power. They lost more money than any other creditors and were unable to recover all their investment. They accepted the compromise settlement under the threat of protracted and prohibitively expensive litigation from Rodman's suit. Such litigation would have depleted the estate and prevented the banks from recovering any of their investment, because Chapter XI provides for payment in full of the legal fees incurred in the settlement of bankrupt estates. The banks' acceptance of a partial recovery demonstrates the limits of bank power and illustrates the difference between bank control and bank hegemony. Control implies absolute power. Thus bank control theory is a static description of power as a trait accruing to banks. By contrast, bank hegemony is a process of relative power that depends on structurally unified action (here in a lending consortium) activated in the context of struggle.

Conclusion

The case of W. T. Grant's bankruptcy demonstrates the power of banks to socially construct a corporate crisis. Through their collective control of capital flows, Grant's banks were able to prevent a serious cash flow problem from becoming an actual bankruptcy for two years by increasing the loans and lines of credit to the retailer to a total of $700 million. When they decided to pull the plug and define the cash flow problem as a crisis, they simply refused to advance any more capital to the firm. Even though Grant management's assessment of the situation differed from that of the banking community, the banks' hegemonic control of capital flows enhanced their ability to enforce their definition of crisis.

The banks were aware as early as 1974 that they were the firm's only source of capital, because the commercial paper market was closed to Grant. Although there is compelling evidence that the banks knew of Grant's deepening problems, they chose to continue to pour money into the retailer, thus postponing the crisis. Evidence indicates that they did so in a bid to increase the size of Grant's estate in bankruptcy. Grant's financial vice president, John Sundman, suggested that the banks used their control of capital flows to keep the firm alive long enough to get as much of their money as possible (*Forbes*, 1 Feb. 1975, 18), to the detriment of other participants in the case, particularly Grant's employees, its unsecured creditors, and the Illinois and Michigan teachers' pension funds. Jacob of the Securities and Exchange Commission angrily said that the banks "took a big public company which should have been a Chapter X proceeding and ran it into the ground" (*Business Week*, 19 July 1976, 62). The banks' collective ability to delay Grant's bankruptcy is consistent with Nelson's (1981) finding that it is common for financial institutions to engage in such behavior to improve their secured position in bankruptcy. Moreover, banks sometimes push firms into liquidation when it would be more appropriate for these firms to reorganize. Grant's bankruptcy case supports this finding. After closing half its stores, the firm had accumulated about $160 million in cash. The banks could either support the firm's continued reorganization efforts (and wait to recover their investment) or force the bankruptcy they had long delayed (and begin the struggle to muscle other claimants aside). They chose the latter course. Most important, only the banks collectively had the power to determine both the timing and the outcome of Grant's bankruptcy.

Although it may be tempting to view the banks' decision as a last-resort remedy to a serious problem, such an analysis is not appropriate here. W. T. Grant was well on the way to restructuring and rehabilitating itself under a Chapter XI reorganization program when the banks cut the capital flows. Apparently, less extreme measures to address the firm's cash flow shortage and its managerial problems were working, if slowly. Clearly the decision to force the firm into liquidation was not selected because less extreme measures had failed. Rather, Grant's banks chose liquidation because of their secure position in the priority claimant list established in bankruptcy.

The large banks (particularly Morgan Guaranty, Chase Manhattan, Citibank, and Manufacturers Hanover) demonstrated their organized power to discipline the small recalcitrant banks into continuing to advance credit lines to Grant. Although the case reveals some conflict within the financial community, the large banks' success in disciplining the small banks shows how banks develop coalescence and present a unified position to the business community. This unity is crucial to the relative power of the banking community. The control of capital flows by individual competing banks would not translate into power, because competition would enable individual firms to bargain and negotiate favorably with individual banks by exploiting the implicit threat of taking substantial corporate business to another bank (see Herman 1973). In contrast, unity transforms the banking community into a cooperative oligopoly. The financial community has structural mechanisms to resolve and moderate conflicts and achieve coalescence. Moreover, banks strongly discourage non–banking community intervention in the formation of bank unity.

Evidence indicates that Grant's banks freely communicated with each other about the retailer's situation, contradicting any notion of bank isolation. Indeed, Grant's interlocks with the banks (through DeWitt Peterkin, Jr., of Morgan Guaranty, and Joseph W. Chinn, Jr., of Wilmington Trust) functioned as one-way information networks, facilitating the flow of information from the retailer to Morgan Guaranty, Wilmington Trust, and many other banks in Grant's consortium.

The day-to-day consultation between lenders is significant in two ways. First, such consultations contradict the notion of the invisible hand of the marketplace as the natural controling mechanism disciplining corporate existence. Apparently, the invisible hand can be guided forcefully by the very visible hands of the banking community. Second, such consultations also contradict the notion of competition in the banking community. The standard practice of friendly consultations indicates cooperation and planning between banks rather than free competition (the hallmark of the invisible hand).

Taken together, the lack of competition between banks and the consequent failure of the invisible hand to rationally and objectively discipline the market suggest inaccuracies in the traditional view of American corporate life. The conventional view of business structure assumes free and open competition to ensure that only the most efficient firms survive (see, e.g., Herman 1973; Chandler 1977; Kaysen 1957; Rose 1967). Critical analyses similarly suggest that competition would mitigate the banking community's ability to establish unity and thus provide the state (and presumably nonfinancial firms like W. T. Grant) with relative autonomy from the lenders (see, e.g., Poulantzas 1968, 1973). But day-to-day consultations between banks are inconsistent with both of these viewpoints. The structural arrangement of the banking community necessitates cooperation rather than competition among banks.

Noteworthy is the divergence of interests between Grant and its banks and the extensive day-to-day participation of the banking community in Grant's decision-making processes. Finance capital is unique as a resource in that it is the prerequisite for the purchase of all other resources. Lending consortia develop because of the legal and financial inability of single banks to provide the increasingly large borrowing needs of corporate America. The structure of the consortia increases access by individual banks to the lucrative business of corporate lending. It also spreads the risks of such loans among many banks, organizes the banking community to mitigate competition, and facilitates cooperation and consultation between banks. Schroeder referred to W. T. Grant's consortium as the "whole family of banks," suggesting a unified group of financial institutions (Schroeder, in *Morgan v. Grant*, 10). By fusing the interests of financial institutions, structural developments such as lending consortia produce bank hegemony and thereby facilitate bank constraints on nonfinancial corporations' decision-making processes.

Similar processes in the social construction of corporate crisis can be seen in the 1969 collapse of Penn Central Corporation. As in W. T. Grant's bankruptcy, there is ample evidence that the banking community knew of the railroad's worsening liquidity problems. And as with Grant, the banks delayed publicly acknowledging Penn Central's grave problems until a time they deemed more advantageous. Meanwhile they contributed to the fiction of a healthy, profitable railroad by hiring a prestigious accounting firm to perform some "creative accounting" procedures and by declaring a series of hefty dividends for stockholders (Fitch and Oppenheimer 1970, pt. 2, 81). The delay in acknowledging Penn Central's real difficulties gave the firm's bankers ample time to quietly sell off their holdings of Penn Central stock even as they told security analysts such investments were sound (*Wall Street Journal*, 25 Sept. 1970, 5). The banks' collective control of capital gives them the discretionary power to time the public disclosure of a firm's liquidity problems and the ability to socially construct corporate reality. This power is inaccessible to all other stockholders and most corporate managers. For example, because nine of the ten largest shareholders at Penn Central were commercial banks (which collectively held 22.1 percent of the firm's total stock), banks dominated Penn Central's board of directors: eleven of the thirteen directors created fourteen interlocks with twelve commercial banks (see Patman 1970, 22632–22638).

The difference between the bankruptcies of W. T. Grant and Penn Central illustrates the variety of sources of organized bank power. Grant's banks derived their power from their common presence in a huge lending consortium, whereas Penn Central's banks derived their power from their collective impact as the railroad's major shareholders.

Chapter Three

Chrysler Corporation: Bailing Out the Banks

Really, as much as bailing out Chrysler . . . we [the federal government] are helping those financial institutions [that] assumed a certain amount of risk. When we come in, we are picking up the risk and we are bailing them out, as well as we are, for example, the other social concerns [labor, state and local governments, and so on], which we all feel deeply about.
—Congressman Bruce F. Vento

Even when a corporation's cash flow shortage becomes problematic, the banking community may choose not to define the situation as a crisis. Instead, banks threaten to impose that definition unless the federal government infuses cash or guarantees further loans by the banks. Indeed, the federal government has helped bail out over four hundred corporations with cash flow difficulties. In so doing, the federal government is often constrained to bail out banks' investments in large, economically critical firms (see Iacocca 1984, 199–200).

Chrysler Corporation's battle for a bailout provides insight into the definitional process of the social construction of corporate reality. Like W. T. Grant Company, Chrysler had a long history of short-sighted managerial decision making that produced a serious cash flow shortage. And like Grant, Chrysler had long-standing lending relations with the banking community. But Chrysler did not go bankrupt. Instead, it was bailed out by a federal loan guarantee that the financial institutions insisted was absolutely essential before they could make any further commitments. How did the banking community elicit a federal bailout of Chrysler? What was the source of relative power in this case, and how did collective control of capital flows contribute to this power?

Setting the Stage: Managerial Decision Making, the Economy, and the Banks

Until the mid-1970s Chrysler did relatively well. It enjoyed a healthy share of the domestic market as one of the three firms dominating the U.S. auto industry. Its sales increased from $3.01 billion in 1960 to a peak of $16.71 billion in 1977. Its profits grew from $32.1 million in 1960 to $209.7 million in 1968, peaking at $423 million in 1976 (U.S. Congress, House 1979a, 487, 488). By 1978 Chrysler was the tenth largest firm in the United States, employing 250,000 workers (*New York Times*, 12 Aug. 1979, F15). Its market share in the automobile industry for 1976–1978 averaged 12 percent (U.S. Congress, House 1979a, 25). Yet in 1978 the corporation reported a loss of $205 million and began pleading for aid from the federal government.

By 1979 Chrysler laid off 23,800 blue-collar and 5,000 white-collar workers (*New York Times*, 12 Aug. 1979, F15). At the close of that year, the firm reported an annual loss of $1.1 billion, with $4.75 billion owed to more than four hundred banks and insurance firms (Iacocca 1984, 240). The first quarter of 1980 looked similarly bleak, with a loss of $449 million (*New York Times*, 29 June 1980, F2). Chrysler's share of the market declined as well, dropping from 16.3 percent in 1968 to 13.6 percent in 1974 and skidding in 1979 to 9.3 percent (U.S. Congress, House 1979a, 476). The firm blamed federal regulations for its financial difficulties. Chrysler's chairman, John J. Riccardo, cited "federal standards for fuel economy, clean air and safety in the 1980's" as the source of Chrysler's "serious problems in raising $8.5 billion to redesign its vehicles to meet" these standards (*New York Times*, 14 Aug. 1979, D3; see Dramatis Personae 2). Chrysler asked the fed-

Dramatis Personae 2. The Chrysler Bailout
(in order of appearance)

John J. Riccardo	Chairman, Chrysler Corp. (1974)
Elinor Bachrach	Aide to Senator William Proxmire
Congressman Stuart B. McKinney	Member, House Committee on Banking, Finance, and Urban Affairs
Congressman Richard Kelly	Member, House Committee on Banking, Finance, and Urban Affairs
Lee Iacocca	President and chief executive officer, Chrysler Corp.
Lynn A. Townsend	Chairman, Chrysler Corp. (until 1974)
Michael Blumenthal	Treasury secretary (until 1979)
G. William Miller	Treasury secretary (1979–1980)
John F. McGillicuddy	Chairman, Manufacturers Hanover Trust
Senator William Proxmire	Member, Senate Finance Committee
Gerald Greenwald	Executive vice president and senior financial officer, Chrysler Corp.
Tom Killefer	Chairman of the board, U.S. Trust Co. of New York
Congressman Bruce F. Vento	Member, House Committee on Banking, Finance, and Urban Affairs
Congressman Norman D. Shumway	Member, House Committee on Banking, Finance, and Urban Affairs
Congressman Norman E. D'Amours	Member, House Committee on Banking, Finance, and Urban Affairs
Congressman Ron Paul	Member, House Committee on Banking, Finance, and Urban Affairs
David W. Knapp	President, American National Bank and Trust Co.
Rodney E. Rohrbaugh	Executive vice president, American National Bank and Trust Co.

Douglas A. Fraser	President, United Auto Workers
Senator Robert C. Byrd	Senate majority leader
Senator Russell Long	Chairman, Senate Finance Committee
Alfred E. Kahn	Chairman, Council on Wage and Price Stability (1979)
Congressman James J. Blanchard	Committee on Banking, Finance, and Urban Affairs
Lane Kirkland	President, AFL-CIO

eral government for a two-year reprieve from compliance with the standards.

In 1978 Chrysler realized that it was going to suffer an annual loss of $200 million. Riccardo made another trip to the White House to plead his firm's case and to ask for $1 billion in tax credits. He proposed that Chrysler defer its 1980 taxes, which it would pay at a future date from the profits the firm's management assumed they would have in 1981 and 1982. Elinor Bachrach, Senator William Proxmire's aide, called the proposal "an appeal for a thinly veiled grant" (Moritz and Seaman 1981, 272). The Treasury Department's Domestic Finance Capital Markets division was assigned to "keep track" of Chrysler's situation, but the federal government took no concrete action at the time (*New York Times*, 14 Aug. 1979, D3).

Chrysler continued to argue that federal regulations and standards had "imposed a disproportionate burden on the smallest of autodom's Big Three." The firm claimed that compliance with such regulations cost it $620 per car, compared, for example, with $340 for General Motors, because the top two manufacturers could "spread the cost" of these regulations "over the larger number of cars sold" (*Newsweek*, 13 Aug. 1979, 53; see also Iacocca 1984, 197). Furthermore, Chrysler claimed that compliance with federal regulations would cost $1 billion more in 1979 and 1980 (*Business Week*, 20 Aug. 1979, 103; Iacocca 1984, 197). "Because the government has helped bring Chrysler to its knees," the company argued, "the government now has an obligation to bail it out" (*Newsweek*, 13 Aug. 1979, 53).

Despite Riccardo's insistence on government responsibility, it appears that managerial decisions within Chrysler helped produce the company's financial difficulties. For example, in 1976 Chrysler decided not to invest in the costly construction of a four-cylinder engine plant for its Omni and Horizon models. Instead, the company decided to make a contract with Volkswagen to purchase 300,000 engines a year (*Newsweek*, 13 Aug. 1979, 55). But the small cars became extremely popular, and Chrysler found that 300,000 cars could not satisfy the demand. The soonest Chrysler could receive more four-cylinder engines was early 1981—a delay that severely restricted the number of small cars the company could produce, left it unable to meet the surging demand for small fuel-efficient cars, and caused it to lose a great share of the market to its competitors. Had Chrysler made the correct decision, it would have improved its market position and had more research-and-development money for the future. In his opening statement for the House Subcommittee on Economic Stabilization hearings for a Chrysler bailout, Congressman Stewart B. McKinney named poor management rather than the burden of regulation as the cause of the firm's financial difficulties:

We could probably ease all of the regulations that Chrysler objects to and the company would still not be able to survive in today's market. Chrysler chose to make big cars, trucks and vans when the competition decided to concentrate on smaller and lighter cars. Chrysler continued to produce cars without orders while the competition produced to meet orders. Chrysler used outside suppliers for its components while the competition manufactured its own. (U.S. Congress, House 1979a, 5)

Congressman Richard Kelly concurred:

Chrysler is in trouble because through a long series of bad judgments it has rendered itself non-competitive. . . . In 1969, before any of the Federal regulations being blamed by the company were in place, a failure to downsize its automobiles caused Chrysler to suffer a drop in earnings of almost 70 percent, while its long-term debt soared almost 400 percent. . . . These factors are in no way attributable to government regulations. (U.S. Congress, House 1979a, 6)

Moreover, results of a National Highway and Traffic Safety Administration (NHTSA) study contradicted Chrysler's assertion that regulations placed a disproportionate burden on the smallest of the Big Three automakers. The study concluded that regulations actually imposed higher costs on the larger automobile firms: "Total investment costs tend to be roughly proportionate to sales volume. This occurs because although compliance costs may be equal per model, or per engine or per transmission line, the larger firms have more of these than the smaller ones." The study also rejected the argument that compliance with regulations was more expensive per car for the smaller firms: "In fact, the exact opposite is the case. Historically, GM's capital investments per vehicle were about 15 percent higher than Ford's. Ford's were at least that much higher than Chrysler's, and Chrysler's were several times more than American Motors" (U.S. Congress, House 1979a, 451–452).

Finally, although Chrysler argued that fuel efficiency standards forced the firm to invest in expensive retooling, consumer demand for fuel-efficient cars (after the 1974 fuel disruptions) was forcing the firm to retool as a marketing strategy: "According to recent statements made by . . . GM and Ford, the market is now demanding more fuel economy than current regulations require, thus mitigating the investment effect of fuel economy standards" (U.S. Congress, House 1979a, 453). Even Iacocca admitted that the Big Three automakers ignored the public's demand for small cars, pursuing instead the higher profits derived from the sale of big cars and producing poor-quality small cars (such as the Ford Pinto): "We owe the public a little more than we've been giving them" (*Business Week,* 22 Sept. 1980, 84; see also Iacocca 1984, 151–166, 217). Thus federal regulatory standards were largely irrelevant. "Any regulatory relief would have failed to provide Chrysler with what it needed most: hard cash" (Moritz and Seaman 1981, 270).

Other managerial decisions dating back as far as 1949 contributed to Chrysler's financial difficulties. Before 1949 Chrysler had steadily cultivated a "reputation for sound engineering" and by 1946 enjoyed a 25.7 percent share of the national market (*Newsweek,* 13 Aug. 1979, 58; see also Iacocca 1984, 148–149). An NHTSA study pointed out that between 1949 and 1953 the firm "had no funded debt and maintained a rate of dividend payout which averaged about 65 percent of earnings (identical to GM)." Yet in 1950 Ford overtook Chrysler's position. The NHTSA study listed "poor market acceptance" of Chrysler's revamped 1953 models as a factor contributing to its loss of market share, which "dropped from 20 to 13 percent [by 1954]—a position never to be recovered" (U.S. Congress, House 1979a, 505–506). Chrysler's management decided to focus on style rather than engineering to defend its share of the U.S. market, but its position continued to slip.

The NHTSA study revealed a number of strategies from this period that backfired on Chrysler:

In the mid-1950s, Chrysler's passenger car divisions had nearly the same number of total dealer franchises as GM, even though Chrysler had only one-fourth the sales of GM. This plan was originally intended to maximize Plymouth sales; however, it resulted in smaller dealer margins as well as poor dealer-manufacturer relations. (U.S. Congress, House 1979a, 506)

Despite these problems—and the disappointing profit performance of its expensive foreign subsidiary, Simca—Chrysler decided to maintain a high dividend payout rate and to raise investment capital through debt financing. By 1957 "Chrysler's capital structure included 34 cents of funded debt for each dollar of shareholder's equity," compared with 5 cents for GM and 9 cents for Ford (U.S. Congress, House 1979a, 506). This high debt-to-equity ratio laid the foundation for Chrysler's later cash flow shortage.

In an attempt to compete with Ford and GM, Chrysler's chairman, Lynn A. Townsend, decided in the 1950s to "match every Ford and GM product line with one of his own." But this emphasis on matching styles in short-term competitiveness for market share produced long-term hazards. "Chrysler neglected to update its core facilities," and this neglect eventually pushed Chrysler's production cost per car 10 percent higher than GM's (*Newsweek*, 13 Aug. 1979, 58). Moreover, the decision to produce models similar to the other auto manufacturers' placed Chrysler in "more direct competition with GM and Ford" (U.S. Congress, House 1979a, 507). Chrysler could not hope to prosper in this head-to-head confrontation in the market, since the other two manufacturers had already staked out substantial market shares.

Chrysler's production strategy also differed from GM and Ford's, a choice that was to haunt Chrysler later. GM and Ford built vehicles strictly by order from dealers. "By doing this, the companies are immediately paid as the cars roll off the assembly line" (U.S. Congress, House 1979a, 502). Chrysler produced cars for its inventory rather than as a response to orders, and this strategy resulted in enormous stockpiles of unsold cars.

Chrysler had been adhering to this practice since the 1960s as a means to store cars in slow periods and quickly take advantage of anticipated market surges. Although this procedure worked for awhile, it started to backfire during the early 1970s when sales growth was low. In the recession of 1975, Chrysler had a backlog of 60,000 cars in its "sales bank" . . . and 110,000 units in June 1979. (U.S. Congress, House 1979a, 502–503; see also Iacocca 1984, 162–164)

In another critical strategy that set Chrysler apart from GM and Ford, Chrysler's management purchased parts from outside suppliers rather than vertically integrating as GM and Ford had done. By 1964 Chrysler's outside purchases amounted to 64 percent of revenue, compared with 52 percent for GM and 62 percent for Ford (U.S. Congress, House 1979a, 508).

Between 1968 and 1970 Chrysler gambled by stepping up its investment program during an economically unstable period, "basing its decision on factors such as strong growth in population, rising incomes and improved highways. This decision, unfortunately, coincided with the 1969–70 recession" (U.S. Congress, House 1979a, 508). Meanwhile, Townsend decided to expand the firm's focus from the U.S. market to the world market, constructing factories in Europe, South America, South Africa, and Australia. This move further eroded the company's available resources to compete on the domestic market (*Newsweek*, 13 Aug. 1979, 58; see also Iacocca 1984, 154–155). Moreover, Chrysler's attempt to become a multinational came too late, long "after Ford and GM had acquired the best operations" (U.S. Congress, House 1979a, 912). Chrysler's rate of profit dropped dramatically from 5.8 percent in 1950 to −3.4 percent in 1958. The firm's global expansion marked an effort to raise its falling rate of profit and to compete effectively with GM and Ford. But the expansion seriously "drain[ed] the corporation of funds, depleting monies for domestic investment and creating for the company a huge and unmanageable debt burden" (Detroit Socialist Collective 1980, 8, 23).

Finally, in 1974 Riccardo replaced Townsend as chairman and proceeded to pare down Chrysler's staff to reduce costs. But by then the damage had been done, and Riccardo faced the additional problem of the recession of 1974–1975. Despite his efforts to reverse Chrysler's problems, the firm lost $260 million in 1975. Moreover, many observers argue that Riccardo's drastic paring down of staff caused Chrysler to get "a late start on redesign of new products" after the recession, "and it was that late start that really hurt them the most" (*Newsweek*, 13 Aug. 1979, 58). Chrysler's vulnerability at that time was clearly a result of poor management decisions. The company had decided not to produce a subcompact car "to compete with GM's Vega and Ford's Pinto, both introduced in the 1971 model year." Townsend decided instead to "redesign Chrysler's big cars," which were marketed in the fall of 1973, "just months before the Arab oil embargo destroyed the market for gas guzzlers" (*Business Week*, 20 Aug. 1979, 105). Whereas GM responded to the gas crisis with a major shift in product emphasis, Chrysler responded by laying off "hundreds of engineers, which obviously set the company back further in terms of planning future projects." According to Howard J. Symons, staff attorney for Public Citizen's Congress Watch, by 1974 Chrysler had "laid off 80% of its engineering staff" (U.S. Congress, House 1979a, 171, 913). When gas prices doubled once more in 1979, Chrysler was pummeled again for its emphasis on large cars, recreational vehicles, vans, and motor homes as sales on these gas guzzlers plummeted. Van sales, for example, fell by 50 percent (Iacocca 1984, 183). Thus Chrysler was hardly the innocent victim of circumstances; poor management decisions made it especially vulnerable to economic recession and fuel disruptions.

By the time Chrysler reentered the compact car market with its Volare and Aspen models in 1976, sales of intermediate-size cars had already begun to slow down. In addition, these models were poorly made in the rush to get them to market. "More than three and a half million cars were brought back to the dealers for free repairs—free to the customer, that is. Chrysler had to foot the bill" (Iacocca 1984, 160). Over this long series of decisions management was clearly out of touch with the market and with consumers.

Chrysler wanted government assistance because it could not get assistance from normal business sources—mainly the banks. The firm therefore contrived a set of arguments to justify a federal bailout. The rationales Chrysler offered for the various strategies it adopted or attempted reflect the inherent constraints on nonfinancial corporations that need to access capital flows. Chrysler first pursued government assistance by claiming that the government was responsible for the automaker's deepening financial difficulties.

When this claim was refuted, Chrysler appealed instead for loan guarantees from mostly hostile congressional banking committees. Chrysler was in for a long struggle.

The Loan Agreement

In 1979 G. William Miller replaced Michael Blumenthal as Treasury secretary, and Chrysler found itself struggling anew for some relief. Miller based his strategy for handling the Chrysler situation on the hope of wringing "major concessions from the company, its suppliers, its bankers, and its union" (*Business Week*, 27 Aug. 1979, 36).

After frustratingly slow progress, the federal government finally conceded. In November 1979 the Carter administration endorsed a maximum federal loan guarantee to Chrysler of $750 million (*New York Times*, 29 June 1980, F1). But the threat of a coming recession forced the government to double this figure to $1.5 billion. The plan called for Chrysler to raise $1.5 billion from sales of its assets and from concessions made by its workers, suppliers, dealers, and bankers. It is not clear why the federal government determined to rescue Chrysler; what is clear is that it ultimately succumbed to the enormous lobbying efforts on the firm's behalf.[1]

Carter's endorsement did not secure $1.5 billion for Chrysler. The loan guarantee still needed congressional approval. After lengthy hearings, Congress offered a proposal for a federal loan guarantee on the condition that the United Auto Workers (UAW) concede $1.2 billion—"the equivalent of a three year wage freeze for union and non-union employees." The proposal also required a total of $1.43 billion in concessions from Chrysler's dealers,

---

1. Rogers-Millar and Millar (1979) have suggested that power involves a situation in which the participants in a conflict share a common perception of one another's resources and one another's ability to use those resources. This version of Thomas's (1928) definition of the situation may be seen at work in Chrysler's struggle. The federal government perceived real power in the financial community's collective control of capital flows. The government also considered the U.S. economy unable to withstand the shock and reverberations of a Chrysler bankruptcy (see Iacocca 1984). Regardless of the validity of that perception, the Carter administration endorsed the loan guarantee, setting in motion the long struggle over concessions. Although the process of federal involvement in and commitment to rescuing Chrysler is important and interesting, it is beyond the scope of this research.

suppliers, and banks, and from state and local governments (Moritz and Seaman 1981, 285). The stage was now set for a great struggle between Chrysler, its workers, the banks, and the federal and state governments.

Conditions of the Loan Agreement: The Struggle

The Banks

John F. McGillicuddy, chairman of Chrysler's lead bank, Manufacturers Hanover Trust, expressed the sentiments of the banking community when he said that further loans to Chrysler were "not feasible" without federal loan guarantees and policy changes in the firm (*New York Times,* 31 Oct. 1979, A1). Several bankers told Congress that such loan guarantees were necessary for the private creditors to lend more money to Chrysler. McGillicuddy told Congress that U.S. and foreign banks had provided Chrysler with $4.8 billion in credit lines and loans. Furthermore, Manufacturers Hanover had acted as agent for 102 banks in providing a $567 million line of credit, of which $408 million was currently outstanding. Another 36 domestic banks had provided $64 million to the firm, all of which was outstanding (U.S. Congress, House 1979a, 824, 333). If Chrysler went bankrupt, the federal government would be required to pay all outstanding debt owed to the banks (*New York Times,* 2 Nov. 1979, D4). Meanwhile, to garner congressional approval the loan guarantee would have to stipulate more favorable terms for Chrysler—a stipulation that did not please the banking community at all (*New York Times,* 29 June 1980, F19).

The banking community also struggled with Congress on the issue of governmental control of Chrysler. The banking community pressed for a greatly scaled-down firm rather than the full-line producer Lee Iacocca envisioned. But Senator Proxmire's intent to restrict the firm to the production of only small cars was apparently too scaled down for the banking community. Furthermore, both Chrysler and the banking community recognized the need to retool and automate if the firm was to continue to compete (although the banks did not want to fund such efforts).[2] One of Chrysler's key bankers threatened: "If we wind up with a real Christmas tree of a bill that gives the company no operating room, then a rescue would be impossible. . . . None of the third parties would want to put additional money into the company." Another banker claimed, "Somebody is going to have to back down . . . and it may be the government" (*Business Week*, 3 Dec. 1979, 42). Because of the standoff between the government and the banking community, many feared that if the loan guarantee package was not passed before Congress recessed for Christmas "there [might] be nothing left to save" when Congress reconvened in January. By then "Chrysler would have gone past the point where aid would be successful" (U.S. Congress, House 1979a, 1190). The threat implicit in the power of the banking community was clear: "If the bailout legislation stumbles badly in Congress, the lenders may run out of hope or patience, and any one of a multitude of creditors could force Chrysler into involuntary bankruptcy" (*Business Week*, 10 Dec. 1979, 36, 37).

The stalemate helped the banking community scare Congress into passing the bill: although "the banks could easily withstand the financial consequences of a Chrysler bankruptcy," the federal government did not think the U.S. economy could (*Business Week*, 10 Dec. 1979, 37). In testimony before the House subcommittee, McGillicuddy held the federal government responsible for action:

When you are talking about a company that is part of an industry, that is part of the mainspring and fiber of the United States, that has tremendous implications in terms of employment, both within their own company as well as the suppliers—I think that you are at a point where the implications are such that you who are sitting here today in hearings . . . have to make a judgment. That is a task that is yours and not mine. (U.S. Congress, House 1979a, 836–837)

McGillicuddy argued that the loan guarantee was needed "promptly" for the banking community to act, emphasizing that "a sign from the Federal government in terms of whether they will

2. Ironically, automation would later eliminate most of the jobs suspended after the union's concessionary bargaining (see *Business Week*, 23 May 1983, 168–170).

or will not act really can't come too soon in terms of the general group [of creditors]." Chrysler's executive vice president and senior financial officer, Gerald Greenwald, testified: "It is clear that the banking community today would not increase its loans to Chrysler in the absence of a firmer program involving Federal aid." And Tom Killefer, chairman of the board of U.S. Trust Co. of New York, stated: "I believe the banking community will continue to show . . . support of . . . [Chrysler] in the future, but quick action by the government is essential in order to assure this" (U.S. Congress, House 1979a, 839–840, 290, 822).

The banking community enjoyed the power to define and create a corporate crisis out of Chrysler's cash flow difficulties and to force the state to make concessions to the banks: "Chrysler's future depends on the willingness of some private lenders to come up with that money. Its major institutional creditors—banks and insurance companies—have been taking a hard line, in hopes that the government would provide interim assistance" (*Business Week,* 31 Dec. 1979, 32). Consequently the stalemate between the banking community and the state was finally resolved in favor of the banks. The Treasury Department proposed a bill with "less stringent terms than it would have liked" because time was running out: "The company was sinking fast, and a House Banking subcommittee was ready to push out a bill with or without the [Carter] Administration's concurrence. As a result, much of the government's leverage over the existing creditors evaporated. And because no single bank [was] owed more than $30 million by Chrysler, the banks had little to lose by forcing a bankruptcy" (*Business Week,* 19 Nov. 1979, 47).

Congress finally approved the loan guarantees for $1.5 billion in late December 1979. But passage of the bill produced a great deal of anger and resentment over the force and pressure the banking community exerted. Congressman Bruce F. Vento complained that the federal government had absorbed the financial institutions' risk in extending credit to Chrysler:

Really, as much as bailing out Chrysler . . . we are helping those financial institutions because they had no basis when they went forward and they are getting 12 or 15 percent interest. They assumed a certain amount of risk. When we come in, we are picking up the risk and we are bailing them out, as well as we are, for example, the other social concerns, which we all feel deeply about. (U.S. Congress, House 1979a, 314)

Congressman Norman D. Shumway pointed out the incongruity that the banking community (traditionally in the business of taking risks) refused to take any further risk with Chrysler while insisting that the federal government take that risk:

Chrysler proponents claim that once Federal assistance has been granted the corporation will soon return to the ranks of the profitable. If this is so, I can't understand why private lenders are not jumping at this opportunity to extend credit—a nice rate of return—to a firm that is surely going to be profitable. If this is not the case, if private lenders do not believe such loans could necessarily be recovered, I just have to wonder how much more confident we in the Federal government should be. (U.S. Congress, House 1979a, 819)

Congressmen Norman E. D'Amours and Ron Paul were more bitter. D'Amours argued, "So in point of fact we are asking the taxpayers to take a risk that the banking community which is in the business and has the expertise to make loans . . . is unwilling to take." Congressman Paul noted that the existing loans the banks had extended to Chrysler would be secured by a federal loan guarantee: "I can't see how this can be construed as anything but an aid to the banks" (U.S. Congress, House 1979a, 838, 847).

Laments about the relative helplessness of the state to resist the power of the banking community in its bid for a bailout echoed in congressional hearings to increase the U.S. quota in the International Monetary Fund (IMF) to bail out the debt burdens of developing countries. Bank representatives and some federal officials insisted that such an increase amounted to a "jobs bill" for American workers, since the IMF would bail out countries that were major importers of American goods. But many members of congress continually expressed anger and frustration in their analyses that bailing out a country's debt is in fact bailing out poor or unmanageable bank investments (U.S. Congress, House 1982, 1983b, 1983c; Senate 1983a, 1983b). This sentiment is precisely the one articulated in Chrysler's case.

The banking community wanted the federal government to assume the risk of granting the future loan guarantees to Chrysler, thus bailing out the banks' investments and protecting them from further risk. Because banks make a substantial proportion of their money from commercial lending, their profitability was threatened by the prospect of a Chrysler bankruptcy (although the threat was less problematic for each individual bank than for the federal government, which was struggling to achieve a healthy economy in an election year). The federal loan guarantee capped that risk, thereby guaranteeing bank profits.

A second objective of the banking community was to force Chrysler to become a pared-down, limited-line automaker. This objective appears to have been instrumental in accomplishing the banks' first objective of maximum risk-free recovery of investment. If Chrysler had to sell off some of its operations, the proceeds from the sales could reduce Chrysler's debt burden to the banks. Although this may have been sound advice for the automaker in the short run, it would have long-term deleterious effects on Chrysler's competitive position. The banking community does not typically involve itself in day-to-day corporate decision making and thus could do little to demand a reduced product line directly. Instead the banks forced the state, which has the legitimate power to enforce conditional legislation such as a loan guarantee, to impose and implement operational modifications and restrictions on the automaker. Requiring a limited product line as a condition of a bailout restricted Chrysler's managerial discretion to make fundamental decisions on production. At the same time, it assured the banking community's first objective: a risk-free recovery of investment.

Now that Chrysler had been granted a federal loan guarantee, the firm "had to raise $1.5 billion in private capital and meet a series of tough conditions that would give the government tremendous control over the company" (*New York Times*, 29 June 1980, F19). For example, the loan guarantee required Chrysler "to submit each purchase contract of more than $10 million to the Chrysler Loan Guarantee Board, created by Congress. That means that many of the contracts to purchase supplies and parts for auto production must be reviewed by Federal authorities" (*New York Times*, 17 May 1980, D1). This requirement placed the federal government in a position to control the day-to-day management decisions of the firm, including "the most fundamental of market-

ing decisions" (*New York Times*, 27 May 1980, D1). According to
a Treasury official, although the federal government did not dictate
"for instance, what options to make standard on its [Chrysler's]
new cars, . . . 'If we don't agree with their plans, they have to
modify it'" (*Business Week*, 7 July 1980, 22).

This potential governmental role in Chrysler was a concession
the banking community had to make to get the federal loan guarantees it wanted. Although the federal government now apparently
had operational control of Chrysler, the banks still maintained allocative control over the investment capital the firm needed to survive. And whereas the federal government did not enforce its operational power over Chrysler, the banks persistently exercised their
allocative power to constrain the firm's day-to-day decision making.
This pattern of the active exercise of bank discretion as a constraining influence on the operational power of a nonfinancial firm resembles the pattern identified in the W. T. Grant bankruptcy case.

With the loan guarantees in place, and with Chrysler required
to raise a similar amount in unsecured private funds, the banking
community took a more aggressively steadfast position. The banks
had wrung concessions and contributions from the workers, the
suppliers, and several state governments. But "resistance from the
bankers [remained] a huge stumbling block in Chrysler's efforts
to assemble the $2 billion package enabling it to qualify for $1.5
billion in Federal loan guarantees. Chrysler's major domestic lenders . . . steadfastly refused to provide the company with any new
money, on the ground that dealers, suppliers, and others should
ante up first" (*Business Week*, 7 Apr. 1980, 30). Congressman
McKinney repeatedly admonished the banks for their "deafening
silence" when asked to join labor, states, the federal government,
suppliers, and dealers in making concessions and offering aid to
Chrysler (U.S. Congress, House 1979a, 289, 818).

Bankers' resistance to the loan agreement's requirement of more
favorable credit terms for Chrysler was the subject of a meeting
held between Chrysler's major banks and three legislators to gently
but firmly force the banks to accept the terms (*New York Times*,
28 June 1980, F19). The bases of the banks' power were (1) their
strategically unified position in the Chrysler bailout plan, thanks
to their common presence in a huge lending consortium; (2) their
threat not to extend further credit to the firm, despite the antici-

pated severe consequences to the U.S. economy of a Chrysler bankruptcy; and (3) congressional and federal government willingness to accept the banks' definition of Chrysler's situation. The legislators' strong suit was power to pass bank reform legislation, which the banking community wanted. One of Chrysler's bankers attending the meeting felt that "the implicit message of the meeting was clear . . . 'If we wanted the bank reform legislation being considered by Congress, we had better be flexible on Chrysler'" (*New York Times,* 29 June 1980, F19). Congressional arm-twisting was apparently effective. By 24 April 1980 several of Chrysler's banks had finally "been persuaded to purchase shares of stock in the company as one way of providing new cash." The banks had been asked to buy $200 million in preferred stock (*New York Times,* 25 Apr. 1980, D1).

Chrysler's condition continued to worsen. The fear that Chrysler would run out of money by early May prompted a meeting with Chrysler's 325 banks to produce a huge financial reorganization plan. This plan, which enabled Chrysler to begin using the $1.5 billion in federally guaranteed loans, was termed a "bitter pill" for the lenders: "$660 million in interest deferrals and reductions plus a 4-year extension of some $4 billion in debt to Chrysler and its credit subsidiary, Chrysler Financial Corp." The banks reluctantly agreed to the compromise, but only after major concessions had been wrung from the UAW, the suppliers, the dealers, and state and federal governments. It was the lesser of two evils for the banks, which would otherwise have faced "the prospect of getting only 30 cents on the dollar in a protracted liquidation" (*Business Week,* 28 Apr. 1980, 27). The measures provided by the restructuring plan were termed "soft funding."

The bankers found their pill less bitter than it seemed at first. Since the funds raised by the restructuring plan were essentially "soft" (rather than the hard cash provided by new loans), "virtually all of the 'new' money available to Chrysler for refurbishing its product lines and plants [would] come from government backing by Washington, several states, and Canada" (*Business Week,* 26 May 1980, 555). The banks did not provide any new money to Chrysler in the form of new loans. They merely agreed to defer the firm's interest payments. Thus any new money the company needed would come from loans made to Chrysler by the federal and state governments (see the section on state and local governments, below) and by Canada, which agreed to lend $200 million to $250 million in government aid to Chrysler's Canadian division (*New York Times,* 3 May 1980, D1). Moreover, the banks took twelve million Chrysler stock warrants, "good until 1990, which could be exercised if the Chrysler stock ever reached $13 a share" (Iacocca 1984, 244). Since the stock was then selling at $3.50 a share, the banks stood to receive a substantial profit later (which indeed they did). Chrysler's banks thus made far fewer concessions than originally appeared, and they succeeded in forcing the state and labor to bear the greatest burden in bailing out Chrysler: whereas the state provided loans and labor made major concessions, the banks advanced no new money at all.

Despite the banking community's stunning tenacity in refusing to add new money to the Chrysler financial package, the banks suffered a major setback (at least initially): they exchanged loans for equity. Therefore they were at enormous risk to lose a large portion of their investment. But they had already indicated that they were ready to take this risk when they agreed to accept a return of 60 to 80 cents on the dollar. In other words, the struggle with the government did not alter the banks' posture at all, because the government had little leverage over them. The banks and the government both believed that a Chrysler bankruptcy would be a greater blow to the state than to the banks. So even though the banks did not get everything they wanted, they were clearly in the more powerful position.

By June 1980 most of the banks had agreed to the terms of the loan. But in a reprise of a similar drama in W. T. Grant's bankruptcy, the larger banks always insisted that "everyone sink or swim with the company" (*Business Week,* 8 Oct. 1979, 33). The lenders' restructuring plan hinged on an agreement by Chrysler's major banks that "they would participate only if all 400 voted unanimously to join them. . . . Unless all fall into line, the Chrysler Loan Guarantee Board . . . is likely to remain unwilling to authorize the loan guarantees" (*New York Times,* 17 June 1980, D8). Both the large and the small banks depended on the loan guarantees to recover their loans to Chrysler. But the structure of the lending consortium gave the large financial institutions the power to pressure the small banks into accepting an arrangement the small ones did not want.

One of the more compelling reasons why the small banks acquiesced is that the largest, most lucrative loans to corporations require the structure of a lending consortium, because banks are legally barred from lending more than 10 percent of their capital to any one borrower. Since such consortia are standard structures in the commercial loan industry, the small banks rely on inclusion in those structures to gain access to large corporate business. Clearly small banks run the risk of being excluded from future lending consortia if they develop a reputation for deserting the group in a crisis.

One of the more irksome factors for the small banks was that the major lenders alone formulated the restructuring plan with Chrysler. Excluded from developing the plan, the small banks were nonetheless expected "to comply with it," but "they maintained that they would not be dictated to by a third party on how to deal with a customer" (*New York Times,* 22 June 1980, F19). David W. Knapp, president of the American National Bank and Trust Company in Rockford (one of the recalcitrant small banks) complained that "the decision and control rests with the large banks" (*New York Times,* 17 June 1980, D8). Originally about twenty small banks balked at the agreement. Meanwhile some of Chrysler's major European lenders wanted to withdraw their participation and would not renew their lines of credit to the firm (*Business Week,* 8 Oct. 1979, 33). These banks were angered by the loan guarantee stipulation that the federal government would get first lien on Chrysler's assets, "including Chrysler's compensating deposits in their own banks," in the event of a default by the firm (*Business Week,* 23 June 1980, 30). They argued that the large banks had given Chrysler greater concessions than the small banks thought necessary. Furthermore, they felt that they were less likely than the large banks to recover their loans, "regardless of whether Chrysler eventually emerged solvent or bankrupt" (*New York Times,* 22 June 1980, F19).

The large banks and their supporters goaded the recalcitrant banks into agreement. Knapp told the *New York Times:* "We've had calls from Chrysler, from suppliers, asking that we be reasonable. . . . We have calls from other banks and I just told them we're not interested in getting in the agreement. I'm sure I'll get more phone calls." Finally, on 17 June 1980, the deadlock began to break. One of the recalcitrant banks, York Bank and Trust Company of York, Pennsylvania, agreed to go along with the large banks. Rodney E. Rohrbaugh, executive vice president, said that his bank was under "a lot of pressure but our decision is honestly based on our own assessment" (*New York Times,* 18 June 1980, D1, D5). That assessment apparently revealed that the large banks were in a better position to survive a Chrysler bankruptcy than the small banks. Furthermore, Treasury Secretary G. William Miller began to make "a series of personal phone appeals" to the re-calcitrant banks (*New York Times,* 22 June 1980, F19). These "appeals" reminded the small banks that the loan guarantees on which they depended would not materialize unless they acqui-esced. By 24 June 1980 approximately thirty thousand investors agreed to lend Chrysler $500 million in ten-year notes at 10.35 percent interest (*New York Times,* 29 June 1980, F2; see also Iacocca 1984, 241–248).

The unification of the financial community is the main source of bank power. Individual banks' control of capital flows would not necessarily translate into discretionary power, whereas hegemonic or unified control does. To minimize or eliminate points of conten-tion that might undermine the discretionary powers of the banking community, large banks may discipline small recalcitrant banks (as they did in both the Chrysler and W. T. Grant cases). This ac-tion solidifies the collective control of capital flows and conse-quently banks' relative discretionary powers.

The restructuring agreement did not express the banking com-munity's confidence in Chrysler's financial future. Rather, it was a way for the banks to protect their investment: "Many skeptical lenders view the reorganization as no more than a stopgap to allow for an orderly sale of Chrysler Financial Corp. . . . which would insulate the bulk of their loans from what many fear will be the inevitable demise of Chrysler when the federal guarantees run out in 1983" (*Business Week,* 7 July 1980, 22). Indeed, the sag-ging U.S. automobile market in 1980–1981 caused more finan-cial difficulties for the already beleaguered firm and forced it to turn once again to the federal government for the needed capital.

Chrysler had already used $800 million of its $1.5 billion in federally guaranteed loans and was now asking for $400 million more.

To convince the federal government of its need for more loans,
Chrysler asked its lenders "to convert $572 million in loans to pre-
ferred stock. It . . . pleaded with suppliers to forgo December payments worth some $233 million. It [was] pressuring the United
Auto Workers to generate an additional $250 million in conces-
sions beyond the $446 million given so far by Chrysler's UAW
workers" (*Business Week*, 29 Dec. 1980, 43). The firm's banks resisted the idea of converting their loans to preferred stock, "claiming that the company's most immediate problem [was] not net
worth" but "cash" (*Business Week*, 19 Jan. 1981, 29). This was an
ironic position for the banks to take, given that they had previously refused to provide any new hard funding to the firm and instead forced the other participants (including the UAW and the
government) to provide greater concessions and cash. Ultimately
the banks agreed to the conversion as a necessary trade-off for the
bank deregulation they wanted.

The United Auto Workers

In August 1979 Iacocca asked the UAW for aid in the form of an
exemption for the firm in the union's contract negotiations and "a
two-year freeze on both wages and fringe benefits. [UAW president
Douglas A.] Fraser promptly rejected the proposal." Chrysler's
workers had already aided the company by buying $37.3 million
of its common stock, which was at its lowest value in 1979 ($7.63
per share), when Chrysler approached the UAW for contract concessions (*Newsweek*, 13 Aug. 1979, 52, 61). Moreover, by 1980
more than 210,000 workers had lost their jobs (*Business Week*,
24 Mar. 1980, 79), with no guarantee of job protection in sight.
Some observers were angry at the UAW's stand, arguing that the
workers had a stake in Chrysler's survival. Arnold R. Weber suggested in a *New York Times* column (24 Aug. 1979, D2) that the
UAW "could use a substantial portion of the [union's $300 million
strike] fund to take an equity position in the company." Congressman Kelly argued that "instead of striking to further depress conditions of production in the United States, they ought to use [the

strike fund] . . . to try and save the jobs of the UAW members that are involved with Chrysler" (U.S. Congress, House 1979a, 248).

The union refused to consider the proposal on the grounds that such an investment would severely undermine their bargaining position against Ford and GM. In addition, Fraser pointed out that using the union's strike fund for other purposes would violate the union's constitution: "Under the terms of our constitution . . . there are several restrictions on [the use of the strike fund]. . . . There is a question in my mind whether you can take money that is supposed to protect all of the workers in our union in times of strike and give that money to one section of our union" (U.S. Congress, House 1979a, 290). Instead, the union suggested that it could offer some aid in contract negotiations in exchange for "representation on the Chrysler board of directors and participation in the management decisions at all levels of the corporation" (*New York Times*, 24 Aug. 1979, D2). Worker representation on a corporate board had no precedent in U.S. labor history.

By October 1979 the prospects of worker representation on the board and employee stock ownership in exchange for union concessions to Chrysler looked promising. Both the union and key members of the Senate (such as Majority Leader Robert C. Byrd and Senate Finance Committee Chairman Russell Long) became convinced that any federal aid "ought to be conditioned on Chrysler's workers' being able to win a chunk of the corporation, or at least to influence decisionmaking 'at all levels of the corporation'" (*Business Week*, 1 Oct. 1979, 46). Senator Donald W. Stewart entered a statement into the *Congressional Record* on 10 October 1979 supporting the notion of an employee stock ownership plan and asserting that such stock should carry voting rights for the employee-owners to facilitate worker participation in management decision making: "If we are to achieve the revitalization of Chrysler, each employee must be sure that he [*sic*] has some voice in the future of his [*sic*] company." Several members of Congress argued: "If the current owners are asking employees to make sacrifices, it is important that the employees gain something in return, such as an increased ownership share and participation in the company" (U.S. Congress, House 1979a, 333, 327).

One of the most important levels of participation the UAW demanded was in pension investment decisions—an implicit recognition of the power afforded the controllers of pension funds and the political implications of worker participation in pension fund investment decisions (see Rifkin and Barber 1978). The UAW's plan would have given workers a voice in the control of those capital flows derived from their own deferred wages and a strong weapon in the class struggle. For example, the UAW and Chrysler "agreed that, in the future, part of the company's pension contributions will be used to fund 'socially desirable projects,' rather than to buy common stocks or government securities, as in the past." Such projects might include

home mortgages, health maintenance centers, and nursing homes in communities with Chrysler plants. . . . In a related provision, the union won the right to name up to five companies each year whose stock it wants the pension fund to shun because of their involvement in South Africa and their failure to endorse the "Sullivan principles" of racial equality. (*Business Week*, 12 Nov. 1979, 93)

Note, however, that the agreement to fund such projects did not include labor participation in determining the actual projects to ultimately receive funding or the amount each project would get. The union also demanded worker participation in decisions concerning plant closings. As of 1987 Chrysler's pension contributions had not funded any of the "socially desirable projects" the union had suggested. Indeed, in February 1982 the firm asked the union to allow it "to defer for a second time payments of $187 million to [the union's] pension fund" (*New York Times*, 22 Feb. 1982, D1).

The Carter administration looked favorably on the use of employee stock ownership plans to aid the ailing firm. The struggle over contract concessions in exchange for labor representation on Chrysler's board, worker participation in decision making, and profit sharing for workers became key issues in Chrysler's attempt to persuade workers to bail it out. In March 1980 Fraser was elected to Chrysler's board of directors at its annual stockholder meeting (*New York Times*, 4 Nov. 1979, F19).

In mid-October 1979 Fraser offered Chrysler a "package of possible contract concessions," including the deferral of $200 million in pension fund payments for 1979 and a lower wage and benefit package than that offered Ford and GM workers. This offer represented "a departure from the [union's] 42 years of history and practice and tradition" (U.S. Congress, House 1979a, 288, 275; *New York Times,* 18 Oct. 1979, D5). Fraser also suggested that the UAW would "be willing to lend virtually all of the union's $850 million in pension funds to Chrysler, provided the loan was fully guaranteed by the federal government to protect the worker's benefits" (*New York Times,* 20 Oct. 1979, 31). But Fraser still refused to lend Chrysler any money from the union's strike fund. He further insisted that although Chrysler workers were willing to negotiate a less advantageous contract with Chrysler than with GM or Ford, they must have parity with the workers of the other two firms by the end of the three-year contract. The wage and benefit concessions meant that Chrysler workers earned $2,000 less than their counterparts at Ford and GM over the three-year contract (*Business Week,* 12 Nov. 1979, 93).

The union's concessions to Chrysler made up the bulk of the $500 million worth of concessions the automaker had to raise from its "constituents and employees" in its bid for federal aid (*Business Week,* 5 Nov. 1979, 55). The company's survival plan included $203 million in UAW wage concessions and the union's $200 million pension fund rollover for Chrysler (U.S. Congress, House 1979a, 318). Fraser acknowledged the union's lack of enthusiasm for the concessions it made to the firm, saying, "We're doing what we have to do" to save members' jobs (*Business Week,* 5 Nov. 1979, 55). He urged the federal government to provide loan guarantees to the firm.

Workers' concessions to Chrysler were considered insufficient when the House Committee on Banking, Finance, and Urban Affairs approved the federal loan guarantees for $1.5 billion. Alfred E. Kahn, chairman of the Carter administration's Council on Wage and Price Stability, suggested that the government was guaranteeing worker's wage increases and argued that the contract concessions made by the union "'should not . . . be considered adequate' to satisfy the legislation's requirement that workers and other parties with a stake in Chrysler's future make sacrifices to help the company survive" (*New York Times,* 16 Nov. 1979, D13). Yet by the end of the House subcommittee hearings, Congressman James J. Blanchard pointed out that although the point of the loan guarantee legislation was to ensure that all interested parties with a stake in the firm make concessions, "the UAW is the only party, thus far, that has made any form of concession" (U.S. Congress, House 1979a, 1395).

When the Senate Banking, Housing, and Urban Affairs Committee approved $1.5 billion in federal loan guarantees for the firm, it required the workers to give up wage increases already approved in their three-year contract with Chrysler. This concession would impose a wage and compensation freeze for three years and required that the contract be renegotiated for the company to draw on the loan guarantees. The committee's demand marked "an unusual intervention by Congress in the collective bargaining process" (*New York Times*, 30 Nov. 1979, D1).

The union flatly rejected the three-year wage freeze, "even if [doing so meant] bankruptcy for the company"(*New York Times*, 5 Dec. 1979, D4). Fraser felt that the UAW was being asked to bear the greatest burden in the Chrysler bailout when labor had no voice in the poor managerial decisions that had produced the situation (U.S. Congress, House 1979a, 298).

The union's militant stand forced the Carter administration to acknowledge that the Senate's proposed wage freeze placed an "inequitable burden on the workers" and to suggest modifications to the bill (*New York Times*, 5 Dec. 1979, D4). Even Chrysler sided with the union in denouncing the Senate bill, perhaps out of fear that a complete lack of cooperation by labor would destroy the firm's chances for federal aid.

The union's militancy also confronted the hardened position of the banks. Both groups were important to the survival of Chrysler, because both were required to make concessions to support the firm and enable it to qualify for the federally guaranteed loans. But neither group wanted to "make the first move to rescue the sinking auto maker" (*Business Week*, 1 Dec. 1979, 36). A *Business Week* analysis implied that the banks and the union were equally strong in the struggle (17 Dec. 1979, 32; 16 Mar. 1981, 28). However, labor was hardly the equal of the banking community. The UAW had far more to lose in a Chrysler bankruptcy than the banks. Indeed, the banks' investment would be protected by the federal loan guarantees. Their more favorable position in a bankruptcy, as well as their direct hegemonic control of capital flows, enabled the banks to stall labor, whose only strength was the ability to strike (a strength it could not exercise for fear of job losses if Chrysler went bankrupt).

The UAW relented first when Fraser suggested that the union might be willing to "grant some further concessions to help Chrysler survive" by reopening its Chrysler contract. The union still adamantly opposed a three-year wage freeze. At a 3 December 1979 meeting of the UAW's 233-member Chrysler Bargaining Council in Washington, D.C., "almost to a man [*sic*], they said that they would rather shut down the shop than take a three-year freeze." The union refused to reopen its contract to aid Chrysler without an "'equity of sacrifice' between workers, bankers, and the company" (*Business Week*, 17 Dec. 1979, 31). The search for equity dissolved when the union relented and reopened its contract negotiations with Chrysler, providing the company with "$446 million in concessions from the industry pattern contract" (*New York Times*, 8 Feb. 1980, D2). By now workers had conceded a total of $460 million in wages and benefits. Nevertheless, in December 1980 Chrysler again asked the union for a wage freeze to "persuade the Government to authorize additional loan guarantees for the company." Once again the union bristled. Fraser suggested that the company "go elsewhere first this time." Chrysler planned to ask its banks to convert $500 million in unguaranteed loans to preferred stock, because "a bank that would enter such an arrangement would be unable to make claims against Chrysler if the company failed" (*New York Times*, 13 Dec. 1980, A1, 37). Needless to say, the banks opposed the plan.

In January 1981 the Chrysler Loan Guarantee Board gave the company "conditional approval" to draw $400 million more from its fund. Once again the condition was "major concessions from the United Automobile Workers, the company's lenders, and its suppliers." Chrysler asked the union to give up cost-of-living adjustments and wage increases totaling $622 million, which represented a 13 percent pay cut. Although Fraser had bargained the company down from its original request of $676 million, he termed the wage freeze "'the worst economic settlement' he had ever had to negotiate" (*New York Times*, 15 Jan. 1981, 1, D3). Iacocca (1984, 233) estimated that "over a nineteen-month period, the average working guy [*sic*] at Chrysler gave up close to $10,000."

The union conceded to the wage freeze in the hope of preventing job losses from a Chrysler bankruptcy, which UAW leaders considered the only alternative outcome to the bailout (see Iacocca 1984, 207–208). Bankruptcy would be disastrous for the union, which was already steadily losing members. Although some speculated that a foreign auto manufacturer would have gladly taken over Chrysler's operations (see Schwartz and Yago 1981), a takeover was not necessarily in the best interest of organized labor. Foreign automakers (especially Japanese firms, the most likely takeover candidates) have generally had poor relations with labor unions.

Ironically, labor suffered enormous layoffs even with the concessions. By the end of 1981 Chrysler was operating with 87,825 employees, compared with 133,811 in 1979 (*New York Times*, 29 Aug. 1982, F8). The union's fear of job losses resulting from their refusal to make concessions proved naive.

Chrysler had to give back some of the pension concessions and gave the union "a commitment . . . that it would not close five plants during the life of the contract" (*New York Times*, 15 Jan. 1981, D3). The company also agreed that any further layoffs would include "supervisors . . . in the same proportion as their ratio to union members in the work force" (*Business Week*, 9 Feb. 1981, 30). But this agreement was relatively insignificant, since more than 210,000 union workers had already lost their jobs (*Business Week*, 24 Mar. 1980, 79).

In addition, Chrysler agreed "to consult—perhaps even negotiate—with UAW local committees on all decisions that 'might adversely affect' job security, such as layoffs and plant shutdowns" (*Business Week*, 9 Feb. 1981, 30). Workers also got a profit-sharing plan from the company. But the employee stock ownership plan implicitly placed a further risk of financial loss on workers in the event of a Chrysler bankruptcy. Workers also took on an inequitable burden compared with the firm's principals:

To be sure, Chrysler is a long way from having a net worth of $3.5 billion (the point below which Chrysler has agreed with its banks not to pay out dividends). Thus, shareholders are much more likely to see dilution than dividends in the near future. Disquieting, too, is the fact that Chrysler officers and directors are willing to risk so little of their own money on the company's future. (*Business Week*, 8 June 1981, 103)

Ford and GM, which had been watching Chrysler's struggles from afar, decided that they too would like to squeeze concessions from the union, which had been "one of the nation's leaders in winning wages and benefits for its members." Although these companies were not as financially troubled as Chrysler, they claimed they were unable to compete with Japanese automakers, which operated with lower labor costs. Both firms threatened to "shift more of their production overseas to areas of lower wage costs if the union [did] not accede to their requests" (*New York Times*, 3 June 1981, D1). But neither wanted to make the concessions to the union that Chrysler had made, and the union flatly rejected their demands. By 1982, however, the UAW had given in and made substantial concessions to both firms (see *New York Times*, 1 Mar. 1982, A1; 22 Mar. 1982, A1; 10 Apr. 1982, 1). The UAW's struggle with GM and Ford demonstrated that Chrysler's bankruptcy was not the main threat to labor. Rather, "runaway shops" and the internationalization of production posed the greatest threat. The automakers' ability to shift production to foreign countries with cheaper, nonunionized labor gave the firms a decisive advantage in their dealings with the union. And it undermined Chrysler's and the union's pleas for a federal bailout to avoid massive unemployment.

Of the few concessions the union was able to get from Chrysler in exchange for forfeiting $1 billion in wages and benefits, Fraser was most pleased with the unprecedented representation of workers on Chrysler's board. He argued that the success of the UAW would help spread the idea. Many observers considered Fraser's presence on the board a conflict of interest, criticizing him as a special-interest director representing the needs of a single group in the firm. But as Donald E. Schwartz noted, banks have a long history of representation on nonfinancial corporate boards, and their presence is analogous to the union's (*Business Week*, 19 May 1980, 149). Even Iacocca (1984, 236–237) agreed, adding that labor's presence on corporate boards is "pretty standard in Europe. And in Japan they do it all the time. So what's the problem?"

Where Fraser saw worker representation on Chrysler's board as a ground-breaking development in the labor movement, Lane Kirkland, president of the AFL-CIO, recognized that power derives from the organized command of capital flows and not from corporate directorships. Kirkland argued that corporate boards are unimportant in the development of policy and saw "control over pension, welfare and other funds" as "a far more effective tool for labor unions" (*New York Times*, 16 Nov. 1981, A1).

In this view the struggle over the survival of Chrysler offered the union a small, insignificant development in the class struggle (union representation on Chrysler's board of directors) in exchange for major, unprecedented, and damaging concessions by labor. The banks' intransigent position forced the UAW to bear the largest burden of federally required concessions for Chrysler to qualify for the loan guarantees. Where labor lost $1 billion in wages and benefits and over 210,000 jobs, the banking community traded debt for equity in the firm—a risk from which the banks have subsequently profited. Labor's concessions were not risks but lost battles that it would have to fight again later. Meanwhile, the banks did not advance any new money at all.

State and Local Governments, Dealers, and Suppliers

Chrysler's desperate situation, aggravated by the intransigence of the banking community, was not lost on several northern Midwest states, home to tens of thousands of Chrysler workers whose jobs were threatened. Fearing the strain such a high level of unemployment could impose on local budgets and social programs, Michigan gave a fifteen-year loan of $150 million to help Chrysler qualify for the federal loan guarantees (*New York Times*, 1 May 1980, D1). In addition, Michigan law provided for "the deferral of property taxes on any improvement in industrial facilities designed to produce products already being produced in obsolete plants" (U.S. Congress, House 1979a, 373). Under Michigan Public Act 198, Chrysler was able to invest $200 million to update its Detroit facilities. Indiana approved a $32 million investment in Chrysler (*New York Times*, 1 May 1980, D4). Delaware joined Michigan and Indiana in offering support to Chrysler, for a tri-state total of $190 million (*New York Times*, 20 Aug. 1980, D4). Illinois gave Chrysler a $20 million loan from its lottery revenues (*New York Times*, 15 Jan. 1981, D3).

Suppliers and dealers also made concessions to Chrysler and were involved in a private offering of Chrysler stock to help save the firm. In addition, Chrysler's purchasing agents were busy trying to "shave more dollars of contract with suppliers" (Moritz and Seaman 1981, 298). Furthermore, Chrysler's 3,000 suppliers deferred $200 million in payments due from Chrysler and agreed to freeze prices during 1981 and to "cut prices 5% from that level for the first quarter" (*New York Times*, 2 Jan. 1981, D1; 12 Jan. 1981, D1). Finally, Chrysler secured $36 million in price concessions from its suppliers and continued to negotiate for another $36 million (Moritz and Seaman 1981, 333).

Aftermath

By 1979 the federal government had assumed the risk of guaranteeing $1.5 billion in loans to Chrysler, a risk the financial institutions were unwilling to take. Chrysler's UAW workers had given the firm $622 million in wage and benefit concessions, and its salaried personnel had conceded $161 million. The company's suppliers had agreed to price concessions of $36 million and continued negotiating more concessions (such as extensions of payments due). Several state and local governments had provided Chrysler with loans and tax credits, and the Canadian government had given a $200 million loan guarantee. The financial institutions agreed to convert "$560 million in long-term debt to equity in the form of preferred stock, and the forgiveness, at Chrysler's option, of the remaining debt at 30 cents on the dollar" (Moritz and Seaman 1981, 333). Schwartz and Yago (1981, 202) estimated that this bank concession represented 50 percent of Chrysler's debt to the banks.

Although all those who had a stake in Chrysler made concessions to the firm, it is important to weigh the concessions against the outcome. Chrysler's financial institutions never gave the firm any new money in the form of new loans. Rather, they deferred or converted a portion of Chrysler's debt, initially writing off about 50 percent. In exchange for these concessions, the federal government assumed the risk of bailing out the banks' investments in a firm with a history of poor management decisions. In addition, the banks got what they originally wanted before the struggle over

Chrysler's rescue began (and before the UAW was forced to make unprecedented concessions): a pared-down Chrysler Corporation. The banks considered the new structure more efficient for their short-term imperative to issue positive quarterly and annual profit statements (a goal that often undermines long-term profits). The banking community also insulated itself from further risk—an objective neither labor nor the state was able to attain.

Chrysler's management had stubbornly insisted from the beginning that the firm had to remain a full-range automaker to survive in the long run as a major competitive firm. In addition, it faced retooling requirements for all its cars to meet federal fuel economy standards by 1985 and, more important, to meet the growing consumer demand for small fuel-efficient cars. Chrysler estimated that it needed $13.6 billion to continue its product line and retool its plants, projecting that both efforts would produce a "2.1 billion cash shortage by 1983." Chrysler's banks projected shortages of $4 billion and insisted that "the only alternative to deeper debt . . . is to trim the product program" (*Business Week*, 21 Jan. 1980, 33). But Iacocca remained determined that Chrysler would continue as a full-line producer.

By 1982, however, Chrysler was a shadow of the inefficient multinational that Townsend and Riccardo had built. Iacocca sold its European, South American, Australian, and South African facilities, keeping only the Mexican and Canadian divisions. Chrysler was now a smaller domestic automaker dependent on Japan's Mitsubishi for subcompact cars and trucks and on Peugeot, which along with Mitsubishi provided engines and other parts for Chrysler (Moritz and Seaman 1981; *New York Times*, 20 Feb. 1982, 31; 17 Mar. 1982, D4). It still trails behind GM and Ford in market share. Chrysler emerged from the struggle with a radically limited product line, furthering the financial community's short-run interest in securing the firm's cash flow so that banks could recover their investment. The banks' interests took precedence over Chrysler's long-term interest in maintaining flexibility to respond to changing consumer demands and to remain a competitive automaker among the Big Three.

Ironically, the rationale several sources gave for a federal bailout of Chrysler was the preservation of hundreds of thousands of jobs and the avoidance of a national recession and devastating depres-

TABLE 2. *Employees in the Production of Motor Vehicles and Equipment, 1977–1982*

Year	Employees (in thousands)
1977	734.7
1978	781.7
1979	764.4
1980	575.4
1981	582.8
1982ᵃ	496.7

Source: U.S. Department of Labor (1982).
ᵃThe data for 1982 are for January (the latest available figure).

TABLE 3. *Employees in the Production of Motor Vehicles and Car Bodies, 1977–1982*

Year	Employees (in thousands)
1977	329.6
1978	349.1
1979	340.8
1980	252.8
1981	247.6
1982ᵃ	198.2

Source: U.S. Department of Labor (1982).
ᵃThe data for 1982 are for January (the latest available figure).

sion conditions in particularly hard-hit metropolitan areas (such as Detroit). An example of the drastic drop in the number of jobs in the U.S. auto industry can be seen in Tables 2 and 3. In little more than half a decade (from 1977 to 1982) the number of workers employed in the motor vehicles industry declined significantly. The loss of jobs derived in part from the industry's inability to compete successfully with foreign automobile imports. Yet after the passage of the Federal Loan Guarantee Act,

Chrysler employed less than 60% of the people it had in 1978, only a third of the 250,000 who had worked there in 1977, and its continued survival depended on even more plant closings and consolidations. . . . More than half of the jobs lost through the consolidation process were in Michigan, Ohio, and Indiana. (Moritz and Seaman 1981, 335–336)

Unemployment in Michigan was more than 11 percent by late 1981, and the state was losing tax revenues so quickly that it cut $270 million in badly needed welfare and social programs from its budget (*New York Times*, 23 Oct. 1981, A16). Furthermore, the national recession Congress feared occurred despite the passage of the Federal Loan Guarantee Act. In fact the rate of unemployment in Michigan, Indiana, and Ohio continued to rise until 1984, and for all years between 1981 and 1984 the rate for all three states was higher than the national rate (see Table 4).

Some might argue that Chrysler's workers stood to gain from the federal loan guarantee package in a trickle-down fashion. They would recover their financial losses through future wage increases from a restructured and presumably healthy Chrysler. Indeed, Chrysler has now been operating as a profitable automaker (although the banking community refused to take the risk of financially supporting that restructuring period). By the close of 1983 Chrysler's sales had improved 71 percent over 1981 (*Business Week*, 21 Mar. 1984, 21), and the firm had captured an "impressive" 15 percent of the market (*New York Times*, 8 May 1984, 14). By April 1983 profits had risen to $172.1 million from $149.9 million for the same period in 1982 (*New York Times*, 22 Apr. 1983, D1). Chrysler's annual profit for 1983 was $925 million, "the best by far in Chrysler's history" (Iacocca 1984, 278). By the end of 1983 Chrysler's earnings per share had reached $5.79; first-quarter figures for 1984 indicated that earnings per share were up to $9.46 (*Business Week*, 14 May 1984, 87). The firm had also announced that capital spending for 1983 would increase by 82 percent—from $823 million in 1982 to $1.5 billion in 1983 (*New York Times*, 19 Mar. 1983, 32). As an indicator of the growing optimism of the firm's health, Standard and Poor's raised Chrysler's debt rating from CCC to B in May 1983 (*New York Times*, 24 May 1983, D10). Similar trends emerged for 1984: figures for the first quarter revealed a 59 percent increase in sales and a 310 percent increase in profits over 1983. By comparison, Ford's sales in-

TABLE 4.   *Unemployment Rates for Michigan, Ohio, and Indiana,*
1980–1984

	1980	1981	1982	1983	1984
Michigan	12.4	12.3	15.5	14.2	11.2
Indiana	9.6	10.1	11.9	11.1	8.6
Ohio	8.4	9.6	12.5	12.2	9.4
Nationwide	7.1	7.6	9.7	9.6	7.5

Source: U.S. Department of Commerce, Bureau of the Census, *Statistical Abstracts of the United States, 1988* (Washington, D.C.: Government Printing Office), 384.

creased by 37 percent and its profits by 325 percent; GM's sales increased by 37 percent and its profits by 147 percent. Chrysler's margins (that is, the difference between net sales and the cost of merchandise sold) were up 14.4 percent in that first quarter of 1984, compared with 5.6 percent for the same quarter in 1983 (*Business Week*, 14 May 1984, 87). Financial institutions continued to hold preferred shares in the firm in exchange for Chrysler's debt. They also received $404 million in interest and nearly $67 million in administrative fees (Iacocca 1984, 283).

The federal government also profited from the federal loan guarantee program for Chrysler: The automaker had agreed to pay the loan guarantee board a monthly administrative fee of $1 million. Iacocca estimated that Chrysler's "January payment alone covered their annual expenses, so the next $11 million was pure profit for the Treasury." All told, the federal government received $33 million in administrative fees by the time Chrysler paid off its loans. In addition, Chrysler had issued 14.4 million stock warrants to the loan board in 1980 as collateral for the guaranteed loans. At the time the stocks were worth about $5 per share. By 1984 their value had increased to about $30 per share, giving the federal government a profit of more than $311 million. One member of Congress suggested that the windfall be used to "retrain unemployed autoworkers" to "help the guys [sic] who lost their jobs when Chrysler had to cut back." But the state was "not interested," and the money went into the general fund (Iacocca 1984, 256, 283, 285). The state thus profited handsomely from bailing out the banks' investments, while refusing to share that profit with the workers who had paid for the bailout with their jobs.

Despite Chrysler's obvious good health, labor had still not recovered the losses it incurred at the concessionary bargaining table. Chrysler's UAW workers did not reach pay parity with their GM and Ford counterparts as promised until 1985. The three-year 1985 contract between the UAW and Chrysler included a one-time immediate cash bonus of $2,120, an hourly increase of 5.25 percent over the contract's three years, a second-year single payment of $750, and "a new 'profit-sharing' plan" that would pay workers "$500 each in 1987 and 1988, then convert to a formula tied to company earnings in 1989" (*Business Week*, 4 Nov. 1985, 30). Chrysler repeatedly postponed resuming payment of its contribution to the UAW pension fund (*New York Times*, 20 Jan. 1982, D4; 22 Jan. 1982, D9). In late 1983 the firm finally made a $270 million contribution to the pension fund, with another scheduled contribution of almost $500 million in 1984—including a $250 million payment it had postponed since 1980 (*New York Times*, 16 Sept. 1983, D3). This long-awaited resumption of payments to the fund occurred seven months after Chrysler announced that it had substantially increased executive salaries (*New York Times*, 19 Mar. 1983, A32). More important than the delay itself was the motivation behind it. The firm argued that it wanted to keep cash on hand in case it was needed. Apparently the strategy of postponing pension fund obligations was an important part of Chrysler's "wooing back a critical ally: the financial community" (*Business Week*, 2 Aug. 1982, 18). The strategy succeeded. By mid-1982 "39 major banks agreed to a new $500 million financing package for [Chrysler's] subsidiary, Chrysler Financial Corporation" (*Business Week*, 2 Aug. 1982, 18).

In the end the struggle to rescue Chrysler left the banking community and government committees in control of the firm, though not as equal partners. As organized controllers of the lending capital Chrysler so desperately needed, the banks were (and continue to be) in a position to collectively put up or deny money to the firm. Despite the federal loan guarantees, the money invested in the firm came from the banks, which could at any time deny new capital to Chrysler.

The disparity in power between the financial institutions and the federal government in this case clearly demonstrates that the corporate crisis was not produced by the state and its regulatory standards. Rather, a long history of poor management decisions produced a cash shortage at Chrysler that forced the firm to go to its banks for more funds. The banks' refusal to advance more loans forced Chrysler to plead for aid from the federal government, setting in motion the long struggle with the banks, labor, and the state to define Chrysler's situation. The corporate crisis Chrysler experienced was produced by the banking community's steadfast refusal to advance new loans to the firm.

Chrysler was not alone in its financial difficulties. The Big Three automakers all experienced sharply declining sales. To stem their losses both GM and Ford struggled with the UAW for concessions similar to those Chrysler had won. But many of the difficulties at Ford and GM sprang from the same decision-making processes that sent Chrysler to its banks and into crisis. Industrywide decisions to produce large cars and to neglect to develop fuel-efficient small cars at a reasonable price provoked American consumers to turn to foreign competitors. The automakers' shortsighted decisions reflect the internal contradictions of a capitalist political economy. In brief, small cars return a small rate of profit. Managers' stubborn pursuit of the short-run profits of large-car sales ensured financial difficulties in the long run (see Detroit Socialist Collective 1980, 22–23; *Business Week*, 22 Sept. 1980, 84; Iacocca 1984, 154). The only way to avert the effects of declining sales and cash shortages was for Chrysler (and eventually GM and Ford) to go to the banks for rescue, giving the banks great collective power over the automakers.

Assessing the Losses

The Banks

As I argued earlier, banks do not have absolute or unconstrained power. At the conclusion of the struggle over federal loan guarantees for Chrysler, the banks had written off $600 million of Chrysler's debt. All parties involved with Chrysler lost in negotiating the rescue. Labor, suppliers, and local, state, and federal governments all compromised and made major concessions. But the banks lost the least and were able to achieve more of their original demands. They never put up any new money, and they emerged from the struggle with the trimmed-down Chrysler Corporation they wanted, with no risk of losing their money later.

Indeed, in 1983 Chrysler issued 26 million shares of common stock as a strategy to raise $432 million to offer to Chrysler's creditors in an effort to eliminate $1.1 billion in preferred shares held by the banks (*New York Times,* 29 Mar. 1983, D1). Business analysts were quick to point out that

although the value of the new common shares that banks and insurance companies would receive in the transaction would be little more than half the amount of what they were owed by the company . . . the common shares gave the financial institutions a far greater degree of flexibility in attempting to recover their investment than they had with the preferred shares. (*New York Times,* 14 Jan. 1983, D3)

Moreover, Chrysler was able to make its final payment on a $1.3 billion bank debt six weeks early (*New York Times,* 28 Jan. 1982, D4). The firm paid off its entire loan by mid-1983, seven years early (*New York Times,* 13 Aug. 1983, 1; see also Iacocca 1984, 279–280). With the loans repaid, the banks' equity in the firm has produced a healthy profit. And the value of the banks' twelve million Chrysler stock warrants increased from $3.50 per share in 1979 to $35 per share in 1983 (Iacocca 1984, 279).[3]

In addition, the banking community got its long-desired bank deregulation, a concession by the state that greatly benefited large banks and ultimately hurt or destroyed small banks. Most important though, the banks recovered their investment early, thus accomplishing their primary objective—even as the new healthier Chrysler continues to struggle to remain competitive.

Labor

Whereas the banks got the outcome they wanted from the start, labor lost the most. The job losses and contract concessions represented a major setback for the UAW in particular and for labor in

3. Some argue that the real winners in this case were Chrysler's stockholders, not the banks. But although the company's stock grew healthier, the firm has still not paid any dividends to shareholders (*Moody's Industrial Manual,* 1983, 1239). Thus the only shareholders who may have profited are, ironically, those who no longer own Chrysler stock.

general. In exchange labor won the "meaningless symbolism" of representation on Chrysler's board (Schwartz and Yago 1981, 200). Indeed, labor lost more from the Chrysler rescue than it would have from a bankruptcy. Had Chrysler declared itself bankrupt, it would have received protection from its creditors under Chapter XI bankruptcy laws while it reorganized. Such a reorganization would have required (1) producing only the fuel-efficient cars demanded by the market and closing the plants that manufactured the big gas-guzzlers (that is, Chrysler would have had to pare down from a full-line automaker); (2) selling underused plant facilities (most likely to foreign producers anxious to buy existing U.S. facilities at low prices); and (3) "affiliating with another automaker," such as Peugeot or Mitsubishi, which would have given Chrysler "access to European or Japanese designs—thus saving costs—and to its partner's financial resources" (*Business Week*, 24 Dec. 1979, 70–72; Schwartz and Yago 1981, 200). But the firm insisted that it could not survive under Chapter XI and struggled to get the federal loan guarantees, ostensibly to save jobs.

Ironically Chrysler has now undergone most of the changes that would have occurred under the Chapter XI reorganization Iacocca so steadfastly resisted. But because the firm refused to reorganize under bankruptcy, it has had no protection from its creditors. Instead, it has paid enormous sums in interest rates and administrative fees to both the banks and the Treasury Department— money that the firm could have used more productively to retool its facilities. Indeed, Chrysler's federal bailout actually led to more plant shutdowns and unemployment by allowing the firm to remain a full-line producer. Chrysler then tried to increase its cash flow quickly by overpricing its K-cars (the cars expected to restore Chrysler's profitability). Strong consumer resistance slowed sales, forcing plant shutdowns and more job losses. Under Chapter XI reorganization, Chrysler would have been able to market its K-cars at extremely competitive prices, thus avoiding further labor sacrifices.

Conclusion

Many observers argued that the predicament of the American auto industry was caused and aggravated by foreign intrusion (particularly by Japanese manufacturers). But U.S. auto industrialists are "surprisingly willing to concede that their problems are largely their own doing. Studies of the Japanese auto industry, including those conducted by U.S. car companies, lay much of the blame for Detroit's predicament on sloppy management methods, not labor costs" (*Business Week,* 14 Sept. 1981, 97; see also Iacocca 1984, 151–166).

The industry's self-assessment attests that managers can produce internal problems and financial difficulties for a firm at the operational level. (Pahl and Winkler [1974] call this ability "operational power".) But the processes of managerial discretion occur in a historical context—in an advanced capitalist political economy where the imperatives of short-term profit seeking (and the prevention of subsequent falling rates of profit), growth, and expansion delimit the range of alternative decisions. This environment constrains management to make short-term decisions detrimental to the firm in the long term (see Detroit Socialist Collective 1980; Iacocca 1984, 154). Thus managers make decisions within the structural limitations of the political economy, increasing the reliance of nonfinancial firms on the banking community. These structural constraints also contribute to the financial community's power as organized controllers of lending capital.

The major banks' ability to force the small recalcitrant banks to accept the loan agreement illustrates the process of hegemony formation, whereby the banking community unites around common interests. As in W. T. Grant's bankruptcy, bank hegemony seriously hampered other participants in their struggle to counter the power of the banking community.

The banks' ability either to elicit a federal bailout of Chrysler or to force it into bankruptcy demonstrates their power to define corporate crises. Although many bankers acknowledged that Chrysler might still go bankrupt when its federal loan guarantees ran out in 1983, the large banks were in the position to force labor, the state, and recalcitrant members of the banking community to bail out the firm, thus protecting the banks' investments. Iacocca (1984, 241) noted that the banks were "far less inclined to compromise than our [Chrysler's] suppliers and our workers. For one thing, their survival didn't depend on our recovery. For another, the sheer number of banks was overwhelming." Had the banks refused to agree to the federal loan guarantee requirements, their decision would have defined Chrysler as a corporation in crisis and precipitated its bankruptcy.

Chrysler's lead bank acknowledged this power to construct corporate reality. McGillicuddy, of Manufacturers Hanover, testified that "the banks, in effect, have acted to protect Chrysler from being in a default position." When asked if the banking community had the power "to foreclose on Chrysler at this particular point or to initiate bankruptcy proceedings against them," McGillicuddy replied, "Yes" (U.S. Congress, House 1979a, 848). His testimony acknowledged the power of the banking community to choose whether to support a firm with massive investments (in the form of loans and stocks held in pension and trust funds) and agreements to defer payments of existing loans, or to force that firm into bankruptcy. Even a seemingly semantic exercise can have real consequences in the definitional process. During congressional hearings on international debt, William J. McDonough, executive vice president and chief financial officer of the First National Bank of Chicago, indicated that the banking community often refers to problematic loans in developing countries as "substandard," "doubtful," and "loss" as euphemisms for default (U.S. Congress, Senate 1983b, 235). Using labels other than "default" (which creates a liability or loss for the banks) enables the banking community to define the situation as current business (which is an asset for banks). The unified control of capital flows empowers banks to impose the label of their choice.

The power of banks to force concessions from the state contradicts a capture theory of the state (Miliband 1969). Banks do not need representatives in positions of political power in the government; their power is economically based and can overrule the political power of the state. In the Chrysler case the banking community's structural bases of hegemony enabled it to constrain the relative autonomy of the state without participating directly in state decision-making processes. Moreover, the collective power of the banks exceeded their ability to produce economic disaster at federal and local levels. Senator William Proxmire pointed out that "since the bankers are community leaders who frequently either contribute or lend large sums to members of Congress to finance election efforts, bankers are listened to with great respect in Congress" (Proxmire 1979, 99).

The banking community was able to capitalize on its power over Congress and on Iacocca's unwillingness to trim Chrysler's operations under a Chapter XI bankruptcy reorganization. Iacocca insisted that such a bankruptcy proceeding would destroy rather than help the company's chances of recovery: "Consumer psychology" would "produce fears of loss of warranties, parts, and servicing in the future, and cause consumers to refrain from buying a Chrysler product" (U.S. Congress, House 1979a, 86, 90–91, 164; Iacocca 1984, 209–210). Although many firms have reorganized successfully under Chapter XI (for example, Allied Supermarkets and Toys R Us), Congress did not press Chrysler to follow suit. The reason for congressional reluctance is clear. If Chrysler had taken Chapter XI protection from its creditors, the banks would not have collected on their existing loans. And according to Proxmire's analysis, members of Congress have good reason not to cross the banking community.

Under a bankruptcy procedure, some argue, "no further raids on the public treasury would have occurred." Indeed, the relative burdens and benefits of a bankruptcy can be summed up as follows:

A bankrupt Chrysler would have been smaller (thus decreasing the power of its executives), its stock would have been less valuable (thus producing massive capital losses for investors) and its enormous debt would have been only partially repaid. . . . None of the developments would have hurt most Americans; instead, only executives, stockholders, and bankers would have suffered. It is no wonder, then, that Chrysler management has saddled the American people with a bail-out-or-bust choice. (Schwartz and Yago 1981, 201)

It is also no wonder that Chrysler's bankers, with the power of collective purse strings, forced the state to bail out their investment in the firm with federal loan guarantees.

The state's pressure on the UAW to grant ever more concessions attests to the relative power of the banking community. When a stalemate developed between the workers and the banks, the state coerced the weaker of the two: labor (which faced graver consequences in a Chrysler bankruptcy). The state acted as the only social control agent with the legitimacy to enforce concessions from labor on behalf of the banks. We will see similar patterns of state relations in later chapters.

Although many observers believe that the bank's behavior made prudent business sense, it is crucial to remember that only the banks had the ability to protect what they saw as their best interests. The state, labor, suppliers, and dealers were unable to counter the collective control of capital flows and therefore were less able than the banks to protect their interests. Moreover, the banks' threat to push Chrysler into bankruptcy was not a last resort to remedy a serious cash flow shortage. Less extreme efforts (such as requiring changes in corporate policy far earlier than 1979) were never tried. Rather, the threat of bankruptcy was part of a power struggle to force the state to bail out the banks' investments in a company with a thirty-year history of questionable managerial decisions.

Chapter Four

Leasco Corporation Versus Chemical Bank: The Political Crisis

As institutionals buy and sell ever larger blocks of stock, they develop greater power in corporate affairs—power they occasionally exercise with the impact of a sledge-hammer.

—Business Week

I always knew there was an Establishment. . . . I just used to think I was part of it.

—Saul Steinberg, chief executive officer, Leasco

Sometimes the banking community defines a firm's economic situation as a crisis even when the firm's original cash flow position is not problematic. In such instances, the corporate crisis has political rather than economic roots. If an otherwise financially healthy firm engages in policies or actions that contradict the banks' interests, the banks can use their collective control of capital flows to sanction the offending firm. By defining the situation as a crisis, the banks set in motion a herd effect that in fact produces a crisis. Leasco Corporation's struggles with Chemical Bank illustrate a politically motivated crisis definition.

By all conventional standards Leasco was a healthy growing firm. Founder Saul Steinberg quickly developed a reputation on Wall Street as an acquisitive whiz kid—a young, brash, but bright

Dramatis Personae 3. Leasco's Struggle with Chemical Bank
(in order of appearance)

Saul Steinberg	Founder, president, and chief executive officer, Leasco Corp.
William S. Renchard	Chairman, Chemical Bank
Thomas B. Stanton, Jr.	President and director, First National Bank of Jersey City (Leasco's bank in the Reliance takeover)
J. A. McFadden	Chief loan officer, Chemical Bank
Richard A. Corroon	Director, Reliance Insurance Co.
Edward S. MacArthur	Director, Reliance Insurance Co.
Donald M. Graham	Chairman, Continental Illinois
Howard McCall	President, Chemical Bank
Robert Lipp	Vice president, Chemical Bank
Richard Simmons	Lawyer, Chemical Bank
Senator John J. Sparkman	Chairman, Senate Banking and Currency Committee
Nelson Rockefeller	Governor of New York

businessman (see Dramatis Personae 3). Wall Street's admiration matched Leasco's steady growth. When Leasco went public in 1965, it sold $750,000 worth of stock within three months. Assets soared from $7.5 million in 1965 to almost $19 million in 1966; profits increased more than eightfold from 1966 to 1967. Wall Street, which was enjoying a lively market, clearly liked the small company, then traded on the New York Stock Exchange. By December 1968 mutual funds held 2,153,762 shares of Leasco stock (U.S. Congress, House 1969, 540).

Despite these positive indicators, Leasco evoked the banking community's anger by attempting to take over Chemical Bank of New York. What followed provided a glimpse of the political process of the social construction of corporate crisis as a sanctioning mechanism.

Steinberg realized the enormous growth potential of his firm and began a successful acquisition campaign that included the hostile takeover of Reliance Insurance Company. Steinberg had decided that the acquisition of a fire and casuality firm was just what

Leasco needed at that time. Because insurance firms are notoriously conservative in their financial policies, they usually hold huge reserves over and above those legally required to cover their policy risks. New York State regulations strictly limited the fire and casualty firms' use of that cash. Reliance Insurance therefore posed attractive possibilities for someone like Steinberg, who could legally use the redundant capital if he acquired the company (Brooks 1973, 36).

Despite Reliance's opposition, Leasco gained control of almost 97 percent of Reliance within five months (Brooks 1973, 36). The successful struggle provided Steinberg with a solid acquisition strategy: quietly accumulate enough of the target firm's stock to make an aggressive tender offer (usually much higher than the market value of the stock) that is difficult for the unwilling target firm to fight. The lure of large profits for the stockholders (should they accept the offer) is often difficult to resist, and the target firm can rarely afford to make a more attractive counteroffer.

The acquisition of Reliance increased Leasco's equity capital from $70 million to $236 million. According to one observer, the acquisition also pushed up Leasco's stock: "As of Dec. 31, 1968, the price of Leasco stock had, over the five years preceding, appreciated by five thousand four hundred percent, making it the greatest percentage gainer of all the five hundred largest publicly owned companies during that period" (Brooks 1980, 260).

In 1968 Steinberg decided that "nothing could stop him" (*Forbes*, 15 May 1969, 182). He tried to acquire a bank to diversify his holdings. His target was Chemical Bank of New York, the sixth largest bank in the United States, with assets of $9 billion. Like Reliance, Chemical clearly did not want to be acquired by such a young, relatively small nonfinancial corporation. But unlike Reliance, Chemical's resistance had a disastrous effect on Leasco's stock. Leasco was trading for $140 before February 1969, just before Steinberg's intention to acquire Chemical became known. By the end of the month the stock had fallen to $99. Stock that had increased 5,400 percent since 1965 lost 33 percent of its gains in just a few weeks, and 95 percent of its gains when it fell to $7 by the end of May 1969 (U.S. Congress, House 1969, 537–540). At that point Steinberg halted his efforts to acquire Chemical. What caused a corporation with steady rapid growth to plunge suddenly to the depths of disaster within such a short period of time?

The Struggle

In November 1968 First National Bank of Jersey City, which had helped Leasco take over Reliance Insurance, began to buy Chemical stock for Leasco. By 6 November Leasco had gained control of 50,000 shares of Chemical stock "without giving rise to untoward rumors of market disruptions" (Brooks 1973, 39). Furthermore, Reliance, Leasco's new subsidiary, held more than 100,000 shares of Chemical. With a total of 150,000 shares, Leasco held more than 1 percent of the outstanding shares of Chemical without any contact with Chemical executives and without any apparent breach of secrecy (U.S. Congress, House 1969, 93).[1]

In early January 1969 Leasco drafted a tender offer to Chemical's stockholders but did not release it. Leasco had not yet decided to go ahead with such an audacious acquisition bid. But at this point the secrecy was breached. William S. Renchard, chairman of Chemical Bank, told the House of Representatives investigating committee: "On January 31, we received what you might call solid intelligence to the effect that Leasco was the leasing company that wanted the Chemical Bank." Renchard apparently was not surprised by Leasco's intentions. Internal memos from Chemical Bank subpoenaed by the House Anti-Trust Subcommittee suggest that Chemical was carefully monitoring Leasco's acquisition activities as early as December 1967—a full year before Leasco began to buy Chemical stock (U.S. Congress, House 1969, 116, 477, 479–484).

When the confirmation of Leasco's bid to take over a bank came on January 31, Renchard wasted no time developing his strategy. He announced, "We intend to resist this with all the means at our command, and these might turn out to be considerable." Renchard "compared his battle plan to the authority of the President [of the United States] to order retaliatory attack should 'any unidentified

1. The control of more than 1 percent of a firm's stock is significant, because wide dispersal makes it possible to control the firm with as little as 5 percent (Burch 1972; Chevalier 1970; Larner 1970; see Zeitlin 1974 for a lengthy discussion of this issue).

flying missiles appear'" (*New York Times,* 6 Feb. 1969, 52). Despite Steinberg's boast that nothing could stop him, "Chemical did—with a vengeance" (*Forbes,* 15 May 1969, 182).

Leasco's takeover bid generated the unheard-of prospect of a major bank's becoming "a mere division of an unseasoned upstart. . . . In established banking circles, the thought bordered on sacrilege" (Brooks 1973, 39). Since Chemical had been monitoring Leasco's acquisition activities for over a year, Renchard knew of its relations with First National Bank of Jersey City. To get the best possible intelligence on Leasco's intentions and activities, he called on fellow banker Thomas B. Stanton, Jr., president and director of the New Jersey bank. Renchard wanted to know "what was going on," and Stanton reported that Leasco was scheduled to have a board meeting to discuss the "possible acquisition of 'a major commercial bank'" (Brooks 1973, 40). Renchard moved quickly to establish a battle plan: he appointed J. A. McFadden (Chemical's chief loan officer) as director of an eleven-member committee to generate a defense strategy against possible takeover attempts.

Corporate board interlocks are often used as informational networks crucial to the control of capital flows. Stanton sat on Leasco's board of directors, forming the interlock between Leasco and First National (as did Samuel H. Bellam, Jr., of Fidelity Bank of Pennsylvania). That interlock with Stanton also facilitated the flow of information on Leasco from First National Bank of Jersey City to Chemical Bank. But the information network was not mutually beneficial, nor did it facilitate joint economic planning among all members. Rather, it fortified the joint efforts of the financial firms to the disadvantage of Leasco. At no time did Leasco participate in that joint planning. Important information traveled in one direction only—from Leasco to the banking community. Although the information network served Chemical's needs well in developing its strategy against Leasco, it would not have been as useful without the organized control of capital flows.

The consultation between Renchard and Stanton apparently occurred without Steinberg's knowledge. Leasco continued purchasing large amounts of Chemical stock with the aid of First National Bank of Jersey City. By then Leasco held 170,000 shares of Chemical Bank. Renchard was still uncertain about Leasco's intended offer to Chemical's stockholders, but he acknowledged: "We knew well enough it would be tough going persuading our stockholders not to accept" Steinberg's anticipated generosity (Brooks 1973, 40). Chemical needed a strong defense. Renchard's first strategy was "to force Leasco's intentions into the open" (*Business Week,* 22 Nov. 1969, 89). Chemical knew of Leasco's intentions before the newspapers reported Leasco's rumored bid. Apparently Renchard planted the story as part of his defense strategy.

The news story forced Steinberg out into the open, a move that clearly benefited Chemical. Steinberg was accustomed to slow, methodical, and largely concealed takeover invasions; he was not ready to show all his cards or to publicly announce a tender offer. Although he had intended to wait a few months longer, the story forced Steinberg to admit his intentions immediately and push ahead.

On 6 February 1969 Renchard called another strategy conference to discuss Chemical's battle plan. McFadden reported in a memo that "there is some question about the breadth of the market on Leasco stock and it might be possible to attack its value if need be." When asked what he meant by "breadth of the market" Renchard replied, "It could mean that [a good proportion of the Leasco shares were concentrated in a few hands] . . . and also that there was a heavy concentration in some of the large funds" (U.S. Congress, House 1969, 507, 128). The memo, along with Renchard's testimony, indicates that Chemical was preparing to manipulate Leasco's stock by "making sales or short sales of Leasco stock over an extended period [and hitting] Leasco where it lived, since its high stock price was the source of its power, and above all, of the possibility of its taking over a firm . . . like Chemical." Such a "bear raid" (or concerted and deliberate sale of large blocks of a firm's stock) violates securities laws against stock manipulation. Yet as Brooks so perceptively pointed out, "The undeniable and striking fact is . . . that on that very day Leasco stock, which had been hovering in the stratosphere at around a hundred and forty, abruptly began to fall in price on large trading volume" (Brooks 1973, 40).

Tables 5, 6, and 7 document institutionals' simultaneous dumping of Leasco stock. Table 5 shows drops in price concurrent with large sales of Leasco stock from 3 to 20 February 1969, the period of Leasco's most disastrous decline. Table 6 shows large sales of

TABLE 5.   *Total Sales of Leasco Stock and Stock Prices,*
3–20 February 1969

	Leasco stock price	Shares sold (in round lots)
3 Feb.	135	9,300
4 Feb.	135¼	11,100
5 Feb.	139⅝	31,600
6 Feb.	—[a]	40,000
7 Feb.	133	27,500
11 Feb.	127¼	27,200
12 Feb.	129	16,600
13 Feb.	129¾	8,900
14 Feb.	123	29,700
17 Feb.	115	31,000
18 Feb.	112¼	63,500
19 Feb.	110¼	34,600
20 Feb.	106	47,100
Total sales		378,100

Source: New York Times, cited in U.S. Congress, House (1969), 537–538; American Stock Exchange.
[a]Congressional records did not provide the stock price for 6 Feb. 1969.

Leasco shares by brokerage firms over the same period. Although brokerage firms were selling on behalf of unnamed clients, only institutionals typically hold such large blocks of stock in any one firm. Table 7 indicates that mutual funds sold massive blocks of Leasco stock during the first quarter of 1969, which includes the period during which Leasco and Chemical struggled (U.S. Congress, House 1969, 538–540). These data attest that stock dumping substantially lowered the value of Leasco stock and suggest simultaneous activity by the institutionals. What makes this activity so remarkable is that "rumors of impending mergers, particularly between titans, customarily drive a company's stock price up, not down" (Brooks 1973, 40). Moreover, Chemical's struggle was not a rational effort to prevent its own stock price from falling; an internal Chemical memo demonstrates that a merger with Leasco

TABLE 6.   *Brokers with Sales of 5,000 Shares of Leasco Stock,*
3–20 February 1969

	Shares sold (in round lots)
Oppenheimer & Co.	79,700
Bregman & Co.	54,700
Dishy, Easton & Co.	40,000
Shields & Co.	31,400
Merrill Lynch, Pierce, Fenner & Smith	15,600
Reynolds & Co.	14,400
Moore & Schley	11,200
White, Weld & Co.	7,900
Goldman, Sachs & Co.	7,400
Blair & Co.	6,000
Oliphant (Jas. H.) & Co.	6,000
O'Neil (William) & Co.	5,800
Bear, Stearns & Co.	5,500
Andrews, Posner & Rothschild	5,200
All other brokers	87,200
Total sales	378,000

Source: U.S. Congress, House (1969), 539; American Stock Exchange.

would have increased the market value of Chemical Bank stock by
86 percent (U.S. Congress, House 1969, 486).

Although Renchard was reticent about Chemical's role in the
dumping of Leasco stock, he acknowledged that one of the strategies suggested at Chemical's meetings was "multiple flogging,"
which "seemed to be a fancy new name for an old-fashioned bear
raid" (Brooks 1973, 42). Experienced veterans of takeovers and of
Wall Street struggles know there are many ways to conceal a bear
raid from legal observers, and they know the difficulty of legally
proving deliberate, coordinated action.

Steinberg insisted that up to this point the only hint of pressure
on Leasco came from Continental Illinois National Bank and Trust
Company. Not only was Continental one of Leasco's leading lend-

TABLE 7. *Securities and Exchange Commission Table of Sales
of Leasco Common Stock by Registered Mutual Funds,
First Quarter 1969*

	Holdings (31 Dec. 1968)	Sales	Holdings (31 Mar. 1969)
Putnam Growth Fund	325,000	200,000	125,000
Keystone Custodian Fund, Series S-4	187,000	187,000	0
Polaris Fund	62,500	62,500	0
O'Neil Fund	62,250	39,000	23,250
Constitution Exchange Fund	37,500	37,500	0
Omega Fund	35,000	35,000	0
Financial Industrial Fund	25,000	25,000	0
Essex Fund	17,500	20,500	2,000[a]
Axe Science Corporation	20,000	20,000	0
Moody's Capital Fund	—[b]	19,400	15,600
Financial Dynamics Fund	17,500	17,500	0
Convertible Securities Fund	0	8,500	650
Pennsylvania Mutual Fund	0	6,000	17,500
Fidelity Capital Fund	187,500	5,000	182,500
Channing Securities	45,250	3,750	41,500
Investors Research Fund	1,812	312	1,500
Hedge Fund of America	23,000	100	22,900
Total	1,046,812	687,062	432,400

Source: U.S. Congress, House (1969), 540; Securities and Exchange Commission.
[a]Includes additional shares purchased during this period.
[b]Figure not included in congressional documents.

ers, but it also held an enormous block of Leasco stock. When Leasco acquired Reliance Insurance in 1969, Reliance directors Richard A. Corroon and Edward S. MacArthur refused to accept Leasco stock in exchange for their considerable Reliance holdings. They held the largest blocks—14 percent—of Reliance stock. Instead, a group of institutionals led by Continental Illinois and Chase Manhattan purchased the Reliance stock from Corroon and Mac-

Arthur for $57 million, exchanged them for Leasco stock, and held this major block (about 10 percent) in their trust accounts (*Forbes*, 15 July 1970, 30). If they dumped these huge institutional holdings, Leasco's stock price would plunge. And it did just that, tumbling from $140 to $99 in just two weeks and ultimately forcing Steinberg to cease his takeover attempt.

The banks had access to the power of loan refusals, customer cancellations, bank refusals to sell Chemical stock to Steinberg, and—most damaging to Leasco—stock dumping. All these strategic mechanisms derived from the banking community's collective command of capital flows.

The free exchange of information and easy communication between banks illustrate the conscious unification of the banking comunity. Renchard testified: "I spoke to Mr. [Donald M.] Graham [chairman of Continental Illinois] and he told me he was planning to meet with the officials of Leasco. I suggested to him that he might consider discouraging them in their thinking about acquiring the Chemical Bank." Continental concurred with Renchard that Leasco's takeover of Chemical was disadvantageous for the banking community (U.S. Congress, House 1969, 125, 106). Graham conveyed this sentiment to Steinberg on 7 February 1969, together with the warning "that his bank [Continental Illinois] valued its association with Leasco highly and expected it to continue" (Brooks 1973, 42).

That Renchard could freely call on both First National Bank of Jersey City and Continental Illinois for information, advice, and support illustrates that cooperation, not competition, characterized the relations between financial institutions. Corporate board interlocks involving financial representatives on nonfinancial boards of directors can help preserve a market the financial institutions consider "rational."

Documents the House of Representatives made public testify to the development of bank coalescence. A Chemical memo asserted that mergers could be resisted by attempting "*to discourage the lending of funds to the* potential *acquirer.* Through banking and other financial contacts the company officials may be able to prevent the company making the offer from obtaining sufficient funds to finance the purchase of shares tendered" (U.S. Congress, House 1969, 495; emphasis in original). Another Chemical memo included a list of all the banks involved in Leasco's $80 million in outstanding loans (U.S. Congress, House 1969, 531). These suggest that the banks tried to frustrate the takeover by refusing or withdrawing Leasco's borrowing capacity. Such a strategy depends on the united, coordinated action of the banking community.

This sense of lender unity is reinforced by the many letters Chemical received from financial institutions in the United States and Europe offering to support Chemical in its fight against Leasco. They included

1. offers to purchase Chemical stock to "keep it in friendly hands" (U.S. Congress, House 1969, 508)
2. promises (from Continental Insurance) to refuse to sell Chemical stock to Leasco (U.S. Congress, House 1969, 510)
3. the open-ended vow (from Shearson Hammill and Co.) to be "ready at any time to do whatever we could to be of assistance to you [Chemical] in the event that the threat [of Leasco's tender] became a reality. By assistance, I mean not only time and effort but also hard cash if needed" (U.S. Congress, House 1969, 511)
4. the promise (from the chairman of the Bank of London and South America) that if a firm like Leasco "were to acquire an important bank such as the Chemical, then I should at once close our account" (U.S. Congress, House 1969, 513)

An internal Chemical memo stated that

on the matter of reaching institutional investors whose shares stand in the name of bank nominations, Mr. Flom [Chemical's lawyer] noted that in his experience, most banks were quite cooperative in arranging meetings between institutional shareholders for whom they act as nominee and companies whose shares are owned by such investors. (U.S. Congress, House 1969, 720)

Apparently bank cooperation and coalescence are routine, rather than unique to this particular case. Moreover, such coalescence exceeds the confines of corporate boards or interlocks. The cooperative meetings referred to above occurred outside corporate board meetings. Furthermore, the participants do not necessarily have to sit on nonfinancial boards to attend these meetings. But they must be in control of capital flows (that is, they must make investment and divestment decisions as nominees for trust and pension funds) to participate. This cooperation between banks suggests that networks of interlocks may not necessarily be the most salient source of bank power. Other aspects of the organized control of capital flows—the control of loan capital and pension fund investment decisions—seem even more important.

Because Chemical Bank could call on other financial firms for assistance, it had great flexibility in mounting a counterattack. The final decision was made at a meeting on 8 February 1969 at Chemical's headquarters in Manhattan.[2] "By coincidence, that same weekend was the occasion of the American Bankers' Association's annual trust conference, and consequently New York City was swarming with hundreds of important bankers from all over the country" (Brooks 1973, 42). Many important financial institutions, all sympathetic to Chemical, were represented at the strategy meeting, and several actions were proposed.[3] Word of Chemical's strategy session leaked out that evening to bankers at the ABA conference and became a topic of conversation at their informal and formal gatherings. Renchard conceded: "I can't rule out the possibility of having a casual conversation [with other bankers] at one of those gatherings that I referred to earlier [namely, cocktail parties and dinners of the ABA convention]. Undoubtedly, there were representatives of some of these banks [Leasco's creditors]" (U.S. Congress, House 1969, 147).

Confident that the power of the banking community was behind him, Renchard made his next move. On 11 February Chemical's president Howard McCall asked for a list of Leasco's creditors, and several of the banks on the list were checked off. The House subcommittee never fully established the exact meaning of the check marks. Brooks (1973, 48) points out that "at about that time Steinberg began to feel 'pressure' from the banking business, in the form of calls from Leasco's two investment bankers—Lehman Bros. and White Weld—informing him that they would refuse to participate in any Leasco tender offer for Chemical." The two investment bankers admitted that several banks pressured them to

2. The meeting took place on a Saturday, outside ordinary banking hours, underscoring the seriousness with which Chemical regarded Leasco's intentions.

3. One of the proposals included a plan to "get state or federal legislation introduced, through the banker's friends in Albany and Washington, in order to make a Leasco takeover of Chemical illegal" (Brooks 1973, 42).

refuse to help Leasco—"a ticklish situation since Lehman is a heavy borrower of bank money" (*Business Week*, 26 Apr. 1969, 144). Steinberg noted, "I'm told they [Lehman and White Weld] got more pressure than we got" (*Forbes*, 15 May 1969, 82).

At the same time, "major customers of Leasco were said to have threatened to cancel their contracts with the company if Mr. Steinberg did not call off his attempt. Commercial banks were said to have intimated that Leasco would have trouble obtaining financing if it went ahead" (*New York Times*, 21 Feb. 1969, 65). The compelling power of the threat did not derive solely from Chemical Bank or other individual commercial banks, but from their collective monopoly over capital flows.

Meanwhile, Chemical held further strategy sessions during which defenses less devastating to Leasco were discussed. Chemical considered altering its holding company charter to legally preclude a Leasco takeover or acquiring its own fire and casualty firm so that a Leasco takeover would violate anti-trust laws (U.S. Congress, House 1969, 486). These actions would have prevented the takeover without necessarily debilitating Leasco. But apparently Chemical intended to do more than merely fend off an unwanted takeover. It wanted to punish Leasco for what was viewed "in established banking circles" as "sacrilegious" aggression against the banking community as an example to other nonfinancials that might consider going after a bank (Brooks 1973, 39).

Chemical next undermined Leasco's resources for the acquisition of the bank. It placed the two leading proxy-soliciting firms, Dudley King and Co. and Georgeson and Co., on retainer, thus denying Leasco access to their talents (*Forbes*, 15 May 1969, 32). An internal memo written by Chemical Vice President Robert Lipp explained that the bank wanted to obtain "the best proxy solicitation firms both for Chemical's use and to deny these firms from the opposition" (U.S. Congress, House 1969, 486). Meanwhile, Leasco's stock continued to fall steadily.

Chemical also activated a legislative counterattack. In early February 1969 Chemical's lawyer, Richard Simmons, "began devoting himself full-time to the Leasco affair. He concentrated his attention on drafting a law specifically designed to prevent or make difficult the takeover of banks similar to Chemical by companies that resembled Leasco, and on getting a copy of this into the hands of the Senate Banking and Currency Committee, in Washington" (Brooks 1973, 50). This proposal was sent directly to Senator John J. Sparkman, chairman of the committee. Simmons testified before the House Anti-Trust Subcommittee that Sparkman asked him to draft the bill. Simmons also testified that he "did it on time billed to Chemical" (*Business Week*, 22 Nov. 1969, 92).

The bill was introduced on 28 February, and although no action was taken on it, Steinberg began to comprehend the depth and breadth of Chemical's power and influence beyond Wall Street. He discovered that Chemical had friends in the New York State legislature in Albany as well as in Washington. Governor Nelson Rockefeller, whose family had longstanding ties to Chase Manhattan Bank, "urge[d] the New York State legislature to enact a law enabling the state to prevent any takeover of a bank by a conglomerate from occurring within its boundaries" (U.S. Congress, House 1969, 620–621, 719). The bill, identical to the one considered in Washington, passed in June 1969.

Chemical also appeared to have friends in the Department of Justice, which sent a warning letter to Steinberg on 18 February indicating its awareness of Leasco's intentions to take over the bank: "Although we do not suggest that such a transaction would violate the anti-trust laws, questions under these laws are raised thereby." The applicability of the Clayton Act to the Leasco-Chemical case is uncertain at best. Although no reliable information has emerged about why the Justice Department became involved at that point, an internal Chemical memo suggested a defense strategy of "creat[ing] a roadblock in terms of the Justice Department looking into any takeover attempt by Leasco" (U.S. Congress, House 1969, 330, 491). The Justice Department's involvement was certainly premature and occurred at Chemical's behest.

Formidable forces were marshaling against Leasco. Chemical Bank, itself a powerful opponent, numbered among its powerful and influential supporters a united banking community; the Federal Reserve Board; the Wall Street law firm of Cravath, Swaine, and Moore, which provided Simmons's legislative drafting talents to Chemical; the two leading proxy solicitors; the New York State legislature; the New York governor; the U.S. Senate; and the U.S. Department of Justice. Together these forces waged an effective legislative and financial offense against Leasco on Chemical's behalf, without the aid of corporate board interlocks. "The nation's big banks, rocked by the thought of one of their number being taken over, did cluster together to create what one banker calls 'a massive groundswell of opposition that was felt in Washington and Albany.'" One Wall Street source said, "Chemical didn't have to do very much. It had so many friends, and everyone wanted to help" (*Business Week,* 26 Apr. 1969, 144).

Throughout the struggle Leasco's stock continued to tumble until 20 February 1969, when Steinberg announced that Leasco had "no plans to acquire control of the Chemical New York Corporation" (*New York Times,* 21 Feb. 1969, 63). Although Chemical had access to several mechanisms to undermine Leasco's acquisition efforts, none was as effective as the banks' ability to divest its pension and trust funds of Leasco stock.

Dun's Review (March 1970, 69) reported that "the Establishment, which banked at the Chemical, cut the ground from under Steinberg." A Wall Street friend of Steinberg's said, "Saul found out there really is a backroom where the big boys sit and smoke their long cigars" (*Business Week,* 26 Apr. 1969, 144).

Conclusion

The conflict between Leasco Corporation and Chemical Bank is an example of a corporate crisis based on political rather than economic considerations. Crisis functioned here as a sanctioning mechanism. Chemical not only fended off a hostile takeover but soundly thrashed Leasco for trying it. The most powerful disciplinary weapon was the banks' ability to dispose of stockholdings in their trust accounts. Chemical's many friends among the institutionals unloaded their holdings of Leasco so quickly that the company's stock dropped from $140 to $99 in a few weeks in February 1969 and, because of the herd effect, to $7 by May. The authority to buy and sell stocks for trust fund accounts is a large source of power for banks: "As institutions buy and sell ever larger blocks of stock, they develop greater power in corporate affairs—power they occasionally exercise with the impact of a sledgehammer." The sledgehammer came down hard on Leasco as "bank trust departments and perhaps other institutions dumped their shares [apparently] to protect Chemical" (*Business Week,* 25 July 1970,

53). Stock dumping by institutionals is so common that Wall Street analysts hold it responsible for any sudden radical drops in stock values (*New York Times,* 17 Dec. 1976, D2). Banks' concerted activity around similar pension and trust fund investment portfolios enhances their organized power—a power that derives from their ability to collectively dispose of stocks.

This case illustrates that ultimate control over the survival of corporations lies not with individual boards of directors, their shareholders, or even their corporate board interlocks, but rather with those financial institutions that administer massive blocks of stock in pension and trust funds. Whereas the board of directors enjoys day-to-day control over a firm—voting on how to use capital the firm already possesses and in that sense exercising some discretionary power over the firm's operations—financial institutions, as organized controllers of capital flows, possess allocative control of social capital, determining which nonfinancials will receive investment capital and which are unworthy of financial backing in the form of stockholdings (Pahl and Winkler 1974). As a result, the banking community is structurally empowered to generate a corporate crisis in an otherwise healthy firm.

Here, as in the two preceding cases, the power of the banking community derived from its unified control of capital flows: in the Grant and Chrysler cases, from the banks' common presence in large lending consortia; in the Leasco case, from the common profiles of the banks' pension and trust fund portfolios. That commonality empowered the banking community to enforce the definition of Leasco's situation as a crisis despite the firm's obvious good health. The banking community's behavior then created an actual crisis for Leasco. The concerted dumping of Leasco stock permanently damaged the firm's business trajectory. Leasco has never fully recovered from this definitional process and its consequences. Major bank trust departments abandoned their positions in Leasco "all over the United States" (*New York Times,* 11 July 1972, 44).

Steinberg has attempted to prevent similar definitional processes and consequences in the future. By the end of 1973 Leasco's stock was still struggling to recover, having reached a maximum value that year of $19¼ and a low of $8¼. Steinberg sought to protect his firm by making it a subsidiary of his Reliance Group, Inc.

(*Moody's Bank and Finance Manual*, 1982, 2: 5909). On the day he did so, Leasco's stock was an anemic 10⅞ (*Barron's*, 17 Dec. 1973, 42). He has also been buying up Leasco and Reliance stock in an effort to make his firms private. If he succeeds, "he will no longer be subject to the pressure from Wall Street" (*Business Week*, 27 July 1981, 79).

Chapter Five

The Default of Cleveland: Constructing Municipal Reality

The Cleveland situation . . . is a reminder of the power of commercial banks. The credit powers, alone, can be literally life or death for business enterprises and individuals and, as we have learned in New York and Cleveland, for large municipalities as well. When these credit functions are enhanced by trust investments, linked directorships and other ties, the potential for control and power is awesome.
— Congressman Fernand J. St. Germain

Commercial banks hold nearly one half of the municipal debt in the nation . . . [and] are an increasingly important source of short-term credit for hard-pressed cities across the nation. . . . With the importance of credit to local governments, the decisions of loan officers and the board of directors of financial institutions are critical, at times carrying far more impact than the decisions of thousands of citizens of a municipality.
— House Subcommittee on Financial Institutions Supervision, Regulation, and Insurance

Like corporations, municipal governments increasingly rely on external sources of finance capital. Inflation, recession, federal and state budget slashing, increasing social welfare expenditures, and declining tax revenues since the mid-1970s (and particularly since the new federalism of the 1980s) have forced local governments to seek loans from the private banking community. These loans are often necessary for local governments to meet their normal operating costs as well as for investments in economic development and growth. They become the lifeblood of the city. Losing or renegotiating loans often leads the municipality into a major crisis and even default. Where loans from the private banking community are critical to municipal survival, nonelected economic elites may essentially run the city government. Cleveland in 1978–1979 is a case in point.

Cleveland is an old industrial city on the southern shore of Lake Erie in northeastern Ohio. Its economy relied heavily on commerce and industrial production, most notably iron and steel manufacturing and Great Lakes shipping. Like many other old northern industrial cities, Cleveland's industrial base began to decline in the late 1940s, a victim of recession, foreign competition, mechanization, and devastating plant closings, and the lack of offsetting fixed capital investment (Swanstrom 1985, 72). The city's economic and political troubles solidified in 1978 and 1979, when, locked in confrontation with an antagonistic banking community, Cleveland defaulted on $15 million in loans. What pushed the city to default, and why did the banking community steadfastly refuse to roll over or renegotiate the loans? What was at stake in the city of Cleveland?

The Storm Clouds Build

Cleveland became the center of national attention in 1977 with the election of Dennis Kucinich, at age 31 the youngest mayor of a major city, on a promise to preserve public control of the municipal power system (U.S. Congress, House 1979b, 6; see Dramatis Personae 4). The son of a Croatian-American truck driver, Kucinich studiously maintained his working-class allegiance and life-style. He saw himself as something of a maverick, a populist who championed the interests of the city's working class, which formed the basis of his political power. Some observers point to this populist activism as the cause of the business and banking communities' antagonism to his administration, arguing that these economic elites (led by Cleveland Trust Company, Cleveland's largest bank) tried "to capsize it through default" (Branfman 1979, 44). Others

Dramatis Personae 4. The Default of Cleveland
(in order of appearance)

Dennis Kucinich	Mayor of Cleveland (1977–1979)
Richard D. Hongisto	Police chief of Cleveland
M. Brock Weir	Chief executive officer and chairman, Cleveland Trust Co.
Ralph Perk	Former Mayor of Cleveland (1971–1977)
Carl Stokes	Former Mayor of Cleveland (1967–1971)
George Forbes	City council president
Ralph Besse	Former chairman, Cleveland Electric Illuminating Co.; advisory director of Cleveland Trust Co.
Claude MacClary Blair	Chairman, National City Bank
George V. Voinovich	Former lieutenant governor of Ohio; mayor of Cleveland (since 1979)
James A. Rhodes	Governor of Ohio

fault Kucinich's aggressive, strident manner for the city's contentious relations. Indeed, Kucinich's periodic clashes throughout his term were frequently reported as interpersonl struggles touched off by his abrasive style. But much evidence indicates that the conflicts and struggles were politically and economically motivated by powerful vested interests in the city.

Fierce attempts to remove Kucinich from office with a special recall election laid bare the fusion of the electoral political process with powerful economic interests. The recall movement was financially supported by the banks and the Greater Cleveland Growth Association (GCGA), a business organization composed of the city's large businesses. In addition, the banks' officers and directors personally helped finance the recall (see Table 8): "When an effort to recall the Mayor [in the summer of 1978] was underway . . . [m]uch of the banking fraternity—from which the Mayor was seeking an extension of the city's credit—lined up to support his ouster."

Four of the six banks and the GCGA provided a total of $20,228 to various campaign committees formed to recall Kucinich. The officers and directors of four of the six banks also contributed at least an additional $8,750 to these committees, as did the wives of two other directors of National City Bank and the wife of an ex officio board member of GCGA (U.S. Congress, House 1979b, 4, 772–773).

The list of contributors to the recall campaign was a Who's Who of corporate Cleveland. Many donors had corporate connections to Cleveland Electric Illuminating Company (CEI), an investor-owned utility. For example, White Consolidated Industries had officers sitting on CEI's board of directors. A partner of Squire, Sanders, and Dempsey, the law firm representing CEI, was a former chairman of CEI and an advisory director of Cleveland Trust Company. Another partner sat on Central National Bank's board and a third on CEI's board. Jones, Day, Reavis, and Pogue were the legal representatives of Ohio Edison (codefendants with CEI in Cleveland's anti-trust suit). Partners of this law firm sat on the boards of Central National Bank, National City Bank, and Cleveland Trust (U.S. Congress, House 1979b, 207). Together with the banks and GCGA, these major business interests contributed 31.3 percent of the total $128,681 in recall campaign funds. The remainder of the recall campaign contributions came primarily from suburbanites, prominent businesspeople, and other corporations (see *Plain Dealer*, 28 Sept. 1978, 22 Apr. 1979).

In contrast, much of the $102,000 raised to defend Kucinich's job came from the city's working class and unions and from the law firm Hahn, Loeser, Freedheim, Dean, and Wellman, which represented Cleveland in its anti-trust suit against the utilities (*Plain Dealer*, 28 Sept. 1978; see Table 9). Together labor and legal groups contributed 71.6 percent of the campaign funds raised in support of Kucinich. This evidence undermines the widely held argument that a ground swell of popular opinion forced the recall election. On the contrary, the citizens and their representatives appeared to rally to Kucinich's defense against Cleveland's corporate power brokers.

Of the six banks in Cleveland's lending consortium, Cleveland Trust Company (CTC) has been identified as the city's dominant power broker. In addition to its web of interlocking directorate re-

	Contributions	Percentage of total funds	Number of directors contributing	Number of top officers contributing
Directors and top officers of banks				
Central National Bank	$1,150	0.9%	9	1
Cleveland Trust	3,100*	2.4	17	5
National City Bank	3,000	2.3	13[a]	1
Society National Bank	1,500	1.2	8	0
Total contributions of directors and top officers	8,750	6.8	—	—
Corporate and organizational contributions				
Case Western Reserve University Board[b]	5,075	3.9	23	—
Cleveland Electric	1,775	1.4	10	6
Cleveland Trust	7,103	5.5	—	—
Greater Cleveland Growth Association	4,375*	3.4	28[c]	—
White Consolidated Industries	5,000	3.9	—	—
Arter and Hadden	1,050	0.8	—	11
Jones, Day, Reavis, and Pogue	2,000*	1.5	—	8
Squire, Sanders, and Dempsey	4,725	3.7	—	53
Thompson, Hirie, and Flory	400	0.3	—	7
Total corporate and organizational contributions	31,503	24.5	—	—
Total recall campaign funds[d]	128,681*			

Sources: U.S. Congress, House (1979b), 772–773. Cleveland *Plain Dealer* (22 Apr. 1979); denoted with asterisk (*).
[a]Wives of two other directors contributed.
[b]Three family members contributed.
[c]Wife of one ex officio board member contributed.
[d]Includes other unspecified corporate contributions in addition to the contributions listed above.

TABLE 9. *Political Contributions to Defend Kucinich*
in Recall Campaign, 1978

	Contributions	Percentage of total
United Auto Workers	$30,000	29.4
Cleveland City Workers	20,595	20.2
American Federation of State, County, and Municipal Employees	2,500	2.5
Hahn, Loeser, Freedheim, Dean & Wellman	20,000	19.6
Total from organizations	73,095	71.7
Total defense campaign funds	102,000	

Source: *Plain Dealer* (28 Sept. 1978).

lations, twenty-four of its twenty-six directors were executives of firms whose single largest stockholder or principal stockholder was CTC. A 1968 congressional investigation noted that CTC, together with Cleveland's other major banks, "is probably the single most influential element in the entire economy of the area." Other bankers widely acknowledged the dominating influence of CTC. As one banker asserted, "No one can ignore the voting power they hold" on corporate boards. One businessman grumbled that CTC's dominating influence was "one of the greatest deterrents to the economic growth of Cleveland," an assessment with which many other businesspeople in Cleveland agreed (U.S. Congress, House 1979b, 195a, 196). During congressional hearings a businessman testified that CTC and its chief executive officer and chairman, M. Brock Weir, did not hesitate to exercise this power in determining the city's political leadership:

There's enough conviction in the financial community of Cleveland and enough resources to fill the short-term need with their own resources, provided we have confidence in whom we're dealing with. I have said I would personally undertake a program to develop an enthusiasm for the banks to recognize the possibility in the right circumstances of putting together a consortium that could provide up to $50 million. (*Financier*, Apr. 1979; cited in U.S. Congress, House 1979b, 196–197)

Clearly the banking and business communities had much at stake in the recall effort; in pressing their agenda, they contradicted any notion of the electoral process as a simple expression of the will of the people. But despite their powerful opposition, Kucinich prevailed by a slim margin in the special recall election (*New York Times*, 15 Aug. 1978, 127; 18 Aug. 1978, 30).

While Kucinich's political troubles brewed, Cleveland's economic problems continued. Part of the city's woes could be traced to a national trend of runaway shops. Many industries that had operated in the northern Midwest and Northeast of the United States were moving to the South and Southwest or overseas.[1] Since 1969 this trend had cost Cleveland 17,000 jobs a year. The city's population was declining at a rate of 20,000 annually (*New York Times*, 13 Nov. 1978, 1). Consequently, city tax revenues were also in decline.

Despite these signals of economic erosion, Cleveland's default was not necessarily inevitable. Most damaging to the city were the spending habits of the previous administration of Mayor Ralph Perk (1971–1977). Perk responded to the city's revenue loss by using "bond funds, borrowed to pay for capital improvement projects, to finance daily operating expenses" (Marschall 1979, 54). This policy left the Kucinich administration with the task of replacing $52 million in missing bond funds. Although an earlier city administration under Mayor Carl Stokes had also used federal funds to pay for Cleveland's operating costs, Perk's spending "more than doubled that of . . . Stokes" (Whelan 1975, 72). City Council President George Forbes admitted in 1978 that the city was paying for the Perk administration's misuse of bond funds and implied that the council could have "brought the city to a halt then instead of today" (*Plain Dealer*, 3 Aug. 1978). Perk also quadrupled Cleveland's short-term debt, from $22 million to $88 million, in an ill-conceived attempt to generate revenues (Marschall 1979, 54). These short-term notes, issued in 1972 and 1973, were required by law to be transferred to bonds in 1978 and 1979, foisting Perk's excesses onto the Kucinich administration.

1. Because unions have made few inroads in the Sunbelt states, labor is generally cheaper there than in the northern tier, where organized labor is strongest and most militant.

In addition to the misuse of federal project grants to pay for Cleveland's operating expenses and the shortsighted escalation of the city's debt, Perk granted costly tax abatements for the construction of two new office towers, one of them for National City Bank. The potential revenues lost to the city because of these abatements totaled almost $35 million (Marschall 1979, 26; Clavel 1986, 78). Taken together, Perk's unsound fiscal practices set the stage for Cleveland's financial woes under the Kucinich administration. Oddly enough, the banks did not monitor Perk's spending and accounting practices.

By December 1978 the city appeared to be headed for default on $15.5 million. Kucinich recommended that voters approve a 50 percent city income tax increase. But the city council steadfastly opposed the proposal, as they opposed all proposals except the sale of the city's Municipal Electric Light Corporation, called MUNY (*New York Times*, 12 Dec. 1978, 18; 14 Dec. 1978, 19).

With Cleveland frustrated in its efforts to avoid default, the city's financial suppliers began to mobilize. Moody's, Standard and Poor's, and the Dreyfus Tax Exempt Fund further downgraded Cleveland's bond rating, which dropped from AA through 1969 to A in 1973–1977, and to BAA on 8 June 1978. Standard and Poor's finally suspended Cleveland's bond rating in July 1978 (U.S. Congress, House 1979c, 507; *New York Times*, 7 Dec. 1978, D2). Because this low rating and ultimate rating suspension forced the city out of the national bond market, the only alternative source of loans was the banks (U.S. Congress, House 1979c, 507; *New York Times*, 7 Dec. 1982, D2). But Cleveland's lead bank, Cleveland Trust Company (which held $5 million in loans due that December) did not approve of Kucinich's proposal for recovery. On the morning of 15 December 1978, Cleveland Trust Chairman and CEO M. Brock Weir and Councilman Forbes told Kucinich that the banks would roll over the city's debt and provide $50 million in credit if Cleveland sold MUNY. Kucinich refused, and Cleveland defaulted on $15.5 million in loans in mid-December 1978 (*New York Times*, 16 Dec. 1978, 1).

The Carter administration compounded Cleveland's problems by refusing Kucinich's request for an advance on the city's revenue-sharing funds (*New York Times*, 17 Dec. 1978, 25). Federal officials insisted that the city caused its fiscal crisis by allowing expenditures to exceed revenues. Therefore, they argued, the city's fiscal problems should not be the responsibility of the federal government but should be resolved locally (*New York Times*, 19 Dec. 1978, 9). Ohio law left Cleveland essentially on its own, since it stipulates that the state may not intervene in the affairs of chartered cities such as Cleveland "without formal invitation." Fearing a loss of local control, Cleveland's officials did not want the state of Ohio to intervene (*New York Times*, 24 Dec. 1978, 12). The refusal of state and federal governments to respond on their own initiative locked Cleveland in a localized struggle with a hostile banking community.

The Banks, CEI, and MUNY

MUNY, the city-owned electric utility, became a political bone of contention in the struggle to resolve Cleveland's fiscal crisis. Cleveland's community relations and economic condition suffered as a result, particularly when Kucinich refused to honor the Perk administration's tax abatement to banks and businesses to build office towers.

Cleveland chose to create its own power system in 1905 rather than rely on existing private systems (the more common approach). MUNY—which provided relatively cheap electricity to 20 percent of the city's residents and to all municipal buildings and streets— had competed with Cleveland Electric Illuminating Company (CEI), a private utility, ever since. The demand for MUNY power had always exceeded capacity (especially during peak hours), forcing MUNY to purchase power from CEI or from utilities outside CEI's customer area. The situation worsened over the years as demand grew and MUNY's operating plants deteriorated. The public utility's decline owed much to CEI's interference, particularly in lobbying the city council not to maintain MUNY facilities (Bartimole 1977). Whichever option MUNY chose for obtaining more power (and it eventually bought all of its electricity from outside sources), an interconnection with CEI was critical because of the prohibitive cost and logistical difficulties of constructing separate transmission lines.

Although CEI could not legally deny MUNY's request for interconnection, its response was a more important factor than the city's inefficient expenditure policies in producing Cleveland's cash flow shortage. After years of contentious negotiations CEI formed an interconnection but often provided inadequate power, causing regular power outages. The Nuclear Regulatory Commission accused CEI of failing to restore electricity immediately after such interruptions and of sending inadequate work crews for repairs and restorations (Bartimole 1977). The continuing problems tarnished MUNY's reputation as an efficient, reliable power system. "CEI took advantage [of this situation] . . . through its aggressive campaign to take customers away from MUNY." When the campaign failed, CEI sought to eliminate the public utility by purchasing it outright. In response Cleveland filed an anti-trust suit against CEI and other regional utilities in 1975 (U.S. Congress, House 1979b, 205). Cleveland lost that suit and had to pay its overdue bills to CEI in full. These bills mounted under the Perk administration, which left the debt unpaid. This debt was the primary cause of the city's serious cash flow shortage.

Proponents of the sale of MUNY to CEI, particularly the Greater Cleveland Growth Association, cited the public utility's decaying physical plant and the perception that MUNY represented a financial liability for Cleveland (U.S. Congress, House 1979b, 208). GCGA's position was not surprising: CEI helped create the association in 1962 (Clavel 1986, 61). Kucinich ardently opposed the sale of MUNY or any other city assets to balance the budget and countered the GCGA's analysis of MUNY as a fiscal drain:

The operation of MUNY has been stabilized. It is no longer draining the city treasury. In fact, with the MUNY Light debt [to CEI] paid off, we can expect MUNY to earn several million dollars a year for the city, as well as continuing to furnish us with low-cost street lighting, which saves Cleveland's taxpayers hundreds of thousands of dollars yearly. (U.S. Congress, House 1979b, 209)

The American Public Power Association, a trade association of public utilities, corroborated Kucinich's analysis and joined the mayor in opposing the sale of MUNY, arguing that the benefit to the public of MUNY's cheaper rates should not be dismissed lightly (U.S. Congress, House 1979b, 209).

The battle to preserve MUNY became a rallying point in what is often described as Cleveland's class war (Branfman 1979, 43).

Kucinich and his working-class followers fought to maintain the publicly owned utility. The business and banking communities tried to force the sale of MUNY to CEI, which would then have a monopoly on Cleveland's electricity. Indeed, Kucinich went before Congress and charged the banking community with deliberately throwing the city into default to aid its business allies by making the sale of MUNY to CEI a precondition for the renewal of Cleveland's loans (U.S. Congress, House 1979c, 5–13). Kucinich charged that "the decisions of the banks concerning extension of credit to the city [were] . . . influenced by massive conflicts between the banks' loan-making functions and their direct and indirect ties to other interests in the Cleveland area" (U.S. Congress, House 1979b, 1). Kucinich specifically named M. Brock Weir of Cleveland Trust, the dominant bank in Cleveland and Ohio's biggest bank (with assets of $4 billion).

The renewal of notes had been predicated by Cleveland Trust on the sale of the city's publicly-owned electric system—MUNY. . . . The Mayor also charged that Cleveland Trust had innumerable links to the neighboring private utility company—Cleveland Electric Illuminating Co.—and that denial of credit was leverage exerted by the bank to force sale of the publicly-owned system to CEI, an admitted long-standing corporate goal of the private utility. (U.S. Congress, House 1979b, 2–3)

Why would Cleveland's banking community be interested in the demise of MUNY? Because of their enormous investments in CEI, it was in the banks' collective interest to eliminate any cost competition for the private utility. Congressional investigations uncovered strong links between the city's six major banks (all of which were involved in Cleveland's lending consortium) and CEI.[2] These relations were based on loans and lines of credit to CEI, shares of CEI stock that the banks held in trust and pension accounts, stockholders' voting rights, corporate interlocks between CEI and the banks (including direct representation of the banks on CEI's board), the banks' management of CEI pension funds, and major CEI deposits at the banks (see Table 10). For example, four of the six banks provided CEI with a total of $74 million in lines of

2. The six banks were Cleveland Trust Company (the lead bank in Cleveland's lending consortium), National City Bank, Central National Bank, Society National Bank, Euclid National Bank, and Capital National Bank.

TABLE 10. *Cleveland Banks' Interests in CEI, 1978*

	Lines of credit to CEI (in millions)	Shares held in CEI	Number of voting rights	Corporate interlocks with CEI board	Representatives on CEI's board	CEI pension funds (in millions)	CEI compensating balances, 15 Jan. 1979	Loans to CEI, 1974–1978 (in millions)
Cleveland Trust	$47	802,844[a]	555,712	60	4	$70[b]	$2,247,839	$37.8
National City Bank	12	776,395	268,934	63	3	0	415,634	41.2
Central National Bank	10	175,295	155,000	38	2	0	133,564	3.0
Society National Bank	5	37,474	34,474	33	1	0	1,997	0.5
Euclid National Bank	0	7,337	7,337	0	0	0	0	1.0
Capital National Bank	0	—	—	11	0	0	0	0.5
Total	74	1,799,345	1,021,457	205	10	130	2,799,034	84.0

Sources: U.S. Congress, House (1979b), 6–7, 50, 183, 372–375; House (1979c), 10.
[a] CTC's holdings may actually have been higher, since the annual report from which the data were originally taken included shares registered in the name of only one of CTC's two primary nominees.
[b] Remaining pension funds administered elsewhere (by other, perhaps national-level, banks).

credit, and the two largest banks (CTC and National City) together provided $79 million in loans to the utility between 1974 and 1978 (U.S. Congress, House 1979b, 372–374).

CEI kept compensating balances at four of the six banks totaling almost $2.8 million. Five of the six banks held almost 1.8 million shares in CEI (Capital National Bank did not provide figures), including more than 2 million with voting rights (U.S. Congress, House 1979b, 375, 50). Cleveland Trust and National City together held almost 4.5 percent of CEI's stock and 2.9 percent of the voting stock (U.S. Congress, House 1979a, 46; 1979b, 47). These same six banks shared 205 corporate interlocks with CEI and had 10 representatives sitting on CEI's board (U.S. Congress, House 1979b, 183). Cleveland Trust alone managed $70 million of the $130 million in CEI pension funds managed by banks (U.S. Congress, House 1979c, 10). In addition to these sources of direct common interest between the banking community and CEI, there were indirect connections between them through the law firms representing the defendants in Cleveland's anti-trust suit against CEI:

The firm representing CEI is Squire, Sanders and Dempsey, a major law firm in Cleveland with 78 members and 95 associates. One of the Cleveland partners is Ralph Besse, former chairman of CEI and an advisory director of Cleveland Trust Company. Squire, Sanders and Dempsey also has a partner sitting on the board of Central National Bank and another on CEI's board. Representing Toledo Edison in the case was Jones, Day, Reavis and Pogue. That firm has 60 members and 58 associates in Cleveland and 63 members and associates in its Washington office. Partners of Jones, Day, Reavis and Pogue sit on the boards of Central National Bank, National City Bank, and Cleveland Trust Company. Contributions to campaign committees supporting the recall of Mayor Kucinich in August 1978 included 8 Jones, Day, Reavis and Pogue members and 53 Squire, Sanders and Dempsey members. (U.S. Congress, House 1979b, 207)

Together these structural arrangements unified CEI and Cleveland's banking community in their struggle to force the city to sell MUNY.

Ratcliff, Gallagher, and Ratcliff (1979) note that interlocks between banks and regional nonfinancials tend to diminish the finance capital available to the local community. Because banks give lending priority to their interlocked corporations, they deprive the local area of residential mortgage capital. That capital is key to urban development; without it urban decline, decreased property values, and lost revenue are nearly inevitable. Cleveland suffered these problems because of disinvestment and redlining (U.S. Congress, Senate 1975; 1980). Disinvestment in the municipality contrasts sharply with the banks' investments in and interlocks with CEI and other capital accumulation interests in Cleveland.

O'Connor (1973) suggests that banks influence municipal policy making by refusing to extend loans for activities that compete with private capital accumulation. Since MUNY competed with CEI and other investor-owned utilities, it is not surprising that the banks pressured Kucinich to sell MUNY to CEI. More important, the investor-owned utilities around Cleveland were interested in investing in nuclear power generation. CEI wanted to absorb MUNY to expand its rate base and thus raise the revenues necessary for constructing a nuclear power plant.

CEI had other reasons for wanting to eliminate its competitor. Because MUNY, as a public utility, did not have to produce profits or pay dividends, it could charge lower rates than an investor-owned utility like CEI. The sale of MUNY to CEI would enable the investor-owned utility to charge even higher rates because of the loss of competition. Evidence from other cities indicates that rates rise sharply when investor-owned utilities buy up their municipally owned competitors. In Fort Wayne, Indiana, for example, the private utility's electric rates doubled after the 1974 sale of the public utility (see Marschall 1979, 114).

Why would the banks have any interest in such matters? The bonds of investor-owned utilities are guaranteed as if the utilities were state agencies. The rates a utility charges are guaranteed indirectly and sometimes directly. Indirectly, the precedent set by *Smyth v. Ames* (1898) guarantees a "reasonable return" on capital "used and useful in the public's service" (Bonbright and Means 1969, 63; see also Metcalf and Reinemer 1967, 21–23; Bonbright 1972). The Supreme Court ruled in *Smyth v. Ames* that rates could not be set so low that they forced a private utility into bankruptcy. But failing to pay a bond would force bankruptcy, because the utility's board would otherwise have a sure form of leverage on public service commissions to achieve the rates they desired. The notion of a reasonable rate of return "quickly became a de facto guarantee of income, sufficient to cover operating costs of fixed and variable capital plus debt service and profits" (McGuire 1986, 258).

In other cases, state guarantees of a bond can be applied directly to secure sufficient capital and bond sales in periods of crisis or to fund joint utility-state projects. The bonds are usually tax free (Metcalf and Reinemer 1967; Wasserman 1979; Hertsgaard 1983). Banks then get a guaranteed return on these bonds, with the support of the state, at rates routinely 2–3 percent above those of state-issued bonds (McGuire 1986). Significantly, the total capital costs of the utility industry rose more than 600 percent between 1969 and 1979 (Munson 1979, 349). That represents a major increase in the bond market precisely when other industries were undergoing depression and recession. No wonder banks had an interest in nuclear-power investments: the costs were passed on to consumers and guaranteed by the state.

In addition to the evidence of common interests among the banks, CEI, and the business community, there was a political bone of contention between Kucinich and National City Bank, a member of Cleveland's six-member lending consortium and holder of $4 million of the city's notes. The previous mayor had given National City a $14 million tax abatement to support the construction of a new building for the bank, a move Kucinich "vehemently opposed." Frustrated by their failure to unseat Kucinich in a recall election, the banks apparently pursued default as their next strategy. As National City's chairman, Claude MacClary Blair, put it: "Default, with all its problems, might be the best thing that could happen to Cleveland if it meant the defeat of Dennis Kucinich" (U.S. Congress, House 1979b, 830).

Furthermore, Cleveland Trust's M. Brock Weir pointedly avowed that the city's fiscal difficulties were really not of grave concern to the banks. "The business climate remains healthy," Weir said. "The only problem is the little canker downtown." So although the banks could easily have rolled over Cleveland's loans (the standard operating procedure in similar instances of impending municipal default), the banks and the business community preferred to construct a political climate favorable to the destruction of MUNY as a cost competitor with CEI and to the provision of tax breaks for the banks. According to Weir, "We [the banks] had been kicked in the teeth for six months. On December 15 [1978], we decided to kick back." The congressional investigation report noted, "Clearly the default of the city and the possibility of a forced sale of MUNY would have been a severe kick in the teeth for the Kucinich Administration" (U.S. Congress, House 1979b, 830, 829).

In addition to the banks' efforts, GCGA's taxation committee had been urging the sale of MUNY since 1977. GCGA's position is understandable in the light of a congressional investigation that uncovered strong relations between GCGA, the banking community, and CEI (see Table 11). For example, GCGA's chairman and three of the nine vicechairs were officers or directors of banks involved in Cleveland's default. Of GCGA's twenty-five-member executive committee, nine were officers or directors of banks and two were officers or directors of CEI. Of GCGA's fifty-one-member board of directors, ten were officers or directors of banks and two were officers or directors of CEI. Moreover, five of GCGA's ten-member ex officio executive committee were officers or directors of banks (U.S. Congress, House 1979b, 211–213).

The strong presence of bank representatives at GCGA is all the more significant because the association knew as early as 1975 that Cleveland's budget and accounting books did not accurately assess the city's fiscal condition. A GCGA report recommended that Cleveland refrain from relying on short-term notes and attempt instead to raise operating revenues from the sale of city assets (U.S. Congress, House 1979b, 214). Yet the banks continued to lend short-term money to Cleveland until 1978 without demanding greater accountability or improved ledger management. Apparently motivated by CEI's major interest in forcing the sale of MUNY, the banks' easy lending policy and tolerance of the city's fiscal mismanagement placed the city at their mercy three years after the association's report. Kucinich repeatedly charged that Cleveland Trust insisted on the sale of MUNY as a precondition for renewing Cleveland's loans and rescuing the city from default.

Faced with Cleveland's deteriorating economic prospects, Kucinich offered to put the MUNY sale issue on a referendum ballot. Part of that proposal also called for an increase in the city income tax from 1 to 1.5 percent. After much battling, the city council approved Kucinich's referendum proposal. When the referendum came to election, voters agreed to raise the city's income tax by 50

TABLE 11. *Greater Cleveland Growth Association's*
Ties to Banks and CEI, 1978

	Bank officers	Bank directors	CEI officers	CEI directors
Chairman	1	0	0	0
Vice chairs (9)	0	3	0	0
Executive committee (25 members)	1	8	1	1
Board of directors (51 members)	3	6	0	2
Ex officio executive committee (10 members)	1	4	0	0

Source: U.S. Congress, House (1979b), 211–213.

percent but rejected the sale of the public utility (*New York Times,* 20 Dec. 1978, 16; 23 Dec. 1978, 1; 28 Feb. 1979, 1).

The Struggle Continues

While intense struggles ensued over the sale of MUNY, Kucinich appealed to the city council to approve an ordinance to get the six local banks to refinance Cleveland's defaulted $15.5 million. Cleveland Trust finally agreed to wait until after 27 February 1979 before instituting measures to collect $5 million on which Cleveland had defaulted (*New York Times,* 26 Dec. 1978, 16; 29 Dec. 1978, 10).

Meanwhile, in a move to raise more revenue, CEI requested a 25 percent rate increase for wholesale power it sold to Cleveland. Kucinich strenuously opposed the request (*New York Times,* 10 Feb. 1979, 8). In a federal setback, the U.S. Supreme Court refused to review Cleveland's appeal in a "dispute over its authority to pay off some electric bills," letting stand the Ohio Supreme Court's ruling that the city did not have the authority to issue bonds to generate revenue for payment of its debts to CEI (*New York Times,* 22 Feb. 1979, D5). This decision made it even harder for Cleveland to access the national bond market and increased the city's dependence on its creditor banks.

The city continued to suffer from the banks' collective definition of a crisis when it lost its largest annual convention. The Pittsburgh Conference, which annually brought 15,800 scientists and around $6 million to Cleveland, decided to hold its 1980 conference in Atlantic City for the first time since 1968 (*New York Times,* 3 May 1979, B8). Furthermore, as Cleveland's image plummeted, more and more firms moved out, including Diamond Shamrock Corporation, which moved its headquarters from Cleveland to Dallas, Texas (*New York Times,* 30 May 1979, D19).

Finally, after protracted feuding over the sale of MUNY almost destroyed the city financially, city council leaders and the Kucinich administration agreed on a six-step fiscal rehabilitation plan to offer to the banks. The plan required that the council approve legislation to establish "an escrow account for income tax money from about 20 of Cleveland's biggest companies," to be used for payments to the banks holding Cleveland's loans (*New York Times,* 10 June 1979, 31).

In July 1979 Cleveland avoided a second default when the city council unanimously passed a measure that gave the city an additional year to repay $7.6 million it borrowed "from its own agencies." Kucinich also requested that the council repeal the city law requiring the approval of a bond lawyer to refinance municipal notes, an approval the bond lawyers had refused to give (*New York Times,* 7 July 1979, 6).

Although the city avoided defaulting on loans by its own agencies, it headed into another default on 31 August 1979. After more squabbling over MUNY's sale, Kucinich and the city council finally agreed on a proposal to begin overdue repayments of loans, and the council approved Kucinich's repayment schedule of $3.75 million to Cleveland's six local banks (*New York Times,* 26 Sept. 1979, 16). The council later approved a plan to refinance $14.4 million in municipal debts, helping the city avoid a third default in less than a year (*New York Times,* 6 Oct. 1979, 11).

Kucinich became the most visible political victim of Cleveland's fiscal crisis when the Republican lieutenant governor of Ohio, George V. Voinovich (heavily supported by business interests), defeated him in a bitter 1979 mayoral election.[3] The election of

3. When Voinovich's daughter was killed in a tragic accident, Kucinich called a two-week moratorium on his campaign attacks against the lieutenant governor

Voinovich smoothed the way to the governor's mansion and access to finance capital: "With Kucinich turned out of office, Governor James A. Rhodes, State Senate leadership, and the City Council [were] prepared to enact legislation that would allow the city to enter the debt market and gain some relief from a series of defaults that [had] plagued it for the last year" (*New York Times*, 8 Nov. 1979, 20). Unfortunately, that cooperation did not come soon enough. Cleveland's officials noted that despite the 50 percent increase in the city's income tax rate, the city ended 1979 with an even larger deficit than the previous year (*New York Times*, 15 Nov. 1979, 26; 18 Dec. 1979, 14).

Shortly thereafter, Cleveland hired a Wall Street banking firm and investment company, Lazard-Freres and Company, as its financial adviser. The firm had a reputation as an effective adviser to cities needing fiscal rehabilitation (*New York Times*, 18 Feb. 1980, D2). But in the fall of 1980 Voinovich announced the disheartening news that Cleveland faced another $7.1 million budget deficit for that fiscal year (*New York Times*, 10 Mar. 1980, D8). Cleveland's Financial Planning and Supervision Commission approved the mayor's financial bailout plan (*New York Times*, 30 Apr. 1980, 20). By June 1980 Cleveland had reached an agreement with the banks to refinance $36.2 million in debt, including the $10.5 million on which the city had already defaulted (*New York Times*, 8 June 1980, 24). In addition, the city council approved Voinovich's agreement to sell $36.2 million in fourteen-year bonds to eight banks to repay the city's overdue debts.

This plan would essentially convert Cleveland's debts from short-term notes to long-term bonds (*New York Times*, 9 Oct. 1980, 22). Ironically Voinovich had to ask voters once again to increase the city income tax from 1.5 to 2 percent to raise revenues to support the city's recovery (*New York Times*, 18 Feb. 1981, 12). These measures apparently worked. Cleveland managed to balance its budget in 1980 "for the first time in years," generating a $3.9 million surplus (*New York Times*, 13 May 1981, 28). Standard and Poor's, which had suspended Cleveland's bond rating in July 1978, resumed the city's bond rating in August 1981 with a

---

and the business interests Voinovich represented. This moratorium and the sympathy created by the accident allowed the Voinovich campaign to build momentum as Kucinich fell behind for good.

BBB (*New York Times*, 16 Aug. 1981, 35). Moody's Investor Service gave a Ba rating to the city's general obligations bonds (*New York Times*, 9 July 1981, D9), up from the Caa rating in 1979 (*Moody's Municipal and Government Manual*, 1979). This made the national bond market accessible to Cleveland once again. Finally, by 1982 Cleveland's downtown had begun to revive along with the "growth of the skilled service industry" (*New York Times*, 5 Feb. 1982, 10). This service sector expansion began well before 1982 and was strong even under Kucinich. The trend suggests that Cleveland's economy was fairly healthy under Kucinich, and that the critical factor in the city's fiscal crisis and default was not simply economics, but political economics.

Conclusion

The struggles between the city of Cleveland and the mayor, on the one hand, and the banking and business communities, on the other, illustrate the power of the unified control of capital flows to compromise the political process and the relative autonomy of the state. When the interests of the business and banking communities lined up against the populist municipal government, the banks' collective control of lending capital was more powerful than legal and electoral mechanisms and resolved the conflict more in favor of the private sector's interests. The power of collective purse strings enabled the banks to collectively define the city's cash flow shortage as a crisis, thereby precipitating Cleveland's default.

Cleveland's fiscal problems were not caused by extraordinarily low revenues or excessively high expenditures. Whereas Beck (1982, 216) speculated that a long history of municipal mismanagement caused Cleveland's default, I argue that the cause was the control of the city's critical capital flows by an organized banking community. Political concerns and interests in the business and banking communities took precedence over the needs and interests of the city and its working-class constituents. Moreover, the behavior of the business and banking communities set the stage for Cleveland's default. In particular, because CEI provided inefficient and expensive interconnections for MUNY, the public utility provided an unreliable and inefficient service to its customers. MUNY's subsequent anti-trust suit against CEI resulted in CEI's countersuit to recover back payment of MUNY's overdue bills to the private utility. The legal tussle pushed the city along the path to default. Cleveland was forced to pay its CEI bills in full, and the payments generated a cash flow shortage. Because of the sharp reduction in cash flow, the city could no longer make payments on its loans. But the downgrading of Cleveland's bonds locked the city out of the national bond market and intensified its dependence on those loans. The banking community, which had significant interests in CEI (including stock ownership, pension fund holdings, CEI deposits, voting rights on CEI stocks, loans, and interlocking directorates) refused to renew or renegotiate the city's loans unless Kucinich agreed to sell MUNY to CEI. Such a sale would have eliminated any further pursuit of the anti-trust suit against CEI and would have solidified the private utility's control of the city's electricity business by absorbing the competition from MUNY.

In an analysis of Cleveland's crisis, Swanstrom (1985) argues that default and urban decline have a political as well as an economic cause (see also Mónkkonen 1984). He also insists that municipal fiscal crises are produced not by capitalist development but by the "political practices chosen by each society" (Swanstrom 1985, 104). His analysis implies a nearly unlimited range of possible practices and urban political leaders with the unbridled discretion to choose among them. Swanstrom ignored the constraints that capitalist relations impose on the range of possible choices. He viewed capitalism as an economic structure separate from the political structure. A political-economy analysis clarifies the limits on political leaders' discretion that render them "able to act only in the terrain that is marked out by the intersection of two factors— the intensity of class struggle and the level of economic activity" (Block 1977, 27). Hence Kucinich's terrain included the struggle over MUNY, the loss of the city's access to the national bond market, and the extent of bank hegemony in Cleveland.

Cleveland's case is consistent with Whitt's assessment that urban elites strongly influence municipal policy formation and expenditure decisions (see Whitt 1979, 1980, 1982). Despite conflicts within the business and banking communities, these urban elites unify around specific issues. The case of Cleveland highlights the structural bases of consensus formation. Elite consensus in Cleveland developed through the structural mechanisms of the lending consortium, GCGA, interlocking directorates between the banks and the business community, and stockholding. Although these structural bases do not necessarily ensure absolute domination of municipal decision making, they have a critical influence on urban policy.

Clearly the banks wielded tremendous influence in Cleveland's fiscal crisis. They made the availability of loans to the city contingent on the sale of MUNY to its private-sector competitor. Although the city's default was a fiscal crisis in that government expenditures exceeded revenues, the roots of that crisis were deeper than simple economics. Cleveland could not meet its expenditures because it no longer had access to finance capital. For political reasons the financial community had cut Cleveland off. Indeed, the coffers opened once again when the business and banking communities unseated Kucinich, and Voinovich took office. Although MUNY remained municipally owned, the new mayor openly sympathized with business and banking interests, and they reciprocated by renewing the flow of finance capital to the city. This result is consistent with O'Connor's conclusion that the financial community enforces the state's role of assisting capital accumulation by influencing the state to allocate funds to activities that do not compete with private interests (see O'Connor 1973).

The banking and business communities never did convince the voting public to sell MUNY to CEI, primarily because Kucinich had successfully identified the issue as a symbol of class struggle. But they still got their money's worth out of supporting George Voinovich for mayor. Part of Voinovich's bailout plan involved an 8 percent increase in MUNY's rates to support CEI's expensive interconnection and electricity service. The new mayor also straightened out Cleveland's accounting procedures and opened the city's books to the banks, laid off 650 municipal workers, and held down the wages of the remaining city employees (*New York Times,* 30 Apr. 1980, 20; 11 May 1980, 24). In other words, the working class paid for the city's bailout in lost jobs, decreased pay, and increased income taxes. Indeed, the increased revenues from income taxes were devoted to paying back the overdue loans instead of preserving workers' jobs and services. So although the collective power of the banks was not absolute, it was strong enough to influence the electoral process and to punish the working class (which had thwarted the banks' ultimate goal) by declaring the city in default and by then pressing for a bailout plan that disproportionately hurt labor.

MUNY's history demonstrates that Cleveland's 1978 default was an extension of political economic issues rather than personality clashes. Turn-of-the-century Cleveland was the mirror image of Cleveland in 1978–1979. Comparable struggles between Cleveland's mayor and the private utilities date back as far as 1905, when Mayor Tom Johnson battled to create a municipal utility (see Rudolph and Ridley 1986). Johnson accused two city council members of accepting bribes from the old Cleveland Electric Lighting Company, which strenuously opposed the proposed municipal utility. Voters supported the creation of MUNY, as they supported the public utility in 1979, but the private utilities managed to convince the city council to vote against it. Johnson's accusations of bribery were significant because "one of the choicest plums of public office . . . was the granting of franchises for electric power, the new industrial heartblood" (Rudolph and Ridley 1986, 23). Johnson based his campaign for mayor in 1900 on a promise to break the utilities' hold on the city council and to take over two major private utilities, including CEI.

Like Kucinich, Johnson fought against formidable corporate opponents. A large, powerful private utility had emerged from the consolidation of many small companies. This large firm was "connected to a regional or national holding company, [and its] board of directors often interlocked with those of banks, brokerage firms, insurance companies, or other interests with whom the city's officials had to do business" (Rudolph and Ridley 1986, 37). For example, Cleveland Electric Lighting was a subsidiary of General Electric and was supported by J. P. Morgan. Faced with such strong opponents, both Kucinich and Johnson turned to the electorate of Cleveland. Frustrated by their failure to turn voters against MUNY, financial interests sought to defeat it by pulling the purse strings. Morgan, for example, tried to choke off the city's access to construction funds by "advising investors not to buy Cleveland's bonds for the [MUNY] plant" (Rudolph and Ridley 1986, 37). But this effort failed, and by 1914 MUNY was providing electricity at rates

70 percent lower than the private utility's. Thus Kucinich's struggles to preserve MUNY in 1978–1979 were a direct extension of Cleveland's earlier struggles to develop the public utility.

Although Kucinich's forceful personality clearly took center stage in Cleveland's later struggle with the business and banking communities, it is inaccurate to conclude that the city's problems arose because of him. Although business interests have long dominated Cleveland's politics, the city also has a long (if inconsistent) history of populist politics in which leaders in community action organizations, unions, and city hall have struggled against business interests (Clavel 1986). In the fight to preserve MUNY, Kucinich had the support of the United Auto Workers; the American Federation of State, County, and Municipal Employees; the Cleveland Planning Commission; the Ohio Public Interest Campaign; and various local community organizations (Clavel 1986; *Plain Dealer*, 28 Sept. 1978). The list of supporters and opponents of the sale of the utility has lead many observers to attribute the struggle to class issues.

Once again the banks' collective action was not a last-resort effort to remedy intractable financial difficulties. As we have seen, Cleveland's economy remained fairly good throughout the crisis. But default *was* a last-resort effort to remedy a political problem: a populist mayor who stubbornly opposed business and banking interests.

Municipal cash flow shortages do not necessarily lead to default, as they did in Cleveland. When New York City suffered a similar shortage in 1976, the banks bailed it out. The critical difference between Cleveland and New York was the willingness of the cities' mayors to comply with the banks' definition of appropriate austerity programs. Whereas Kucinich steadfastly resisted selling MUNY, New York City Mayor Ed Koch sold valuable city property to private interests, sharply reduced the city's work force, slashed social welfare expenditures, and forced the municipal workers' pension funds to purchase "Big Mac" bonds (that is, municipal bonds) to support the bailout (see Lichten 1980, 1986; Tabb 1982). New York allowed a "significant transfer of public power to the private sector" by creating the Emergency Financial Control Board, through which "the major banks and corporations were granted a direct veto over government decisions," including the negotiation of municipal workers' contracts (Berkman and

Swanstrom 1979, 297). In contrast to Kucinich's refusal to compromise the interests of his working-class constituents, Koch instituted an austerity plan that hurt labor the most. The banks responded to the different mayors with different definitions of their
cities' situations and different social contructions of municipal
reality. They bailed out New York and pushed Cleveland into
default.[4]

This tale of two cities parallels the tale of two corporations discussed earlier. Chrysler's willingness to make labor bear the brunt
of its austerity program enabled the firm to access federal loan
guarantees. The banks refrained from defining the situation as a
crisis and instead bailed Chrysler out. In contrast, Saul Steinberg's
overt opposition to the banking community's interests set Leasco
against an array of forces that successfully defined the firm's situation as a crisis. These parallels between corporate and municipal
experiences reveal that control over capital flows allows the banking community to socially construct economic reality for governments and corporations alike. Whereas the structures of bank hegemony over corporations include lending consortia, institutional
stockholdings, pension and trust fund portfolio holdings, and interlocking directorates, the main source of bank hegemony over
municipalities is the lending consortium. That loans from a unified
private banking community are the primary source of external
capital for municipal governments empowers the banking community to dominate the affairs of city governments just as it dominates corporate affairs.

4. Cleveland was once again in danger of defaulting on its loans in June 1980.
But this time, with Voinovich still in the mayor's office, the banks quickly refi-
nanced the debt.

Chapter Six

Mexico's Foreign Debt Crisis: Bank Hegemony, Crisis, and the State

Lending institutions . . . have tended to move from a confident, expansive view of this lending [to developing countries], to a very cautious view in recent months. And there is some danger that an abrupt contraction in this lending would precipitate the very kind of [global and domestic financial] crisis that we want to avoid. . . . International lending does play an important role in the world economy. You just don't want to shut it off abruptly.

—Paul Volcker, former chairman of the
Federal Reserve Board

This chapter will examine international finance capital relations, particularly those revealed in Mexico's 1982 foreign debt crisis. I will analyze Mexico's history of mounting debt, U.S. congressional participation in the resolution of the crisis, and the effect of this participation on Mexico's domestic relations. Finally, I will discuss the significance of these developments for the relative efficacy of theories of the state.

Developing and developed countries have increasingly relied on debt financing to support development and to close balance-of-payments gaps. These capital needs have previously been met through aid and loans from multilateral and bilateral official sources (such as the International Monetary Fund, the World Bank, and the International Bank for Reconstruction and Development). But the international capital market has undergone a structural transformation.[1] Prior to World War II private banks were the predominant source of capital in developing countries; after the war until the mid-1960s developing countries continued to rely on external capital, but the predominant source was direct investment and official bilateral and multilateral aid. Official development aid (ODA) from the international Development Assistance Committee has been declining since the late 1960s: "ODA was 0.44 per cent of [developing countries'] . . . gross domestic product in 1965 and barely 0.3 per cent in 1977" (Dhonte 1979, 6). Private financial institutions have increasingly filled the void created by declining official aid. The debt developing countries owed to private creditors increased by more than 200 percent between 1972 and 1975, whereas their liabilities to official creditors increased by only 60 percent. "The share of official commitments in total lending, which was 55 to 60 per cent until 1972, dropped to 46 per cent in 1975" (Dhonte 1979, 7). Meanwhile, between 1970 and 1976 private debt as a component of total foreign debt in developing countries nearly quadrupled (Lichtensztejn and Quijano 1982, 264).

One indicator of the enhanced participation of private financial institutions in peripheral countries' development is the striking pattern of growth of debt servicing. Debt service burdens for official loans increased by 58 percent between 1972 and 1975, whereas the burden of private loans in that period increased by 87 percent and that for loans from private financial markets increased by 125 percent (Dhonte 1979, 7; see also OECD 1984a; Seiber 1982; Stallings 1982). Thus developing countries owe an increasing proportion of their debt to private banks. Private debt as a share of poor countries' debt grew from 2 percent in 1971 to 6 percent in 1980; for middle-income countries that proportion increased from 14 to 30 percent, and for newly industrialized coun-

---

1. See Corm 1982; Dale and Mattione 1983; Debt Crisis Network 1985; Dhonte 1979; Glasberg and Ward 1985; Lichtensztejn and Quijano 1982; Lipson 1979; Marsden and Roe 1984; Moffitt 1983; OECD 1984b; Sanchez Arnau 1982; Seiber 1982; Wood 1986.

tries, from 38 to 65 percent (Wood 1986, 256). Most important, the proportion of new loans going to service old debt rose from 37 percent between 1970 and 1976 to 88 percent in 1980 (Wood 1986, 269). Consequently increasing proportions of developing countries' gross national product service debts to private banks.

One of the important stimuli for this structural transformation was the fuel disruptions of the early 1970s. The cost of petroleum quadrupled during that time, exacerbating the balance-of-trade problems of non-OPEC developing countries. At the same time OPEC countries enjoyed tremendous profits from the sudden radical increase in petroleum prices. They deposited those petrodollars in core financial institutions. With demand for credit stagnant in the developed countries, banks invested the windfall in the form of loans to developing countries (Seiber 1982; Stallings 1982). Trade dependency in developing countries added to the significance of petrodollars. Trade dependency distorts the structure of the economies of developing countries by forcing overconcentration in the production of particular commodities and a reliance on imported goods for other necessities. The balance-of-payments problems created by the soaring cost of petroleum forced developing countries to rely increasingly on loans to bridge the gap, thus contributing to finance capital dependency (Seiber 1982; Stallings 1982).

Similarly, dependence on transnational corporations forced many developing countries to develop expensive infrastructures. Transnational corporations required the construction of roads, sewers, electric systems, railroads, and airports as prerequisites for locating in peripheral countries. Host countries assumed the cost of this construction, which they financed with loans. Later those countries sought loans to escape from the negative effects of dependence on transnational corporations (Wood 1986).

Fuel disruption, petrodollars, and dependent development were neither the only nor the most important causes of developing countries' increased reliance on private loans. In fact, private banks' largest investment increases in developing countries occurred earlier, in the late 1960s and early 1970s (OECD 1984a; Moffitt 1983). Among other reasons, the return on corporate loans fell sharply during this period, causing banks to search aggressively for new loan customers (Moffitt 1983, 93–97).

Developing countries came to rely on loans from private banks for several reasons. Global inflation and the declining value of the dollar during this period meant that real interest rates were negative (Wood 1986, 243). More important, private bank loans offered developing countries an avenue of "escape from the discipline of the aid regime" of official agencies such as the International Monetary Fund and the International Bank for Reconstruction and Development (Wood 1986, 245). Official aid was generally earmarked for specific projects with strict conditions. Projects funded by official agencies had to be oriented toward attracting private industry. Recipient countries could not use the funds for social welfare expenditures or state-owned or -controlled enterprises. By contrast, Euromarket loans carried few specific conditions (except those affecting repayment and default) and were not tied to particular projects. As long as the loans were repaid (or at least serviced), banks did not care what they were used for. Private banks' continued reliance on the IMF to impose conditions and policy changes on developing countries can be traced to their embarrassing failure at such efforts in Peru in 1976–1977 (Wood 1986; Stallings 1979).

Private bank loans hence enabled developing countries to avoid official agencies' "strategic withholding" of aid. Strategic withholding from particular sectors or projects empowered official aid agencies to influence the development policies of recipient countries (Payer 1974). In particular, official agencies routinely withheld aid from state-owned industries, while more readily funding projects for private industrial development. Developing countries could use commercial loans to maintain and expand state-sponsored industrial development (Wood 1986). Finally, private banks' lack of concern about policies and the use of loans enabled developing countries to expand social welfare expenditures despite mounting fiscal deficits (Reynolds 1978). As a rule, private bank loans enhanced the state's relative autonomy in determining policies, relations with constituents, and the direction of development. Mexico's experience was no exception.

The borrowing market of developing countries offers a fairly attractive investment opportunity to private banks because they receive large commissions from loan placements and interest payments (Gonzalez 1985; U.S. Congress, Senate 1982, 343–345). The ten largest U.S. banks make almost half their total profits from foreign investments (Moffitt 1983, 51). Indeed, Lichtensztejn and Quijano (1982, 203) point out that "international loan operations carry considerable weight in the total profits made by banks. . . . The international gains of the thirteen principal United States banks amounted to 34.2 per cent of total profits in 1973 and 47.7 per cent in 1975, and it is estimated that roughly 75 per cent of the profits of United States banks in 1976 came from their foreign operations."

In addition to the structural transformation in the capital markets for developing countries, there has been increasing concentration in both the lending organizations and the recipient countries: two-thirds of private bank loans are concentrated in five countries and three-fourths in ten countries (Dhonte 1979; Lichtensztejn and Quijano 1982; OECD 1984a; Marsden and Roe 1984; Sanchez Arnau 1982; Stallings 1982).[2] Moreover, in 1975 only six banks provided almost 40 percent of developing countries' debt from private international banks (Dale and Mattione 1983; Lichtensztejn and Quijano 1982).[3]

Meanwhile the trend in international capital markets has moved toward lending consortia, for several reasons:

1. The capital requirements of most developing countries are so high that no single bank could reasonably (or legally) cover them. Lending consortia give banks access to this desirable and profitable business.
2. Lending consortia spread the risks.
3. Such syndicated arrangements enhance the profitability of loans,

2. In 1976 these ten countries were Brazil, Mexico, the Republic of (South) Korea, Argentina, Peru, the Philippines, Taiwan, Colombia, Thailand, and Chile—in order of proportionate reliance on private sources of finance capital (Lichtensztejn and Quijano 1982, 198). By 1981 the list had changed slightly, but the proportionate concentration remained as pronounced. The ten most indebted countries that year were Mexico, Brazil, Venezuela, Argentina, South Korea, Chile, the Philippines, Indonesia, Taiwan, and Nigeria (Moffitt 1983, 103).

3. The six largest private lenders are Citicorp, Bank of America Corp., J. P. Morgan & Co., Chase Manhattan Corp., Manufacturers Hanover Trust Corp., Chemical New York Corp., Bankers' Trust New York Corp., and Continental Illinois Corp. (Lichtensztejn and Quijano 1982, 203; Moffitt 1983, 52; Dale and Mattione 1983).

since consortia charge higher commission fees than individual banks for administration and participation.

Lending consortia thus represent power for the private banking community because they structurally organize and unify the control of capital flows: "Risk-sharing . . . becomes a source of strength [for the private banking community], since a joint commitment by banks in different countries presents a solid front to discourage the outbreak of disputes with debtor States" (Lichtensztejn and Quijano 1982, 205).

These developments have formed a structurally hegemonic international banking community whose collective control of capital flows can constrain the relative autonomy of nation-states. The concentration of international capital flows in fewer and fewer banks and the enormous size of states' lending consortia also give the banking community the potential to socially construct international economic reality.

Shocks to the international financial system in recent years could have caused the system to collapse. Mexico, Argentina, and Brazil were the most significant on a long list of developing countries in danger of defaulting on foreign loans by 1982. Peru has threatened to limit its debt repayments to 10 percent of its exports (*Wall Street Journal*, 31 July 1985, 1). In Africa, where the export earnings for many poor countries are negligible or negative, increasing debt service burdens are creating what Brooke (1987, 11) calls a "financial famine." Meanwhile, persistent inflation and recession continue to erode the balance of payments of developing countries, further aggravating their debt positions. Yet despite the great threat of collapse in the international monetary and financial system, the banking community has weathered the storm and continues to thrive.[4]

Developing countries have not fared so well. Many have suf-

---

4. Some banks recently claimed that they had already lost a substantial amount of money by increasing the reserves to cover future state defaults. For example, Citicorp added $3 billion to its loan reserves in 1987, claiming a $2.5 billion loss (*Chicago Tribune*, 20 May 1987, C1). But this loss is an illusion. The banks have simply set money aside to minimize the risk of loss. They have not really lost money; they have invested less by removing it from the market. Banks' profit rates are high enough that the slightly decreased income still represents a healthy profit.

fered contracting economies, high unemployment, stratospheric inflation rates, devalued currency, and mounting debt. What processes and relations produced the foreign debt crisis? How did the banking community overcome grave difficulties to socially construct international economic reality? What is the basis of the relative autonomy of the state in the world political economy, and how does the control of capital flows affect that autonomy?

To address these questions, I will focus on Mexico's massive foreign debt crisis, which had great significance for the banking community.

Setting the Stage

Mexico's foreign debt difficulties owe much to its previous trade dependency and consequent mass dissatisfaction in the 1960s. Mexicans began to question Mexico's "miracle" of economic growth—averaging 6 percent annually for thirty years with limited inflation—after a violent clash in 1968 between students and the army (*New York Times*, 29 Aug. 1982, E3; Barkin and Esteva 1986; Cockcroft 1983). Protesters criticized Mexico's approach to growth and development, which heightened the already unequal distribution of land and wealth (Reynolds 1978; Kraft 1984; Barkin 1986). Increases in productive capacity during the 1940s and 1950s had stimulated growth and price stability in the 1960s, but productivity gains in agriculture and manufacturing continued to increase underemployment. High underemployment meant decreased state revenues. At the same time, the industrialization of the 1940s and 1950s had encouraged urbanization and population growth, which increased the demands on state capital expenditures. Mexican officials feared that changes in fiscal and exchange rate policies would cause an exodus of private investors that would destroy the Mexican miracle (Reynolds 1978).

In addition, Mexico continued to support and subsidize national industries that competed with multinational firms—an increasingly expensive policy (Davis 1986). Mexican leaders therefore chose to finance the country's deficit with long-term loans. From 1965 to 1970 loans increased at an annual rate of 34 percent, while foreign direct investment increased only 5.5 percent. Interest payments since 1965 have increased fourfold, with debt servicing growing from 35 to 95 percent of new loans (Reynolds 1978, 1007–1008; see also Davis 1986).

The state addressed the popular criticism and reduced the left's radical appeal by becoming more directly engaged in rectifying these imbalances. President Luis Echeverría Alvarez established social, educational, health, housing, and rural development programs (see Dramatis Personae 5). He stimulated new job creation

Dramatis Personae 5. Mexico's Foreign Debt Crisis
(in order of appearance)

Luis Echeverría Alvarez	President of Mexico (1970–1976)
José López Portillo	President of Mexico (1976–1982)
Jorge Díaz Serrano	President, Pemex
David Ibarra Munoz	Mexican finance secretary (1976–1982)
Jesus Silva Herzog	Mexican finance minister (1982)
John F. Beck	Vice president, North American Vehicles Overseas
Paul Volcker	Chairman, U.S. Federal Reserve Board
Jacques de Larosière	Managing director, International Monetary Fund
Carlos Tello	Director, Mexico's central bank (1981)
Fidel Velazquez	President of Mexico's unions
Miguel de la Madrid Hurtado	President of Mexico (1982–1988)
Miguel Mancera	Director, Mexico's central bank (1982)
Willard D. Andres	President, Latin American division of Becton Dickinson and Co.
Angel Gurria	Mexico's public credit director
William S. Ogden	Vice Chairman, Chase Manhattan Bank, N.A.
Congressman Stewart B. McKinney	Member, House Committee on Banking, Finance, and Urban Affairs

Congressman Fernand J. St. Germain	Member, House Committee on Banking, Finance, and Urban Affairs
Congressman Charles Schumer	Member, House Committee on Banking, Finance, and Urban Affairs
Lionel H. Olmer	Under secretary for international trade, U.S. Department of Commerce
Senator William Proxmire	Member, Senate Finance Committee
Marc E. Leland	U.S. assistant secretary of the Treasury for international affairs
William H. Draper	Chairman, Export-Import Bank
Alfred H. Kingon	U.S. assistant secretary of commerce

by supporting tourism and by subsidizing the steel, auto, and chemical industries. These measures pushed the annual growth rate in 1971 and 1972 to 7 percent. But private-sector opposition within the ruling party (Partido Revolucionario Institucional, or PRI) quashed the initial plan to pay for these programs through increased taxation of the private sector. Subsequently inflation, which had kept pace with U.S. inflation, began to rise faster, increasing 12 percent in 1973, 24 percent in 1974, and 15 percent in 1975. Simultaneously the world recession eroded the foreign markets for Mexican exports, seriously damaging Mexico's balance of payments (U.S. Congress, Joint Session 1984; Senate 1983a, 32). By 1976 Mexico had devalued the peso for the first time in decades, from 12.5 to 20 pesos per dollar (Kraft 1984, 33; *New York Times,* 1 Sept. 1976, 49). Devaluation "almost doubl[ed] the real foreign debt (to almost $50 billion)" (Cockcroft 1983, 259).

Echeverría's solution was a stabilization program with the IMF. This plan touched off a great deal of controversy within the government. When Echeverría's term ended in 1976, PRI replaced him with José López Portillo, whose approach to Mexico's problems depended on the country's oil industry (nationalized since 1938). The quadrupling of oil prices in 1973 meant that Mexico's oil could salvage the country from disaster. Indeed, Mexico freed itself from the IMF's program by 1979 primarily through its $4 billion in crude oil exports, which produced a growth boom between 1978 and 1981 (*New York Times,* 12 Sept. 1982, F1; U.S. Congress, House 1983b; U.S. Congress, Senate 1983a). During the boom Mexico had an annual real growth rate of 8 percent, created 500,000 new jobs a year, and had an annual investment rate of 20 percent. Oil became critical to the Mexican economy: 75 percent of Mexico's export earnings derived from petroleum (Cockcroft 1983; Hamilton 1986b; *New York Times,* 12 Sept. 1982, F1). Meanwhile, from 1976 to 1980 Mexico tripled its reliance on imported capital goods to 80 percent (Cockcroft 1983). In addition the green revolution of the 1960s generated increasing inequality, focused agricultural activity on export processing, and reduced Mexico's ability to meet its own basic food requirements. By 1980 Mexico had to import "half of all its basic grain needs" (Barkin and Esteva 1986, 134).

Mexico's rapid growth also produced problems: "The combination of too much money chasing too few goods achieved its usual result—inflation, up from 15 to 35% in 1980" (Kraft 1984, 34; see also Taylor 1984, 148). The rate jumped to over 100 percent in 1982 (*New York Times,* 21 Aug. 1982, 32; 12 Sept. 1982, F1). In 1981 the global oil glut undermined the price of crude oil. Jorge Díaz Serrano (president of Pemex, Mexico's national oil company) attempted to lower the price of Mexican premium crude from $30 to $28 per barrel to stay competitive with other oil producers. Díaz Serrano was overruled by strong opposition from both the radicals, who disliked the oil boom because it enriched the wealthy at the expense of the poor, and the orthodox economists, who disliked the resulting inflation. After his resignation, the price of Mexican crude oil returned to $30 per barrel, with exactly the consequences Díaz Serrano expected. Major customers in the United States, France, and Japan canceled their orders, causing Mexico's oil exports to plunge from 1.5 million barrels per day to 1.1 million. The damage was significant:

By the time the price was restored in September, Mexico had lost at least a billion dollars in projected revenues. Holders of pesos, alert to the trouble ahead, stepped up their conversion to dollars or their purchase of foreign goods. The net loss in foreign exchange was some $5 billion for the year. That constituted a substantial fraction of the payments deficit during the year—$13 billion. (Kraft 1984, 35)

The need to close that enormous balance-of-payments deficit helped push Mexico into debt in the foreign capital market (U.S. Congress, House 1982, 1983a; Joint Session 1984).

Riding the Debt Spiral

Like other developing countries, Mexico became indebted to the private banking community because of its attempts to escape the restrictions of official aid agencies and because of the structural transformation of the capital market (Wood 1986). Both the private and public sectors in Mexico relied heavily on foreign loans to finance the phenomenal growth of the 1970s, because during this period the Mexican economy turned toward import substitution manufacturing of consumer goods instead of the previous industrial production, which depended on capital goods importation. Ironically, the rapid expansion of Mexico's petroleum industry aggravated the dependence on foreign loans because Mexico had to import the technology required for that industry's development. While export earnings soared from $6 billion in 1977 to $19 billion in 1981 (75 percent of which derived from petroleum), imports nearly quadrupled from $6 billion to $23 billion (Hamilton 1986b, 154–155). Earnings from petroleum exports were wiped out by the cost of the imported goods required to support the growth of the oil industry, producing a balance-of-trade gap.

Getting into debt came quickly and easily for Mexico. Pemex borrowed $10 billion in 1981. (Its previous total debt was $5 billion.) Mexico's total debt increased in 1981 from $55 billion to $80 billion (*New York Times*, 17 Aug. 1982, D17). It owed almost $34 billion (60 percent) to U.S. banks, which shortened the maturities on this debt (U.S. Congress, House 1982, 6–7; Joint Session 1984, 46; see also *New York Times*, 21 Aug. 1982, 32; 31 Aug. 1982, D1). In the first half of 1981 only 5 percent of Mexico's debt was due within one year. That proportion climbed dramatically to 22 percent by the end of that year. The majority of the new loans were due in six months (U.S. Congress, Joint Session 1984; Kraft 1984, 35).

López Portillo refused to cut government expenditures or raise new taxes despite Mexico's quickly deteriorating situation (*New York Times*, 9 Sept. 1982, D19). Instead Mexico devalued the peso several times, further eroding its balance of payments (U.S. Congress, Joint Session 1984; Barkin and Esteva 1986; Hamilton 1986b).

In addition, because of internal political struggles Mexico's leaders often made contradictory decisions. For example, only days after announcing a devaluation in March 1982, the government allowed a wage increase that reduced the benefits of the devaluation. Austerity measures that were supposed to accompany the devaluation (including decreases in public spending, increased interest rates, and more price increases to discourage food and oil overconsumption) never materialized. The capital markets responded by raising the interest rate on Mexico's $100 million Eurodollar loan to 18.5 percent (Kraft 1984, 37; see also *New York Times,* 19 May 1982, D8; 25 May 1982, D1).

Although high inflation and interest rates and repeated currency devaluations seriously hurt Mexican industrialists, Mexican bankers benefited from the situation (Hamilton 1986b). Mexico's economic expansion of the 1970s included a significant transformation in its banking community. The number of banks fell from 243 in 1976 to 63 in 1981 as a result of a streamlining program by Finance Secretary David Ibarra Munoz in which many small banks were combined into large ones. At the same time Munoz urged Mexican banks to join major Western banks in lending consortia, thereby increasing their access to international financial resources. The resulting concentration of resources was dramatic: "By 1982, 65 percent of [Mexican] banking assets and 75 percent of profits were concentrated in the three largest banks" (Hamilton 1986b, 155). This concentration and access to foreign capital resources benefited the Mexican banks during the continued devaluations because they earned high interest rates on assets and earned profits from dollar investments ouside Mexico. But Mexican industrialists, who had no access to international financial resources, suffered from the devaluations of the peso and high interest rates on their outstanding debts (Hamilton 1986b).

Further devaluations of the peso and increases in imports produced a flight from the peso. Some foreign banks whose loans were maturing refused to renew them (U.S. Congress, House 1983a; Kraft 1984, 37; *New York Times,* 17 Aug. 1982, D1). Mexico's new finance minister, Jesus Silva Herzog, instituted a series of emergency measures that failed to ease the country's economic crunch. In mid-August 1982 Silva approached the U.S. government for a rescue plan.

Meanwhile López Portillo had another approach in mind. He believed that Mexico's problems derived from the massive transfer of money out of the country by the banks and the wealthy and middle classes. He wanted to plug that drain by nationalizing Mexico's banks and by using exchange controls (*New York Times*, 9 Sept. 1982, D19; Hamilton 1986b). The measures were supposed to produce funds that the government could invest productively. The business community and several Mexican government officials, including Finance Minister Silva, opposed the plan. Silva argued that these measures would not stop capital flight from Mexico, but rather would aggravate it by provoking a loss of confidence in the Mexican government and economy (*New York Times*, 3 Sept. 1982, 2).

On 31 August 1982 López Portillo sought to pacify increasingly militant workers and peasants by signing decrees that nationalized the banks and imposed exchange controls to stop the flight of pesos (Cockcroft 1983). Americans with business investments and fixed-interest dollar documents in Mexico were "angry and alarmed" at the continual devaluation of the peso, the freezing of dollar assets, and the imposition of currency exchange controls (*New York Times*, 24 Aug. 1982, D13). The devaluations also placed Mexican corporations in a debt crisis. Grupo Alfa, Mexico's largest private corporation, was among the hardest hit by the devaluations; it responded by suspending payment on the principal and most of the interest on $2.3 billion in foreign debt (*Business Week*, 23 Aug. 1982, 41; see also *New York Times*, 12 Sept. 1982, F1; Hamilton 1986b).

Currency controls frightened and infuriated the upper classes. Corporations, which could only meet their foreign obligations with dollars, were also angered by the uncertainty about their access to dollars and the rate at which access would be achieved. Groups such as the National Association of Exporters and Importers lodged accusations of governmental incompetence and panicky decision making (*Business Week*, 30 Aug. 1982, 38; Hamilton 1986b). The devaluations and currency controls also worried and antagonized U.S. corporations. John F. Beck, vice president of

North American Vehicles Overseas (a division of General Motors) warned that the devaluations would generate severe price increases that the market would not bear. Many other business leaders noted that if the Mexican government's extreme measures were not temporary, they would be considered expropriation (*Business Week*, 30 Aug. 1982, 38).

The U.S. government, alarmed by the implications of Mexico's debt crisis, arranged a package in August 1982 in which the United States agreed to buy $1 billion of Mexican oil for its strategic reserve at prices well below market value, and to pay in advance (Cockcroft 1983). Mexican steel and cement corporations found eager markets in Texas and other U.S. Sunbelt states that were still enjoying growth (*Business Week*, 13 Sept. 1982, 106).

The Mexican debt crisis and the subsequent currency controls and devaluations also affected U.S. multinational corporations and threatened corporate loans. Many firms had to reexamine their corporate priorities as profits and earnings fell and shipments were interrupted. As one reporter noted, "Many U.S. corporations have Mexican affiliates with substantial dollar debt being placed in overdraft" (*Business Week*, 4 Oct. 1982, 87; see also Erb 1982; *New York Times*, 7 Oct. 1982, D1). Most firms ceased all but the most critical shipments to Mexico, and some companies supplied their Mexican subsidiaries with just enough capital to ensure the subsidiaries' survival. When non-Mexican suppliers to the subsidiaries nervously demanded that the U.S. parent company guarantee payment in advance, most of these corporations refused. The suppliers, meanwhile, risked losing their market shares by refusing to make unguaranteed shipments to long-standing customers. One banker summed up the corporate dilemma: "If you want to continue to do business down there, you have to do it on open account and risk not getting paid" (*Business Week*, 4 Oct. 1982, 87). Interestingly, the banks were unwilling to accept this risk and later struggled for state bailouts of their investments in Mexico (U.S. Congress, House 1983b; Senate 1983a).

The weak peso and uncontrolled inflation sent unemployment soaring in a country where underemployment already stood at 50 percent. More than a million Mexican workers lost their jobs in 1982. Half the layoffs were in construction (Cockcroft 1983; Hamilton 1986b). General Motors had laid off 1,000 of its 9,000

Mexican workers by September 1982. Severe declines in auto sales prompted massive layoffs in Mexico's steel industry (*Business Week*, 13 Sept. 1982, 104). The new layoffs, together with the old underemployment and inflation, seriously eroded Mexican consumer demand. Workers' purchasing power declined because of the labor unions' agreement to support López Portillo's job creation objectives by accepting more modest wage increases during Mexico's more prosperous years (*Business Week*, 13 Sept. 1982, 104). Antagonisms between labor and the state were already heated because López Portillo had recently increased the price of such food staples as corn, tortillas, and bread by 50 to 100 percent and of beans (Mexicans' major protein source) by 265 percent as a means of reducing the subsidy burdens of the crisis-ridden state (*Business Week*, 13 Sept. 1982, 104; Cockcroft 1983; Hamilton 1986b).

Although López Portillo imposed exchange controls to reduce the budget deficit, most social expenditures continued. He argued: "Government spending . . . is the most useful means for achieving the redistribution of income. . . . There has been no squandering of resources. Every program has its own justification" (Kraft 1984, 38–39). These measures made the banking community extremely nervous, and some banks began to take action. They inundated Mexican branch banks in New York with demands for over $70 million in repayments and deposits. At the close of business on 7 September 1982, two major U.S. banks (Chemical and Manufacturers Hanover) found themselves $70 million short, a situation that, left uncorrected, jeopardized the entire clearinghouse system of the banking community (Kraft 1984, 40–41). Paul Volcker, chairman of the Federal Reserve Board, arranged to deposit $70 million into the two banks' accounts from money the Bank for International Settlements (BIS) had advanced to Mexico (*New York Times*, 31 Aug. 1982, D5). But he emphasized that this was merely a temporary solution, since any demand for Mexico to pay all its $6 billion in obligations would absorb all the money advanced by BIS, the United States, and the IMF. An advisory committee told Mexican officials not to pay the demands in full yet.

At this point negotiations between the IMF, Mexico, the United States, and the banking community began to develop an austerity program for Mexico. A great deal of struggling between Mexican officials and Jacques de Larosière, managing director of the IMF, ensued in the negotiations. De Larosière rejected López Portillo's approach, insisting instead that Mexico develop policies to cut government expenditures and hold down wages (U.S. Congress, House 1983a; Joint Session 1984). Mexican officials Carlos Tello (director of the central bank) and Fidel Velazquez (head of Mexico's unions) opposed the IMF's standard austerity program. They advocated an administrative retrenchment program involving "a preset and generally overvalued exchange rate, exchange controls, and import licensing." Mexican leaders viewed this alternative approach as Mexican nationalism, facilitating a reduction in "trade and financial dependence on the U.S." (*Business Week*, 22 Nov. 1982, 55; see also *New York Times*, 9 Sept. 1982, D19). Volcker, Mexico's advisory committee, and Silva all supported the IMF's position.

These struggles and the mounting pressures prior to the August crisis had a political impact. López Portillo and PRI selected Miguel de la Madrid Hurtado to succeed as president. De la Madrid shifted Mexico's economic policy away from the populist alternative toward compliance with the IMF's austerity program. In his inauguration speech de la Madrid announced his plan to reduce the country's deficit, a plan that included a tax increase, cutbacks in public works programs, and the elimination of subsidies on domestic consumer products such as tortillas and gasoline. Indeed, the next day de la Madrid "doubled the cost of gasoline—twice the increase anticipated by most Mexicans" (*Business Week*, 13 Dec. 1982, 55). Whereas López Portillo firmly resisted the IMF in his last days as president, de la Madrid committed Mexico

to cut the budget deficit drastically—from an estimated 16.5% of gross national product in 1981 to 8.5% in 1983. Foreign borrowing was to be reduced by three-quarters—from $20 billion in 1981 to $5 billion in 1983. Inflation was to be cut from roughly 100% in 1982 to 55% in 1983. Subsidies, imports and wage hikes were to be lowered accordingly, and taxes raised. Inevitably growth would be negative for a long time to come. (Kraft 1984, 46; see also *New York Times*, 11 Nov. 1982, A1; Taylor 1984, 147–150)

Silva hoped to use the agreement to raise the banking community's confidence in Mexico. Mexican officials wanted the banks to extend the ninety-day moratorium on payment of principal, granted in late August, for another ninety days (Kraft 1984, 46; see also *New York Times,* 17 Nov. 1982, D9). But the banks refused to agree to the extension unless Mexico satisfied two conditions. First, the banks wanted Mexico to maintain its interbank deposits to ensure that other foreign banks would not gain access to Mexico's finances at the expense of the major banks. If Mexico did not comply, the major banks threatened to declare the country in default. Second, the banking community wanted Mexico to address the debt in the private sector. The currency exchange controls imposed by the Mexican government made it impossible for Mexican firms (including those with healthy balance sheets) to find the dollars necessary to pay off or service their debts. The banks wanted the Mexican government to rectify this situation, which threatened to force the banks to reclassify the loans for nonpayment of interest—a move that would have negative consequences for the banks (Kraft 1984, 47; *New York Times,* 15 Dec. 1982, D2). The banks also wanted Mexico to guarantee the private sector's debt (Wood 1986). Although Mexico basically agreed to establish a mechanism to satisfy these conditions, it hinged on the Mexican central bank's ability to accumulate dollars and on the approval of the U.S. Federal Reserve.

Despite those misgivings the U.S. banking community generally applauded de la Madrid's program to shift the Mexican economy toward a free-market orientation. His approach transferred the blame for Mexico's economic woes from greedy bankers and exploitative industrialized countries to "the Mexicans themselves" (*Business Week,* 13 Dec. 1982, 27; see also Cockcroft 1983). In line with this position, he reinstated Miguel Mancera as head of the central bank and retained Jesus Silva Herzog as finance minister. Both men opposed López Portillo's program of exchange controls and bank nationalization (*Business Week,* 13 Dec. 1982, 27; Hamilton 1986b). Members of the Mexican labor movement and leftists in the ruling party were not among de la Madrid's appointees. The pattern of appointments silenced labor and alternative populist viewpoints in favor of the approach preferred by the IMF and the banking and business communities. Willard D. Andres, president of the Latin American division of the U.S.-based Becton Dickinson and Co., noted, "Business supports this guy, and business is prepared to wait to get some of the fruits" (*Business Week*, 13 Dec. 1982, 28). Business interests had a strong ally in the new state administration, which would work on their behalf in negotiations with the IMF and the banking community. The wait was worthwhile for the business community. De la Madrid denationalized 33 percent of the banking industry in 1983 by selling shares in Mexican banks to the private sector (*Business Week*, 10 Jan. 1984, 40; Hamilton 1986b). He also sold shares in "nonessential" firms held by the nationalized banks (*New York Times*, 22 May 1984, D8; Hamilton 1986b).

The Struggle Intensifies

While Mexican officials struggled with the banking community over the specifics of Mexico's rescue, de Larosière of the IMF had bigger goals in mind: he wanted to develop a model to preserve the international financial system. At a meeting he called with top executives of the banks on Mexico's advisory committee, de Larosière "presented an analysis of Mexico's financial requirements for 1983." They included $1.5 billion for reserves, $2.55 billion to repay loans from BIS and the U.S. Federal Reserve, and a deficit of $4.25 billion, for a total of $8.3 billion (Kraft 1984, 48; see also *New York Times*, 23 Dec. 1982, D12; 24 Dec. 1982, D4). According to de Larosière, the IMF was ready to extend $1.3 billion. He believed the United States and other foreign governments could offer $2 billion. The remaining $5 billion, he told the banks, would have to come from them. To underscore his position, de Larosière informed the banks that he would not recommend that the IMF accept Mexico's program of adjustment without new money from them (Kraft 1984, 48).

The IMF and de Larosière received some support for this approach from Volcker, who implied that the Federal Reserve would not strictly apply regulatory rules against banks that made additional loans to Mexico. Fearing the collapse of the banking community without the support of the IMF, the banks accepted the second ninety-day postponement of Mexico's debt payments. After wrangling over how to raise the $5 billion, the U.S. banking community reached a settlement with the IMF and the European banking community. Under the U.S. banks' prevailing solution, *all* the participating banks were assessed an additional 7 percent over their existing exposure to Mexico (termed the "7 percent solution", see Kraft 1984, 50).[5] The U.S. banks thus structurally unified the international banking community in relation to Mexico.

De la Madrid instituted a series of measures for Mexico's recovery, including the easing of exchange controls, an increase in interest rates, and an arrangement whereby Mexico's private sector could gain access to dollars to make interest payments on their loans. Negotiations had concluded by early December 1982. The new $5 billion loan would be repaid over six years, with a grace period of three years and a fee of 2⅛ percent over the U.S. prime rate, plus a 1¼ percent up-front negotiating fee to the banks. The agreement also extended the 180-day moratorium on the repayment of $20 billion to the close of 1984; repayment would be made over eight years, with a four-year grace period, at an interest rate of 1¾ percent over the U.S. prime rate and an up-front negotiating fee of 1 percent to the banks (Kraft 1984, 51; see also *New York Times*, 16 Dec. 1982, D8; 17 Dec. 1982, D6). Mexico had stepped back from the brink of bankruptcy—at least temporarily.

The Scorecard

We can evaluate the relative power of each of the participants in Mexico's rescue by comparing the benefits received and the concessions made. The Mexican government was able to negotiate for time. It avoided default but agreed to an additional annual interest payment of $150 million for eight years. Mexico also accepted an IMF-imposed austerity program that has a history of undermining economic recovery and development (Girvan 1980; Debt Crisis Network 1985).

In exchange for extending the moratorium on Mexico's debt and providing new loans, the banks received profitable rates: "They raised by half a point the average they were receiving on the rescheduled debt. They got for the new money a half-point more in interest than they had received for the last big commercial loan to Mexico" (Kraft 1984, 51). Although half-point increases may not

5. The European banks and the IMF preferred assessing 9 percent above the total exposure, eliminating the necessity of including every small and European bank to preserve the rescue project. The U.S. major banks preferred the "7 percent solution" because it required all banks to participate.

sound like a great deal, the enormous principal produces millions of dollars. Furthermore, the up-front negotiation fee of 1¼ percent translates into $200 million at no risk. One banker noted that most of the up-front renegotiation fee is pure profit for the banks, because "the administrative costs associated with renegotiating the loans were 'not near' the amount of the fee" (*New York Times*, 10 Jan. 1983, D1). The Federal Reserve conceded that up-front fees may be part of the cause of debt crises in developing countries, because they provide an additional incentive to banks to "seek out international loans in order to boost earnings immediately, and, once this has occurred, to sustain past earnings levels" (U.S. Congress, House 1983c, 134).

In addition, the U.S. banking community reasserted itself as the international heavyweight champion by winning the struggle with European banks over the so-called 7 percent solution. The final agreement with Mexico "set a precedent for similarly advantageous terms with Brazil, Argentina, and other troubled countries" (Kraft 1984, 52; *New York Times*, 25 Feb. 1983, D1). Above all, instead of absorbing massive losses, the banks increased their earnings under the agreement. One Federal Reserve official noted that Citibank's earnings increased by $8 million. As Angel Gurria, Mexico's public credit director, noted: "The banks did fabulously well on the deal. They played the good Samaritan and did their best business. They made 70 to 90% on their capital. Restructuring turned out to be good business for them" (Kraft 1984, 52). Indeed, several banks reported that they could earn a profit of more than $300 million in fees for renegotiating the loans of Mexico, Argentina, Brazil, and Costa Rica alone (*New York Times*, 10 Jan. 1983, D1).

In congressional hearings on U.S. legislation to bail out the banks' investments in Mexico, Volcker indicated that the federal government may have helped precipitate Mexico's crisis. He admitted that the interest rates on Mexico's debt were sometimes as high as 20 percent and that the peak interest rate coincided with Mexico's crisis. Yet Volcker insisted that although "there was no question that when world interest rates went up that added greatly to their [Mexico's] balance of payments problem and helped precipitate their difficulty," the Mexicans would not have been affected by the interest rates "if they [hadn't had] the debts in the first place" (U.S. Congress, House 1983a, 135–136). Volcker's analysis ignores the banks' pressure on Mexico to borrow, federal pressure on U.S. banks to continue to lend to Mexico, and the role of the Federal Reserve in raising interest rates. His refusal to acknowledge the banks' and the United States' responsibility in creating the debt crisis in Mexico infuriated many congressional leaders, who noted the hypocrisy of bailing out the banking industry when the Reagan administration was heavily promoting laissez-faire in the business community.

Disciplining the International Banking Community

Parts of the international banking community were displeased with the U.S. banks' domination of the agreement with Mexico. In particular, Japanese and European banks were angry that previous loans to Mexico served as the baseline in computing the value of the 7 percent solution. Japanese banks argued that they had never made any direct loans to Mexico, but had simply "acquired promissory notes from U.S. banks" (Kraft 1984, 52). Swiss banks claimed that Mexico's baseline numbers included the sale of bonds (which were specifically excluded from the rescue agreement).

Regional and local banks in the United States were equally contentious. They were not as heavily exposed to Mexico as were the major commercial banks. The small banks resented being forced, in effect, to bail out the large banks (Kraft 1984, 52). Regional and local banks were particularly unhappy that the large money center banks made the policy decisions and agreements that all banks had to abide by: "We never participated in jumbo loans to the Mexican government. So we didn't feel we should pay for the mistakes of the money center banks. Just because they decided to put up an additional 7 per cent was no reason for us to do it. 'Who decided what and why?' was the question I kept raising," complained one regional banker (Kraft 1984, 53). But the large U.S. banks had state help to enforce those decisions. When one Florida bank balked at the 7 percent solution, the Federal Reserve got involved. The head of the recalcitrant bank explained:

We made trouble for the big banks on the theory that they might let us out of all the loans just to get us out of their hair. At one point we even made noises about a law suit against some of the Mexican banks. That turned out to be unwise. The threats came to the attention of the Federal

Reserve Board. The Fed is our main regulator, and in fact we need approval for a merger. The bank examiners came around and started asking questions. That was enough for us. We dropped the suit. (Kraft 1984, 53)

The large U.S. banks achieved unity in the international banking community despite the resistance of Japanese and European banks and small regional U.S. banks, which claimed that the so-called 7 percent solution placed an inequitable burden on them to support what was essentially a rescue plan for the large U.S. banks. The mechanism that compelled opponents to comply with the large U.S. banks' solution was the structure of lending consortia. More than 1,600 banks had jointly provided loans to Mexico (U.S. Congress, House 1982, 52). A refusal by the major U.S. banks to renegotiate those loans would have meant a significant loss to all and bankruptcy for some. The sheer size of the large U.S. banks put them in a stronger position than the small banks to flirt with the possibility of a Mexican default without suffering bankruptcy. Their size all but guaranteed the large banks a federal bailout, since the U.S. government has always feared the economic and political repercussions of bankruptcies among major banks.

Although each bank's exposure to Mexico would in theory determine its ability to absorb Mexico's bankruptcy, past congressional action indicated that the size of the bank would be the more important factor. Furthermore, participating in lending consortia is the only way small banks can get access to the lucrative corporate and national lending business. They had to comply with the 7 percent solution or forfeit participation in future lending consortia of all sorts.

The forces of discipline in the international banking community were formidable. In the United States the major commercial banks applied pressure on the regional banks, and the regionals pressured the local banks. Mexico's advisory board (composed predominately of bank representatives) invoked whatever forms of pressure it considered appropriate: "Sometimes we [the board] brought pressure from state or Federal regulators; sometimes from figures in the local community; sometimes from other bankers" (Kraft 1984, 53). Apparently the major banks had little difficulty getting state institutions to apply pressure on their behalf.

Internationally, the U.S. Treasury unofficially pressured the Japanese, French, and Swiss governments to "make their banks see reason on the basic financing formula." British and French bankers visited the Middle East to convince Kuwaiti and Saudi Arabian bankers to cooperate. De Larosière himself promoted the agreement to Italian bankers (Kraft 1984, 53). Finally, the comptroller of the currency in the United States sent a letter to Mexico's advisory board reaffirming Volcker's earlier promise that the Federal Reserve would ease regulations for all banks participating in the loan agreement, as stipulated by the IMF. After much arm-twisting, the major banks successfully disciplined the rest of the banking community into a hegemonic front. The rescue operation was well on its way. What the banks now needed was state support in developing a mechanism to bail out their investments. That effort quickly found a voice in congressional hearings on increased quotas for U.S. participation in the IMF and on new facilities at the Export-Import Bank for Mexico (and Brazil, which had similar problems).

Bailing Out the Banks

Two major proposals before Congress addressed the debt crisis facing developing countries. Heated controversy attended the hearings on the increase in U.S. financial support for the IMF and on new facilities for the Export-Import Bank. Many government and banking industry representatives who testified at the IMF hearings called the proposed increase a form of jobs bill for the United States—the same argument they had used during Chrysler's bailout hearings (see U.S. Congress, House 1983a, 1983c; Senate, 1983b).

Volcker insisted that if the United States did not resolve the debt problems of developing countries (particularly of those most important to the United States, such as Mexico), "the prospects for growth in the industrialized world and then in the developing world and in the U.S. would be impaired. We would jeopardize our jobs and our exports and financial markets if this situation is not managed" (U.S. Congress, House 1983a, 10). Volcker reminded Congress that approximately 5.1 million U.S. jobs in 1980 were export related (U.S. Congress, House 1983c, 7). Mexico, the third largest importer of U.S. goods and services, is a key market for U.S. exports. The foreign debt crisis (and the imposed austerity program) had a profound effect on Mexico's imports; in 1983 imports fell 60 percent below 1982 levels and nearly 70 percent below

1981 levels. The United States suffered a $6.2 billion drop in exports to Mexico in 1982 and another $3 billion drop in 1983; "almost 85% of that decline occurred in the manufacturing sector, and that total translates to almost a quarter of a million lost jobs for American workers" (U.S. Congress, House 1983b, 44; see also House 1983c, 38; Senate 1983b).

Volcker repeatedly denied that the increased quotas to the IMF were designed to bail out the banks, but he could not categorically deny that the increases would benefit them. Indeed, Volcker acknowledged the pivotal role of the banking community in international and national affairs by asserting that the financial stability of the nation and of the world system depended on the health and stability of the banks (U.S. Congress, House 1983a, 14, 15).

Bankers did not deny the benefits to them of the proposed increases and at times were blunt about their power to inflict a world crisis unless they received help from the state. William S. Ogden, vice chairman of Chase Manhattan Bank, N.A., noted, "With one out of five U.S. jobs export-related, and with over one-third of U.S. exports going to LDCs ["less developed countries"], it is an inescapable fact that this country's well-being is vitally affected by the debt problem and by our ability and *willingness* to solve it" (U.S. Congress, House 1983a, 183; emphasis added).

Many opposed increasing quotas to bail out the banks' investments. Congressman Stewart B. McKinney criticized Volcker for equating increased support of the IMF with an insurance policy against the collapse of the international financial system. McKinney was annoyed that the banks had avoided both accountability and concessions while leaning on the IMF as their insurance policy. He argued that banks do not worry when borrowers can't repay their loans, because they assume that "Uncle Sam is going to come across and take care of them" (U.S. Congress, House 1983a, 99; see also Gonzalez 1985, 65). Congressman Fernand J. St. Germain echoed McKinney's anger and frustration: "You and I both know if push comes to shove . . . the Fed will come riding to the rescue. The chariots will be thundering down the streets of Manhattan" (U.S. Congress, House 1983a, 131). Congressional opponents throughout the hearings reiterated that any increased quotas to the IMF represented a bailout of the banks and warned that taxpayers would ultimately pay for defaults incurred by developing countries. Since the banks had made the loans without consulting the taxpayers or sharing their profits with them, congressional leaders did not think that the public should have to share in the losses.

Moreover, some doubted that increased quotas to the IMF would in fact solve the crisis. On the contrary, such increases might have deleterious effects on the United States. Congressman Charles Schumer pointed out that the austerity measures the IMF imposed had potentially negative effects on the United States, since they had a history of depressing imports and retarding gross national product growth. Schumer cited a Morgan Guaranty estimate that "the kind of austerity settlements being imposed would decrease the growth of our own . . . GNP by a full percentage point which is quite significant" (U.S. Congress, House 1983a, 115). Schumer termed the austerity settlements "self-defeating." Without denying the charge, Volcker objected to Schumer's antagonism to the up-front fees the banks charged for renegotiating debts, but he would not respond directly to reports that the fees were higher than necessary. It seemed that Volcker and the banks refused to entertain alternative solutions that were not in the banking community's interest.

Despite the opposition, anger, and frustration expressed at these congressional hearings about forcing U.S. taxpayers to bail out the banks, the state did not cross the banks. The proposal for a 47 percent increase in quotas to the IMF passed (Kraft 1984, 55).

Similar debates and struggles ensued when Congress considered a proposal to establish a special $2 billion facility at the Export-Import Bank (Eximbank) for Mexico and Brazil (see U.S. Congress, House 1983b; Senate 1983a). The Eximbank is a key factor in U.S. exports, providing assistance to foreign countries to purchase U.S. goods and thereby giving the United States a stronger position than other exporters in the world market. The Eximbank was originally created in 1945 to provide an institutional supplement to the private credit market and to offer credit that commercial banks were unwilling to provide because of high risks. Eximbank credit supplements were crucial to the world's recovery from World War II. The proposed new facilities were designed to help the Mexican and Brazilian governments pay for U.S. goods and services by underwriting their trade with the United States. Ultimately, proponents hoped, the new facilities would encourage private banks to "reestablish their trade financing roles with Mexico and Brazil" (U.S. Congress, Senate 1983a, 2). Like the proposal to increase IMF quotas, the Eximbank proposal was cast as a jobs bill. Because Mexico is the third largest export market for U.S. goods and Brazil is the ninth largest economy in the world, Eximbank support of those two countries' imports would preserve U.S. jobs. Lionel H. Olmer, under secretary for international trade, U.S. Department of Commerce, estimated that for every $1 billion of lost exports, U.S. workers lost 25,000 jobs (U.S. Congress, Senate 1983a, 77). He pointed out that the decline in Mexico's importation of U.S. goods might cost as many as 250,000 U.S. jobs (U.S. Congress, Senate 1983a, 8; see also Senate 1983a, 292–297; House 1983b, 3).

Many congressional leaders (including Senator William Proxmire) questioned the appropriateness of the proposal. Because one of the IMF-imposed austerity measures was the radical curtailment of imported goods, the enhanced facility would not help those countries import more U.S. goods and hence would not preserve any U.S. jobs at all. Furthermore, Proxmire asked, are the proposed facilities "really in keeping with the primary purpose of the Bank, which is to assist U.S. exports, or . . . will they function to assist the Governments of Mexico and Brazil to resolve their balance of payments difficulties?" (U.S. Congress, Senate 1983a, 52, 3). In noting that the IMF is the more appropriate source of credit to close balance-of-payment gaps, Proxmire identified the relation between the two proposals before Congress: both sought to bail out the banks' investments.

Marc E. Leland, assistant secretary of the Treasury for international affairs, explained the connection between the proposed guarantees for U.S. exports and debt servicing, noting that both were an integral part of the financial system as a whole:

One simply can't separate one part of this system from the rest. One cannot . . . look at debt servicing and balance of trade as . . . separate problems. Our banks and banks around the world loan these monies. They have every reasonable expectation that these countries, with proper adjustment policies, will be able to continue servicing their debt. (U.S. Congress, House 1983b, 20)

Leland's remarks suggest that austerity programs and programs from the IMF and the Eximbank (which minimize banks' risks) ensure debt servicing and profits to the banks. Indeed, William H. Draper, chairman of the Eximbank, acknowledged that if loans the

Eximbank has guaranteed go into default, U.S. taxpayers would have to pay them off. He noted that the guarantees would cover both principal and interest, and that the Eximbank could not control the interest rates demanded by the private banks. Apparently, with the support of the Eximbank—a state institution—a unified banking community that sets a high interest rate could make a great deal of money at no risk.

The struggles over the proposals to increase IMF quotas and improve the Eximbank's facilities highlight the role of the state in assuring the financial community's interests in international finance capital relations. Previous structural imbalances in developing countries' economies (produced by trade dependency and dependent development) generate balance-of-trade gaps, which lead to increased foreign debt (Delacroix and Ragin 1981). To avoid aid agencies' restrictions, many developing countries seek loans from private banks. Worldwide inflation and recession, characteristic of trough periods of long-wave cycles of economic development (Kondratieff 1979), further aggravate balance-of-trade gaps and jeopardize the ability of developing countries to repay or to service their existing debts. The Eximbank helps the structurally distorted economies of developing countries to continue to import U.S. goods and services while restoring private banks' confidence and profits by guaranteeing a risk-free investment. Similarly, the IMF provides bridge loans to close the balance-of-payments gaps and interim loans between private bank loans. Thus the Eximbank and the IMF, both international state agencies, guarantee private bank loans—mitigating the risks to banks—and actually encourage loans that are of dubious value to U.S. taxpayers but are ultimately profitable to the banks. Austerity programs and assistance programs from both institutions ensure debt servicing and huge profits to private banks. Furthermore, both the Eximbank and the IMF discipline developing countries to focus significant proportions of their gross national products on debt repayment.

No one in the debate over alternatives to the traditional IMF austerity programs raised the issue of increased taxes for the private sector, although such a plan had been proposed and quashed a decade earlier. One alternative to the austerity program might have been an IMF-imposed private-sector tax increase to raise revenues and close Mexico's budget deficit. The bailout program also failed to address the banks' excessive front-end fees for negotiating and renegotiating debt, a practice acknowledged in congressional hearings to have contributed to Mexico's foreign debt crisis (U.S. Congress, House 1983c).

Why would the state and various state agencies do so much on behalf of finance capital interests? The historical process of concentrating finance capital in fewer and fewer hands, coupled with bank unity and the finance capital needs of developing countries, has placed the banking community in a pivotal position in the global economy. Congress expressed great concern during the hearings that a sharp contraction in new credit to developing countries with financial difficulties could have "a cumulatively depressive impact on the world economy" (*New York Times*, 31 Aug. 1982, D5; see also U.S. Congress, House 1982, 72). For example, by 1981 Mexico owed more than $80 billion to more than 1,600 banks around the world (Kraft 1984, 35; see also *New York Times*, 17 Aug. 1982, D1; 20 Aug. 1982, D15). If the state did not bail out the banks, the international financial system could collapse. Leland underscored this insight when he noted that the enormity of the debts of developing countries requires the involvement of governments and their agencies to aid the private banks (U.S. Congress, House 1983b, 20).

Assistant Secretary of Commerce Alfred H. Kingon inadvertently portrayed the process by which banks contribute to the difficulties of developing countries, necessitating a state-sponsored bailout of the banks' investments. He noted that banks were increasingly demanding that all loans be "fully collateralized: titles to real estate, cash deposits, or payment guarantees"—all of which further concentrate capital flows in the banking community. Kingon added that disruptions in cash flows, trade credits, and financing have "undoubtedly complicated attempts by Mexico and Brazil to adjust to their debt burdens and reorder their economies" (U.S. Congress, House 1983b, 34). Ironically, these bank-induced complications threaten the banks themselves. Because of the contradictions inherent in international finance capital relations, the state and its institutions must bail out the banks or risk jeopardizing the world economy (and with it the economy of the United States).

Ultimately, despite the often heated controversy and the critical insight into finance capital relations and processes, Congress approved the proposal to create a special $2 billion facility at the

Eximbank for Mexico and Brazil. Once again the banks appeared to compromise the relative autonomy of the state.

Outcome

The IMF forced the Mexican state into the politically unpopular position of sharply contracting the Mexican economy (see Taylor 1984; Hamilton 1986b). Indeed, there was widespread recognition of the relative weakness of the state. The *New York Times* (29 July 1983, A3) reported: "The administration of President Miguel de la Madrid Hurtado is not controlling its own destiny as far as economics is concerned. The country is under severe strictures from international lending organizations in return for help in paying off its foreign debt of more than $80 billion."

The banks elicited state initiatives to bail out their investments in Mexico. As we have seen, despite strong opposition the U.S. Congress passed initiatives to establish special facilities at the Export-Import Bank for Mexico and Brazil and to join the international community in increased quotas to the IMF (see U.S. Congress, House 1982, 1983a, 1983b, 1983c; Joint Session 1984; Senate 1982, 1983a, 1983b). The fear of chaos in the world economy in general, and in the U.S. economy in particular, prevailed over congressional outrage at bailing out the banks. Significantly, neither bill provided for greater controls on or accountability for the banks' lending practices. The banks' excessive up-front renegotiation fees, identified as a major factor in the overwhelming debt of developing countries, remained untouched. What occurred was a state-sponsored bailout of the banks' investments without any fundamental modifications of the lending practices that contributed to and exacerbated the international debt crisis.

With new special facilities at the Eximbank, new loans—including a $5 billion loan agreement with 530 Western banks (*New York Times,* 25 Feb. 1983, D1; 4 Mar. 1983, D4)—and an IMF-imposed austerity program in place, Mexico began to show signs of recovery by late 1983. The recovery was a mirage. In 1984 Mexico's debt to U.S. banks increased by almost $4 billion (a rise bankers attributed to Mexico's strict austerity program). Although Mexico's balance of trade shifted dramatically from a 1981 trade deficit of $4.5 billion to a 1982 surplus of $6.6 billion (U.S. Congress, Senate 1983a, 22), the improvement was illusory. More than

35 percent of Mexico's export income went to interest payments in 1983 (*New York Times*, 17 Aug. 1984, A14). The changes in the balance of trade reflected "a crippling contraction of imports" and a greatly weakened peso (Weiner 1984, F3; *New York Times*, 29 June 1983, D1; see also Taylor 1984, 148–150). Mexico's export level of $21 billion remained constant between 1982 and 1983, while imports shrank from $24 billion in 1981 to $14.4 billion in 1982 and about $8 billion in 1983. The cost of these drastic cuts in imports to Mexico's economic growth and domestic production was substantial:

The unavailability of foreign-sourced raw materials, machinery, and replacement parts . . . contributed to the decline in the country's output in 1983. . . . However, here is where Mexico is chasing its tail. There can be no real improvement in its manufacturing exports without an increase in the imports of raw materials and equipment essential for production, which in turn would have an immediate adverse impact on the balance of trade—thereby fogging that image of functioning austerity. (Weiner 1984, F3; see also Weiner 1983, A23; Taylor 1984, 152–153; Hamilton 1986b)

Many observers point to the decline of Mexico's inflation rate from more than 100 percent in 1982 to 75 percent in 1983 as a sign of recovery. But again the improved picture disguises the arbitrary and inconsistent measures used to gauge inflation. As Weiner (1984, F3) reported: "While the Consumer Price Index shows an 82 percent increase from December 1982 to December 1983, other estimates of inflation in 1983 exceed 100 percent. And conveniently forgotten by all concerned was the Mexican target of a 55 percent inflation ceiling for 1983." The peso took a beating, dropping by 85 percent since 1982 (*Business Week*, 28 May 1984, 50). The falling peso contributed to the inflation rate in 1983, which depressed real wages in Mexico by 30 percent (*Business Week*, 1 Oct. 1984, 75).[6] Unemployment exceeded 8 percent, and underemployment reached nearly 40 percent (*New York Times*, 29 June 1983, D8). The devastating effect of the austerity program on workers deepened the problems of the Mexican economy. Still under import constraints, Mexico now devoted 40 percent of its

6. Despite the high inflation, wages rose by only 25 percent, causing a dramatic decline in real purchasing power (*Business Week*, 10 Apr. 1983, 9; see also Taylor 1984, 148–149).

budget to debt servicing and imported seven million tons of food in 1983 (after a poor harvest). Consequently, "all major construction projects [were] cancelled or suspended" (*New York Times*, 15 Dec. 1982, D2).

Mexico's illusory recovery illustrates how IMF-imposed austerity programs may undermine the long-run prospects for real recovery. The main objective of the austerity programs is to bail out the banks, because the programs are designed to force the state to curtail imports, economic growth and development, and wages to channel a large proportion of the GNP to debt servicing and repayment.

This process recurred to a lesser extent more recently, when Mexico faced another debt crisis caused by the collapse of world oil prices. Once again the peso lost 30 percent of its value in less than one week, because the revenues anticipated from oil production fell more than $3 billion short of the interest payment due in 1986 on Mexico's debt. And again the forces of collective finance capital marshaled their willing and reluctant allies to deal with the situation. After de la Madrid threatened to limit Mexico's interest payments "to our capacity to pay," the U.S. government, the banks, and the IMF joined forces to produce a new rescue package (*Business Week*, 23 June 1986, 43, 42). In exchange, they pressured Mexico for fundamental economic changes, including the privatization of state-owned enterprises, trade liberalization to open Mexican markets to U.S. manufacturers, and changes in economic policy (such as state subsidies of manufacturing) to promote a more favorable climate for U.S. manufacturers (*Business Week*, 4 Aug. 1986, 35; 25 Aug. 1986, 51).

Whereas the Mexican government had previously nationalized the banks in response to the drain of dollars out of Mexico, the austerity program resulted in the privatization of at least 34 percent of the nationalized banks (*New York Times*, 29 Dec. 1982, D1). Although de la Madrid refused to accept another austerity program (since the first had failed to stimulate a recovery in 1982), the banking community's collective control of finance capital flows empowered it to limit Mexico's relative autonomy to determine domestic policy.

Although it may be tempting to view the banks' behavior as a last resort to a serious problem, that analysis is not entirely appropriate here. The banks had aggressively pursued the placement of loans in Mexico, as they had everywhere in Latin America, demanding highly lucrative up-front renegotiation fees and applying nonconcessional interest rates. In addition, they elicited the IMF's help in forcing Mexico to accept an austerity plan that set the stage for further cash flow shortages and declines in economic development two years later. More appropriate actions would have included more prudent lending, minimal up-front renegotiation fees, and concessional interest rates (none of which would have jeopardized the banks' profits). Furthermore, the IMF's standard austerity package actually damaged Mexico's economic development. Ironically, economic development would have improved Mexico's ability to manage its finances more effectively in the future. The banks' threats to produce a crisis in Mexico did not represent a remedy of the last resort after other, less extreme, measures had failed (or because other remedies were not appropriate). Rather, they represented an extreme remedy to the banks' previous inappropriate actions, which had caused economic problems in Mexico.

Mexico's $20 billion of internal debt and $73 billion of external debt continue to grow. So enormous is this burden that almost 50 percent of state expenditures were devoted to debt repayment in the first half of 1986. Mexico's economy is not growing to absorb this burden; 1986 gross domestic product was down 12 percent from 1981. Decreases in production have caused a combined unemployment-underemployment rate of almost 50 percent. In effect, no new jobs have been created there since 1981. Wage erosion continues to be a serious problem affecting consumerability. Real wages fell almost 14 percent in 1986, to 40 percent below 1981 levels. Indeed, with triple-digit inflation in 1986, real wages in Mexico hit "their lowest point in 50 years" (Schmitt 1986, 11). Continued reductions in state subsidies of food staples add to inflation and the decline of real wages. Prices soared in 1986: tortillas went up 150 percent, eggs 104 percent, cooking oil 110 percent, beans 201 percent, and bread 280 percent. Reductions in state subsidies of transportation have had similar results: Mexico City's metro fare increased 2,000 percent and bus fares 700 percent.

Mexico suffered from the drop in world oil prices, which "cost . . . almost 6 percent of its gross national product" in 1986. Many observers (including de la Madrid) cite this drop as the cause of Mexico's latest round of economic problems. But a Wharton Econometric analysis blamed Mexico's economic program for the nation's spiraling debt problem. The study cited "continued upward revision of prices for government-supplied services, the elimination of price controls, the acceleration of the 'slide' in the peso's value in the controlled market, the peso's downward volatility in the free market, high interest rates and the large public debt" (Schmitt 1986, 11). In sum, the Wharton study cited precisely those elements of the IMF's austerity program that were supposed to ensure recovery.

What is most interesting about this latest crisis in Mexico is that it is happening to a government that has already complied with the IMF-imposed austerity program of 1982—a program hailed as the path to economic recovery and the model for other developing countries' debt restructuring. Yet the stunning failure of the austerity program in Mexico is not extraordinary; these programs have had a deplorable record of aggravating poverty and inequality, hindering economic development, and ultimately intensifying debt crises. Why, then, does the IMF continue to impose them? Considering that debt restructuring is such a lucrative business for the banking community, we should not be surprised that the banks insist on austerity measures, even though they are counterproductive in the long run and contrary to the interests of the target state's political leaders and political economy.

Class and Intraclass Conflict

Mexico's foreign debt crisis involved several layers of conflict. One pervasive element was the banking community's collective intrusion into Mexico's class struggle, a move that ultimately compromised the relative autonomy of the state. The net effect of the banks' collective control of capital flows was the social construction of Mexico's political and economic reality (before and after the debt crisis). Mexico originally relied on foreign debt to pay for its "miraculous" development and growth, the green revolution, Echeverría's job creation program, and the enhanced social welfare expenditures of the early 1970s. Mexico's leaders turned to the oil industry to fund the country's plans for recovery and development. But the sharp drop in the price of oil on the global market in the mid-1980s pushed Mexico once again into a serious cash flow shortage.

The State Versus Labor and the Poor

An ongoing historical struggle between the state, on the one hand, and labor and the poor, on the other, preceded Mexico's 1982 foreign debt crisis. Until that time the state had participated in broad and fairly extensive social welfare programs, including subsidies of tortillas and gasoline, pro-labor wage and benefit agreements, health and housing expenditures, and the nationalization of basic industries such as oil and petroleum. The onset of the state's foreign debt crisis and the consequent devaluations of the peso and flight of dollars from the country did not entirely dissuade the state from this position. López Portillo nationalized the banks and raised wages after the currency devaluations.

At the same time, the state decreased some public spending, increased interest rates to discourage credit spending, and increased prices of tortillas and gasoline by as much as 50 to 100 percent to discourage overconsumption. All these measures antagonized labor. Because the state-initiated austerity measures failed to curb the rampant inflation, currency devaluations, and rising unemployment that plagued the country, the PRI changed policy direction. López Portillo's successor, de la Madrid, quickly raised taxes, reduced public works expenditures, and eliminated state subsidies of domestic consumer products. These moves more than doubled the cost of tortillas and gasoline. The business community applauded de la Madrid's approach, which balanced the greatest burden of the deficit on the backs of the workers.

Banks Versus Labor and the Poor

What the state failed to accomplish in its political struggle with labor, the banking community achieved with its collective control of capital flows. The state's austerity program was limited by its historical political relations and process of struggle with the labor force. The international financial community had no such constraints and was in a stronger position than the state to impose an IMF austerity program that was far more disadvantageous to labor. This program included the strict curtailment of imports, further reductions in social welfare expenditures, and significant decreases in wages. Despite labor's intense opposition, the banks' collective position remained implacable. There would be no re-negotiation of Mexico's debt without compliance with the IMF's austerity program.

Through these various levels of class struggle over Mexico's foreign debt crisis in 1982, the structurally unified international banking community intruded into Mexico's domestic affairs. The subsidies of food staples and gasoline, nationalization of some in-dustries, rising wages, and increasing jobs that labor had won from the state were all possible because of the availability of fi-nance capital. Later, however, the international banking commu-nity, backed by the IMF, turned back those policies and shifted the political economy to a free-market orientation that assigned a large proportion of the GNP to debt servicing. Thus the servicing of debt and the austerity program compromised the Mexican state's relative autonomy in mediating and managing its own af-fairs. The debt crisis and subsequent austerity program success-fully turned back the clock on class struggle so that labor would later have to struggle once again for gains it had previously won and now lost.

Conclusion

As the history of Mexico's foreign debt crisis reveals, the increas-ing concentration of capital flow relations mitigates the discretion-ary powers of the state on several levels. Developing countries saddled with debt must accede to painful and politically inexpe-dient economic contraction to avoid default. The international community and various national and international institutions are constrained to bail out the banks' loans because default in one of the larger of the troubled developing countries could spell disaster for the world economy. Thus a sovereign government's relative au-tonomy can, and often is, constrained by the goals of international finance capital. These goals often oppose the state's goals of eco-nomic development, health, education, and welfare. Capital flow relations between the state and a structurally unified banking com-munity empower the banks to socially construct the economic and political reality of individual states as well as the global economic system.

Mexico's "rescue" from default bears a striking resemblance to Chrysler's bailout. In both cases a unified banking community elicited state-sponsored bailouts: loan guarantees for Chrysler, and increased IMF quotas and Export-Import Bank special facilities for Mexico. Furthermore, the definitional processes invoked in both cases illustrate two facets of the power of collective purse strings. The banking community's willingness to advance loans allowed Chrysler to operate as a full-line automaker for more than thirty years. The banks' cooperation also enabled Mexico to pay for the development programs of the 1940s and 1950s, the green revolution of the 1960s, and the social welfare programs of the 1970s. Neither Chrysler nor Mexico could have accomplished so much without bank support. But the banking community later turned the same definitional processes against Chrysler and Mexico by defining their situations as crises and then, after the state-sponsored bailouts, as resolvable crises. At each stage only the banks were able to set the definition of the situation.

The structure of the lending consortium unified the banking community in both cases. Chrysler's lending consortium included more than 325 banks. Mexico's involved more than 1,600. The structure of these consortia fused the banks' interests. Moreover, loans to corporations and governments constitute the most lucrative business for banks. Participation in lending consortia is particularly crucial for small U.S. banks, because the law restricts banks from lending more than 10 percent of their assets to a given customer. Since the major commercial banks typically act as lead banks in consortia, small banks depend on good relations with them to ensure inclusion. As we have seen, this dependence empowers the major banks to compel small recalcitrant banks to remain in the consortium and to accept unfavorable terms. This disciplining process guarantees the structural coalescence of the banking community.

The history of Mexico's debt crisis highlights the analytical weaknesses of the pluralist perspective. At no time before, during, or after the crisis was the state a neutral arbiter. Ongoing struggles between private banks, private industry, labor, and the state have always been at the center of Mexico's political-economic processes and have largely determined state policies and practices. Furthermore, participants were clearly unequal in strength and had unequal access to resources. The banking community's privileged access to finance capital enhanced its power over all other actors, including the state. Finally, the state was not insulated at all from the economic sector. Indeed, it participated directly in the economy, thereby undermining the pluralists' assumption of the separation of the political and economic sectors.

The cases of Chrysler and Mexico both raise the question of the relative autonomy of the state. The literature on this issue does not specify the factors affecting the state's relative autonomy and fails to analyze the effect of capital flow relations. Chrysler's and Mexico's cases suggest that the banking community's collective control of capital flows may compromise the state's autonomy. Because the state cannot generate enough revenue to meet its expenditures, the state itself becomes a major borrower. In addition, the reliance on giant corporations for jobs mitigates the state's relative autonomy from corporations, particularly in periods of state crisis. At such times banks may access at least some of the state's discretionary powers to determine political and economic policies.

Additionally, the struggle over Chrysler's bailout produced an unprecedented reversal in U.S. labor-capital relations. For the first time this century, labor was forced to accede to major wage and benefit concessions. These concessions brought on a long period of concessionary bargaining for all unions and undermined the effectiveness of the strike as a strategy for labor. In Mexico the IMF-imposed austerity program produced a similar reversal of historical labor relations. The conditions of the austerity program included the repression of labor with a no-strike agreement, reductions in the size of the labor force, decreases in wages, the elimination of social welfare expenditures, and the privatization of nationalized industries. In sum, both the austerity program in Mexico and the bailout program for Chrysler placed the major burden of debt renegotiation on the backs of the workers.

Finally, Mexico's crisis illustrates the dialectic of lending relations. Although a reliance on private bank loans initially increased the relative autonomy of the state by enabling Mexico to escape the restrictions of official aid agencies, in the long run it had the reverse effect by forcing Mexico to comply with IMF restrictions. This dialectical relation between the state and the structurally unified banking community is the hinge on which the state's relative autonomy turns, propelled by the process of struggle.

I will analyze the similarities and differences between the corporate and state cases in the concluding chapter.

Chapter Seven

The Social Construction of
Economic and Political Reality

Financial institutions are the hub of capital flow relations. They provide or deny massive loans to corporations and states, own or control substantial blocks of stock in enormous pension and trust funds, and sit on so many nonfinancial firms' boards of directors that they overwhelmingly dominate interlocking corporate directorates. Their central position gives banks unique control over a vital resource: finance capital.

In and of itself the control of finance capital by many independent banks does not produce power. Industry, commerce, and governments could easily exploit competition between banks in search of the most favorable capital arrangement. The key to the power of the banking community lies in its structural unification—in large lending consortia, in the strong similarities of trust and pension fund portfolios, and in joint ventures. This structural unification produces bank hegemony. Together with control over capital flows, bank hegemony often empowers the banking community to impose its perception of economic and political reality and its interests over those of all other groups (stockholders, workers, the state, and so on).

What do banks do with this potential power? The case studies in this book illustrate some of the mechanisms banks use to socially construct economic and political reality. W. T. Grant Company plunged into involuntary bankruptcy when the banking community declared it bankrupt and refused to provide further loans.

Chrysler Corporation was saved from bankruptcy when the banks, threatening to deny further loans to the automaker, elicited loan guarantees from the federal government that bailed out the banks' investments. Similar processes led to the rescue of Mexico in 1982 and forced Mexico's political economy to shift from state participation to a free-market orientation. Cleveland was forced into default in 1978 when the banks refused to renegotiate the city's debt as a means to force the sale of the municipal utility to Cleveland Electric Illuminating Company. Finally, a healthy Leasco Corporation quickly fell to disaster in a stock-dumping exercise by banks angered at the firm's attempts to acquire Chemical Bank.

Together these cases shed light on the processes of bank hegemony, the functioning of corporate board interlocks, the relative autonomy of the state, and the social construction of crisis as an economic and political reality.

Bank Hegemony

Under ordinary circumstances, the hegemonic structures that bind otherwise competitive financial institutions do not affect corporations and the state. Financial institutions activate hegemonic processes only when common interests are threatened. The economic and/or political threats the banks perceive need not be real. Yet if banks define the situation as a crisis and act on that definition, the consequences are very real. Then the banks set competition aside and pull together to protect the interests that bind them. For example, when Leasco threatened to alter traditional relations between banks and nonfinancials, the banking community used the considerable resources at its disposal to reinforce and defend its domination. Cleveland's default similarly illustrates the banks' ability to act collectively on their common interests when Kucinich's populist politics threatened to disrupt business and banking's domination of city politics and capital accumulation.

The cases examined here exhibit bank hegemony in several forms. The bankruptcy of W. T. Grant demonstrated the ability of the banking community to coalesce in a consortium of 143 banks against the firm's other creditors, managers, workers, and stockholders. The Chrysler bailout showed how easily the banking community could form a unified position in a struggle with the federal government. Here, as in the case of W. T. Grant, coalescence was structurally produced by the firm's lending consortium of over 325 banks and the reliance of the small banks on lending consortia to access corporate business. Similarly, 1,600 banks fused interests in Mexico's lending consortium.

Consortia do not have to be large to be effective. Although only six banks were involved in Cleveland's default, they were strong enough to push the city around. The six banks were cemented together not only by their common presence in Cleveland's lending consortium, but also by their presence in the lending consortium for Cleveland Electric Illuminating Company, their stockholdings in CEI, and their presence on the CEI board.

Finally, in the struggles with Leasco and Cleveland the banks were capable of deliberate, concerted action because of their collective control of vast capital resources and the strong similarities of investment portfolios for their trust and pension funds.[1]

Coalescence within the banking community is clearly the product of structural arrangements rather than conspiracy or the workings of the "invisible hand." Banks' structural relations (namely, joint investments, common membership in lending consortia, similar stock portfolios managed for pension and trust funds, and so on) cause them to join forces and unify because (1) they know they have to work together in future lending consortia and (2) they have formed long-term relations based on these consortia. This structural unity gives the banking community great power over nonfinancial corporations and the state. Although nonfinancials often have symbiotic relations with one another, these alliances are not necessarily long term and can be replaced by other alliances or alternative resources. In contrast, there is no alternative to finance capital. It alone is the means of purchasing all other resources. And because finance capital is also a social relation, cooperative relations between banks are not easily abridged and are necessarily long term.

The concept of bank hegemony illuminates the subtle but critical difference between power and influence. Power is the ability to fix or change entire sets of alternative actions for other partici-

1. Legally, there is supposed to be a "Chinese wall" separating the trust and commercial departments of a bank to prevent such occurrences. Yet according to *Business Week* (5 Nov. 1979, 87) a major brokerage firm's chief executive officer and chairman said, "No matter what they tell you about their Chinese Walls, they're more like curtains."

pants in a given relation. In contrast, influence is the ability of actors to determine the actions of other participants within the confines of the existing set of action alternatives (Mokken and Stokman 1976). Whereas managers, board members, and political leaders can exercise a great deal of influence on corporations and the state, power belongs to those who command capital flows. Managers and board members in all three cases of corporate crisis were able to exercise a degree of discretion in corporate decision-making processes. Mexican political leaders exercised relative autonomy in some of their domestic policy decisions. Mayor Kucinich exercised some discretion in determining how to respond to the city's fiscal crisis. But all were limited by the power of the banking community to define their situations (Mintz and Schwartz 1983; Glasberg and Schwartz 1983).

The reputation for power achieved through bank hegemony pre-empts corporate and government leaders' consideration of many alternative decisions that might antagonize the banks. For example, W. T. Grant closed more than 50 percent of its stores at the insistence of the banks. At the same time, the banks' reputation for power restricted the alternatives Grant considered and in fact led Grant's management to seek the banks' approval before making decisions. Similarly, the overt conflict between Chrysler and its banks forced the automaker to squeeze unprecedented concessions from its UAW workers. The banking community's reputation for power, based on its unified control of lending capital, forced the federal government to bail out the banks' investment in Chrysler and in Mexico because Congress feared economic disaster if the banks did not get their way. Leasco's struggles with the banking community forced the firm to discontinue its efforts to acquire Chemical Bank. Since that infamous struggle no other nonfinancial has tried to acquire a commercial bank. Finally, Mayor Kucinich's struggles with the banking community set the pattern for future mayors in their attempts to resolve fiscal difficulties.

The Social Construction of Economic Crisis

Institutional theories of organization argue that organizations (such as corporations) "are influenced by normative pressures, sometimes arising from external sources such as the state, other times arising from within the organization itself" (Zucker 1987, 443). These pressures might cause the organization to conform to the expectations they define. The limitation of this theory, however, is that the external source of influence can be other organizations. Institutional analyses often do not emphasize this point strongly enough. In particular, the cases presented here demonstrate that an organized banking community can pressure non-financial firms to conform to the banks' definition of normative behavior. Moreover, the banking community can pressure the state itself to conform to the banks' definition. The major source of influence and pressure is not state laws and regulations (as institutional theory suggests), but rather organized financial institutions' collective control of capital flows. Hence a modified version of resource dependence theory is a more appropriate model for analysis.

Bank hegemony and the control of capital flows empower the banking community to generate economic reality. Banks may advance needed loans to corporations and governments or support a firm with major stock purchases for the pension and trust funds that banks administer. Or they may deny loans to corporations and governments or pull the rug out from under a corporation by dumping its stocks from those pension and trust funds. Thus the banks have the power to define any situation as a crisis, setting in motion all the responses and consequences of a crisis and thereby creating an actual crisis. The banks' definition affects a firm's business trajectory and a state's political trajectory.

The power to make such definitions lies not only in the unified control of capital flows, but also in the increasing reliance of corporations and governments on external sources of finance capital. When W. T. Grant began to experience serious cash flow difficulties, the banking community initially refrained from defining the firm's situation as a crisis and participated at several junctures in restructuring the firm. Ironically, precisely when Grant appeared able to restructure itself into a smaller but more profitable firm, the banking community defined the situation as a crisis. The evidence suggests that the banks timed their definitional process, which permanently damaged the firm's business trajectory and destroyed the firm, to better position themselves to recover their investments. Similarly, Chrysler Corporation experienced severe cash flow shortages and appealed to the federal government for a bailout when the banking community refused to advance further loans. The ensuing struggle revealed the power of the banking community to choose the outcome of the definitional process. The banks repeatedly threatened to force the automaker into bankruptcy unless the federal government bailed out their loans. Once the banks got the loan guarantees and forced labor to shoulder the largest burden of those guarantees, they refrained from defining Chrysler's situation as a crisis, thus saving the firm from bankruptcy. Chrysler is once again a relatively healthy firm. When the Mexican economy experienced serious cash flow shortages, the banks elicited a U.S.-supported bailout through increased participation in the IMF and the Export-Import Bank as a prerequisite for further bank support. They repeatedly threatened the collapse of the international financial markets. Once those bailout supports were in place the banking community resumed loans to Mexico, thus staving off the crisis definition. In fact, Wood (1986, 284) notes that banks sometimes deliberately withhold new loans "in order to force debtor countries . . . to restructure existing debt on terms more attractive to the banks." Finally, when Leasco Corporation, a healthy firm, was defined as crisis-ridden, the ensuing stock dumping generated a real crisis. Of all the participants in each case, only the banks could collectively define the situation and impose their view of corporate and state reality.

Emerson's (1981) analysis of institutionals' last-resort remedies to troublesome situations implies that banks take extreme measures such as stock dumping and loan denials after less extreme measures fail to rectify the situation. Although this analysis makes sense, it is inappropriate here. For example, W. T. Grant was well on its way to restructuring and rehabilitating under a Chapter XI reorganization program when the banks withdrew their support. In other words, a less extreme measure than liquidation was apparently working when the banks chose to institute the measure of last resort. Leasco was a healthy corporation when the banks dumped its stock. Other, less extreme, approaches could have stopped this nonfinancial from taking over a major commercial bank, but the banks did not seriously consider them.

In Cleveland's case, municipal default became a remedy of last resort when the campaign to recall Kucinich and the legal and political efforts to force the sale of MUNY failed. But here the problem the banks perceived was political rather than economic: a populist mayor who stubbornly opposed the interests of the business and banking communities.

In the cases of Chrysler and Mexico, the banking community invoked the power to define crises that they had helped produce. In Chrysler's case, the banks had lent money to the firm for more than thirty years while giving tacit consent to a long series of problematic managerial decisions. They should have required changes in corporate policy far earlier than 1979. In Mexico's case, the banks had aggressively pursued the placement of loans in Latin America, demanding highly lucrative up-front renegotiation fees and applying nonconcessional interest rates. A more appropriate action would have been more prudent lending, minimal up-front renegotiation fees, and concessional interest rates (none of which would have destroyed the banks' profits). In neither case did the banks' threats to produce crises represent remedies of the last resort. Rather, they were extreme approaches to rectify the banks' previous inappropriate actions.

Interlocking Directorates: Sources of Power or Traces of Power?

Although banks predominate in networks of interlocking corporate directorates (Mintz 1978; Mintz and Schwartz 1978; Kotz 1978), and although bank representation on nonfinancial boards may correlate with bank loans and/or major institutional stockholdings, such interlocks are merely traces of power (Mokken and Stokman 1978). The ultimate source of bank power is the hegemonic control of capital flows. As the case studies of W. T. Grant, Chrysler, and Leasco revealed, financial institutions' control of lending capital and pension and trust fund assets can constrain the autonomy of the board.

Sometimes interlocking directorates function as one of several mechanisms that fuse the interests of the banking and business communities. In Cleveland, for example, the strong presence of banks on the board of CEI and in the Greater Cleveland Growth Association made them natural allies. But only the capital flow relations, represented in the banks' stockholdings in CEI and their common presence in lending consortia for both CEI and the city, empowered the banks to determine Cleveland's economic reality. The most important determinant was the lending relations between the city and its creditors.

Corporate board interlocks sometimes facilitate the flow of information between firms—often a one-way flow from the nonfinancial corporation to the banks (Scott 1978). Such information was essential, for example, in the banks' formation of effective strategies against Leasco, as when Continental Illinois informed Chemical Bank about Steinberg's intentions. The presence of bank representatives on nonfinancial corporate boards also gives banks the opportunity to vote on operational decisions. Interlocking corporate directorates are thus symptomatic of capital flow relations between banks and nonfinancial firms.

The Social Construction of Political Reality and the Relative Autonomy of the State

The role of the state in the capitalist political economy has remained an important focus of inquiry for more than a century.[2] But much of this debate has never fully specified the factors affecting the state's relative autonomy (particularly the organized or hegemonic control of capital flows), focusing instead on the internal structure of individual national political economies as if each existed in a vacuum (Rubinson 1977). The relative autonomy of the state in the political economy of internationally organized relations has remained unexplored.

The cases of Mexico's foreign debt crisis, Chrysler's bailout, and Cleveland's default fail to support the pluralist assertion that the state acts as a politically neutral arbiter balancing competing demands. In none of these cases did the state give equal weight to the competing demands of labor, corporations, banks, and the state itself. Indeed, the legitimacy of the demands was not the most important factor in determining the state's actions. For example, although Congress recognized the legitimacy of labor's interests (as well as its own) in the Chrysler and Mexico cases, it reluctantly

2. See, for example, Dahl 1961; Domhoff 1967, 1970; Fitch 1972; Gramsci 1971; Habermas 1975; Lipset 1960; Mandel 1978; Miliband 1969; Mills 1956; O'Connor 1973; Offe 1972a, 1972b, 1974; Poulantzas 1968, 1973; Rose 1967; Weinstein 1968.

acquiesced to the interests of the banks because of economic and political constraints. The relative power of the claimants, not the legitimacy of their claims, was the critical factor in determining congressional decision making. Furthermore, although Kucinich recognized the legitimacy of the interests of labor and the state, he could not completely negate the power of Cleveland's organized banking community.

These cases also illustrate the inadequacies of the capture theory of the state, promoted by instrumentalists such as Domhoff (1967, 1970), Miliband (1969), Mills (1956), and Weinstein (1968). The representatives of the banking community never needed to occupy positions in the state apparatus to have their interests served. Rather, their structurally hegemonic control of capital flows (facilitated by large bank consortia and the imposition of bank discipline) gave the banking community oligopolistic control over financial capital resources that are less accessible to the state without the mediation of the banks. For example, the banks' common presence in Chrysler's lending consortium empowered them to threaten to push the United States closer to economic depression and an almost certain political legitimacy crisis for the Carter administration in an election year. Although the state can generate revenues through taxation, those revenues are rarely sufficient to meet state expenditures, especially under inflationary conditions and during extensive military buildups. State deficit spending increases the debt burden and state dependence on the international financial community.

The cases of Mexico and Chrysler partially support Poulantzas's (1968, 1973) notion of the relative autonomy of the state—that is, the state's autonomy from the control of individual capitalists or sectors of the capitalist class. But although the state may not be controlled by individual capitalists, state autonomy may still be compromised by a sector of the capitalist class, namely, organized finance capitalists.

The organized control of finance capital also enables the banks to intrude in the process of class struggle to accomplish for the capitalist class those goals that the state must set aside to preserve its political legitimacy. Although the banks are not always completely successful, they usually tip the balance of the class struggle in favor of capitalist interests. For example, in Cleveland the banks fought a populist mayor over a working-class cause, with mixed results. Pushing Cleveland into default failed to win the sale of the municipal utility to its private competitor, but the crisis toppled the mayor. With a new mayor sympathetic to business and banking interests in place, the banks quickly renegotiated the city's debt. The banks' collective intransigence also forced a crisis of political legitimacy in Mexico for the somewhat radical President López Portillo. His successor, Miguel de la Madrid, was more sympathetic to banking and business interests; during his tenure the IMF-imposed austerity plan rolled back years of state support for labor in the class struggle.

Mexico's debt crisis highlights a problem with the analytical focus of theories of the state, which implicitly examine the relative autonomy of the state in relation to the internal structure of individual nation-states. Most such research ignores the external factors affecting the state's relative autonomy. The struggle between Mexico, the United States, and the banking community demonstrates that organized international finance capital relations can constrain the relative autonomy of the state—in this case, of both the United States and Mexico. Politically the state-as-debtor is likely to lose control of domestic policy making and may also lose influence in the state's guiding ideology. For example, Mexico's debt crisis undermined the state's ability to maintain nationalized industries, continue social welfare expenditures, and determine the direction of economic growth. Clearly the IMF and the banking community compromised Mexico's domestic policy of state participation in the economy. Indeed, IMF-imposed austerity programs (which typically demand the privatization of nationalized industries) minimize state participation in the economy and promote instead a "free-market" ideology.

Individual cases such as these give insight into the external processes and relations that influence the relative autonomy of the state. Poulantzas's interpretation neglected the dialectical relations between the state and finance capital. With hegemonic control over capital flows, the banking community wields allocative power to constrain the discretionary power of the state. But the banks lack the political legitimacy to enforce these constraints and must rely on the legitimacy of the state and its institutions. For example, the banks could not restrict Mexico's imports, decrease wages, or curtail social welfare expenditures, but they could rely on the legitimacy of state institutions, such as the IMF, to impose such measures. Moreover, the banking community relies on the state to reverse the crisis tendencies of debt cycles by guaranteeing banks' investments. Although the international financial community can ill afford the default or economic collapse of a major state borrower, the state is even less equipped to absorb the worldwide reverberations of such a collapse or the domestic political legitimacy crises that would plague the existing state administration.

Mexico's struggles for economic security and Chrysler's struggle for a bailout support Mandel's (1978) analysis that the state facilitates the fusion of the economic and political sectors in its efforts to regulate the deepening inherent crises of the political economy. With the U.S. and world economies in deep recession (which at times gave way to occasionally weak and temporary "recoveries"), the state had to regulate the "free-market" economy by bailing out the banking community's excessive investments in Chrysler and in developing countries. The threat of substantially increased pressures on an already straining U.S. economy (with rising unemployment) forced the state to capitulate to the interests of the banking community. Thus the relative autonomy of the state both locally and globally may hinge on the capital flow relations forged between the state and a structurally hegemonic banking community.

Conclusion

Although the cases discussed in this book involve corporations and governments in crisis, they reveal a great deal about ordinary relations between banks, nonfinancial firms, and states and about the processes of power within them. Many of the details of these relations become public through litigation and congressional hearings, providing insight into those circumstances under which the potential power of banks translates into real and far-reaching consequences for nonfinancial firms and states. Although I cannot prove that the processes and relations uncovered here are typical in noncrisis situations, I have shown that the banks can activate and exercise that power at will. Moreover, the banking community's power to socially construct corporate reality restricts the everyday decision making of nonfinancial firms by delimiting management's choice of alternative actions.

The cases presented here also demonstrate the dialectics of finance capital relations. Initially loans expand the relative autonomy of the state by removing restrictions imposed by international aid agencies or by compensating for limited tax revenues. Loans also expand the range of discretion of corporate managers (over labor, other corporations, the state, and so on). But in the long run loan relations can restrict the relative autonomy of the state and the range of discretion of corporate managers. The sale of corporate stock forges similar dialectical relations between corporations and financial institutions that manage pension and trust funds holding those stocks. At first the stock purchases increase a corporation's cash flow, thereby broadening its range of discretion in matters such as plant relocation and expansion, merger mania, merger defense, and product development. But again, in the long run large holdings of corporate stock in pension and trust funds can severely constrain managerial autonomy if those holdings are dumped on the market.

Finally, the patterns of bank hegemony and the control of capital flows found in corporate relations also characterize relations between the financial community and governments both domestically and internationally. For example, the collective control of capital flows gave banks the power to declare St. Louis ineligible for mortgage investments, pushing that city into decline (Ratcliff 1980a, 1980b, 1980c); New York City's 1974–1978 brush with bankruptcy and its subsequent struggles with the banking community illustrate similar processes of the social construction of economic reality (Lichten 1986). The experiences of developing countries like Mexico that have tottered on the brink of default demonstrate that huge lending consortia structurally empower banks to construct the political and economic reality of whole countries, sometimes against the interests of U.S. foreign policy (see Girvan 1980; Glasberg 1987). Poland's struggle with the Western banking community in the early 1980s suggests that this power transcends not only national boundaries but ideological differences as well. Indeed, a 1979 article warned that "U.S. Banks Are Making Foreign Policy" by extending loans to foreign governments:

When many of the loans are not repaid as scheduled, these credits . . . will be recognized for what they are—disguised aid to the recipient countries. It will then be clear that foreign policy decisions have been made by private institutions. . . . Private banks are effectively making United States foreign economic policy without public debate or oversight by elected representatives. (*New York Times*, 18 Mar. 1979, F14)

Why should we care about what happens when major elements in the business community do battle or when governments struggle with a collective banking community? Our jobs, our pension funds and IRAs, our financial well-being are threatened by these struggles and the power they reveal. For example, when the institutions managing our pensions and IRAs invest heavily in stocks of firms that go bankrupt or whose stock the banks dump, our funds lose a great deal. Consider that Michigan and Illinois teachers lost their entire pension fund investments in W. T. Grant Company. Workers always lose power when firms and the state struggle with a collective banking community. Mexico's workers lost jobs, wages, consumer power, and bargaining power as a result of the state's struggle with the banking community and the IMF. Cleveland's workers lost jobs and wages when Kucinich lost to Voinovich because of struggles with the banks. W. T. Grant's workers lost their jobs, their pensions, and their severance and vacation pay when that firm went bankrupt. Chrysler's workers lost jobs, wages, pension fund contributions, job security, and bargaining power in the automaker's struggle for a bailout.

The struggles and power processes described in this book also have international consequences. Development may never succeed in countries with mounting debt burdens. Struggles to avoid default invoke the imposition of IMF austerity packages that undermine development efforts as large portions of the country's gross national product transfer from development projects to debt servicing. Reductions in social welfare expenditures leave basic needs unmet. And the austerity package requirement of reductions in imports frequently means that the country cannot import spare parts for industrial production. This pattern suggests that debates on development and growth in the Third World must include an analysis of the role of international finance capital. Those of us in developed countries must also take notice, whether our country is the target or not. Cheapened labor in crisis-stricken countries may undermine workers' bargaining power and jobs in countries like the United States because it attracts runaway shops. In addition, developing countries' reductions in imports could spell trouble for the exports and balances of trade of developed countries, touching off recessions, job losses, and further reductions in labor power. Remember, too, that the United States is now the largest debtor nation in the world. What happens to Third World debtor countries can happen here as well, with the same consequences for labor.

What can we do? The cases described in this book imply a potential source of power and participation for labor. Pension funds represent the single largest source of investment capital in the world (Rifkin and Barber 1978). Right now banks administer this vast pool of workers' deferred wages. Should labor resume control of its own pension funds, it would be able to offer an alternative to banks' hegemonic control of capital flow relations. Consider, for example, how different the resolution of Chrysler's cash flow shortage might have been had the UAW controlled its own pension funds. The ability to offer a competitive source of finance capital would have strengthened labor's bargaining position with Chrysler, the state, and perhaps the banks. The union might have lost far less as a result. Indeed, it might have gained a greater voice in the firm's decision-making processes in exchange for bailing out the firm.

Federal deregulation of the banking industry in the United States has intensified the power of collective purse strings by contributing to the concentration of capital flows, as large commercial banks take over small savings and loan associations and force others out of business. Fewer banks mean less competition and greater hegemonic control of finance capital resources. A return to federal regulation would allow the state to reverse this increasing concentration of capital and power in the banking industry. Regulation and labor control over pension funds could alter capital flow relations and the processes of power, which in turn could alter the consequences of those relations.

Appendix 1
Using Government and Legal Documents

Unlike many other methods, archival historical research does not have a how-to manual to guide the researcher. Those of us who use this method often find ourselves groping in the dark until we develop a sense of the material. I frequently wished there was a tried and proven set of steps I could follow to quicken the pace of my research. In that spirit, I am sharing my trials and tribulations with others who may wish to join in this tedious, time-consuming, but satisfying search. I warn the reader that this appendix is not a handbook for using documents but merely a summary of the approach I took in researching the case studies included in this book.

I began these case studies as part of an attempt to understand the meaning of the statistical evidence on interlocking corporate directorates generated by the MACNET research group at the State University of New York at Stony Brook. I could see that the patterns of interlocking directorates were strong, but what did they mean? Many of the researchers insisted that they indicated power, but I was still unable to follow the empirical analyses to the substantial conclusion. Finally, Michael Schwartz wisely challenged me to look at some cases and see if I could trace the meaning of the interlocks. Thus began the search that resulted in this book. I started with the theoretical framework of the debates concerning interlocking corporate directorates. Later, many of those questions would change as the theoretical framework broadened to include issues of the state and questions of power.

My selection of corporate cases began as an attempt to test Beth Mintz and Michael Schwartz's notion that banks become more central when corporations experience a crisis and then recede when the crisis ends. I also realized that many corporate relations and processes are hidden until a firm runs into a crisis and such information becomes a matter of public record. To untangle this material, I began with a simple typology of the possible sources and outcomes of crisis. This led me to select cases that are generally well known but had not been analyzed in this particular framework. The Chrysler Corporation bailout had received extensive coverage in the business and popular press, as had W. T. Grant Company's bankruptcy and Leasco Corporation's struggle with Chemical Bank. I decided to begin with these materials to get a rough idea of the sequence of events, the major actors in each case, and the location of documents and other materials. Once I was satisfied that I had a reasonable understanding of the information available from these sources, I interviewed several business analysts and lawyers involved in these cases for further insight into the events, actors, and source materials, particularly those not mentioned in the popular and business press. These interviews also alerted me to important elements to watch for in my examination of the available documents. Occasionally I was able to locate documents myself, give them a preliminary examination, and then perform interviews. Later I returned to the documents for a more careful inspection.

The interviews conformed to the professional code concerning research with human subjects. I told all interviewees the purpose of the research, promised anonymity if they wished, and provided the telephone number of the university's office of research administration to call to report any mistreatment they felt they encountered. I sent interviewees a transcript of their taped interview to allow them to identify any remarks they wished to have off the record, to correct any inaccuracies they found, or to add any new information they wished to include.

Armed with a basic outline of the cases, I then visited the government documents section of the library (all government documents used in this research are included in the bibliography). Both the

Leasco and Chrysler cases had gone before congressional committees that investigated and held hearings about these firms' troubles.
Congressional hearings are gold mines of data. When the hearings
end, the Government Printing Office publishes the transcripts of
the entire proceedings, including any documents submitted to the
committees during the hearings. Since the Leasco hearings had occurred almost a decade before my research began, I had to spend
long hours in the library copying notes from the transcripts. I also
spent quite a bit of money copying the pertinent supportive documents included in the volume of testimony. I was luckier in the case
of Chrysler Corporation's bailout hearings. Since those were current and not yet published, I was able to request a copy from the
committees holding the hearings. If you can keep abreast of congressional hearings relevant to your research, you can call the
committee in Washington, D.C., and request a copy of the proceedings. To date, these publications are free and provide an in-
credible amount of research material.

I was far less fortunate in my attempts to access the materials
concerning W. T. Grant's bankruptcy. First, the case was mired in
a long, drawn-out series of litigations that were still going on when
I began my research. Second, the materials were not neatly bound
and available in the library as government documents, but were
lodged in the basement of the United States Southern District
Courthouse in New York City. No one had filed and categorized
them so that I could quickly access the ones I wanted. There were
hundreds of thousands of pages of testimony transcripts, depositions, documents, and legal briefs related to the case, all strewn
about in corrugated boxes in a dusty room.

Sifting through these documents was not quick, but it was dirty.
There appeared to be no rationale behind the storage of documents other than a haphazard tossing of paperwork into the first
available box. I simply had to roll up my sleeves (literally) and dig
in. The first difficulty was getting comfortable with the legal language of many of the documents. Interviews with the lawyers involved in the case helped clarify the meaning of the professional
language. Breaking the code of legalese helped me realize that
many of the documents were simply legal applications for contin-
uances and extensions of the various hearings, real estate leases,
and so on. These were not relevant to the case study and could

therefore be omitted. I still had to untangle the mountain of remaining documents, particularly the transcripts, depositions, and supportive documents. This task took many months of intensive digging, categorizing, copying, and analyzing. I periodically telephoned Grant's lawyers to ask for translations, clarifications, and updates on the status of the case as it worked its way through the courts. They were most generous with their time in telephone conversations and straightforward in their explanations. Their guidance was instrumental in sorting out the complicated pieces of the case. I also tried to keep up with the various hearing dates and attended court sessions for the case whenever possible. The hearings helped me become accustomed to the legal proceedings and the patterns of questions and answers.

Once I had collected the materials for the three cases, I had to work through the problem of coding and analyzing materials that defied quantification. Using government and legal documents does not make a strict coding scheme easy. For one thing, like other qualitative methods, the categorization of quotes, data, and evidence frequently changes as the research evolves. Sometimes the researcher gains new insights, alters her perspective, or modifies her analysis as new evidence confronts previous analyses and interpretations. In addition, since my task was to trace the processes and relations of specific cases, I was concerned not so much with quantifying instances or variables but with uncovering details and telling a story. Hence I cannot provide a codebook by which the reader could replicate my findings. Instead, I will describe the process I used to handle the materials and will provide a sample interview questionnaire and outline of court documents for the W. T. Grant case study (as an example of similar questionnaires used for the other cases). The reader may review these and the publicly available documents to determine if the findings are indeed accurate.

I made copies of all the materials I collected, keeping the original copies for a master file. I kept a file of the bibliographic information for each of the sources on four-by-six-inch file cards. I marked the secondary copies with colored markers representing various issues and concepts: green for managerial decisions, pink for bank hegemony, orange for loans, purple for stockholding, yellow for bank participation in decision making, and so on. (Of course, some markings changed for each case, as the important details in each differed. Only the broad categories were common, such as bank hegemony, loans, and stockholding.) I cut and sorted these marked document pieces into piles of topics and issues, noting their original source in the master file. Later I reshuffled these document pieces into new piles as new ideas and analytical frameworks occurred to me. This sorting and resorting continued until the end of the analysis.

I began each case study by writing a chronology of events and then sorting through and eliminating those events that were irrelevant to the research. Next, using the analytical framework, I broke out of the chronology to categorize events and relations by issue or concept: here was evidence of early bank knowledge of impending problems, there was evidence of bank hegemony, and so on. I revised each case study no fewer than a dozen times to smooth out the analysis.

Later, in reading through the business press, I happened to notice that many of the processes and relations involved in Mexico's foreign debt crisis bore a striking similarity to those I had found in the corporate cases. I decided to keep an eye on the case, and particularly on the congressional hearings. As in the Chrysler case, I was quick enough to catch the hearings before the Government Printing Office published the data and was able to get copies of most of the relevant documents; the rest I got from the government documents section of the library. This time categorizing the materials was easier than it was for the corporate cases. For one thing, I had developed an approach to data management that worked for me. For another, I had developed an analysis that I could now use to categorize the data in this case. I looked for similarities and differences relative to the corporate cases using the master file and colored-marker method.

The process for the Cleveland case study was quicker and smoother than the other cases for several reasons. First, I had grown comfortable with my method of data location and management. Second, there were fewer government documents related to this case than there were for the Mexico case. But the age of the case meant that I had to spend more time in the government documents section of the library than I did for the Mexico case (although surely less than I spent in the Southern District Courthouse in New York). My conceptual framework was clearer, my categories firmer, and my approach more refined than when I first began the project. Both the Cleveland and Mexico cases underwent many revisions before the analyses became tight and clear. Like the corporate cases, both began with the popular and business press accounts for the chronological development, identification of important actors, and location of materials. I continued to look for similarities and differences between the government and the corporate cases. And I continued to re-sort and recode the document pieces until I was satisfied.

I now realize that there must be a way to make a computer do the coding and re-sorting that I did by hand with my colored markers. Yet the process of repeatedly going through the materials to recode them made me see new things each time. Often materials that I had neglected to color code the first time would suddenly become more significant after the second or third reading. I am not sure that would have happened had I left the data management to a computer.

I would have liked to interview the key actors involved in each of the cases. Indeed, I repeatedly wrote to and called several of the corporate actors in an attempt to interview them, either in person or by telephone. Each attempt met the same response: they were not interested. Although many researchers have found managers and executives more than willing to grant interviews, the people involved with these cases were not—and for good reason. These cases are all politically and economically sensitive. An executive with any intention of remaining in the business world, or a government official who wants to remain an effective state leader, must be wary of antagonizing the banking community. Hence my research depended on government and archival documents, business press information, and interviews with business analysts and lawyers.

Although the method I used is time-consuming and tedious, it is also most rewarding. It can produce clear details of relations and processes that remain hidden in statistical analyses. The very tangibility of the material allows us to trace these relations and give life and form to the quantitative data on which speculations of meaning often depend. I found the lack of a road map for the method frustrating but exhilarating—and well worth every minute.

Appendix 2
Sample Outline
of Court Documents for
W. T. Grant Company

The following court document outlines the names of the participants deposed by the court, the documents examined by the trustee, and the location of some of the documents. This listing was invaluable in locating important materials and identifying critical actors in the case.

I. *Persons examined by Trustee pursuant to Bankruptcy Rule 205*

   A. The following bank officers have given approximately 846 pages of testimony:

Name	Position [1]
1. John P. Schroeder	Executive Vice President, Morgan Guaranty; Presently Director and Vice-Chairman of Board (J.P. Morgan and Morgan Guaranty).
2. Robert Dannenbaum	Vice President, Branch Manager, Bank of New York, since January, 1972.

---

1. Unless otherwise indicated, the positions given are those held during the period from July 1973 through October 1975.

      3. John Snyder   Senior Vice President, Morgan Guaranty.

B. The following persons who were directors of both Grant and one of its lending banks have given approximately 753 pages of testimony:

Name	Position
1. DeWitt Peterkin, Jr.	Director, Member of Executive Committee (Grant) (1966–1975); Director, Vice-Chairman of Board (J.P. Morgan and Morgan Guaranty).
2. Joseph W. Chinn, Jr.	Director, Member of Audit Committee (Grant) (1969–1975). Director, Wilmington Trust Company.

C. The following officers, directors or employees of Grant have given approximately 8,000 pages of testimony, much of which reveals information pertinent to the claims asserted in the Adversary Proceeding:

Name	Position
1. Robert A. Anderson	Chief Operating Officer and President from 5/15/75. Became Chief Executive Officer in October, 1975.
2. James Kendrick	Chairman of Board, President and Chief Executive Officer (9/3/74–5/15/75).
3. Richard W. Mayer	Chief Executive Officer, President and Chairman of Board (2/1/68–2/1/74).
4. Harry E. Pierson	President and Chief Operating Officer and Acting Chief Executive Officer (6/30/74– 9/3/74); became

	Executive Vice-President in September, 1974.
5. John Sundman	Joined Grant in June, 1974 as Financial Vice President; elected to Board of Directors 10/22/74.
6. John G. Curtin	Executive Vice President of Finance (2/11/74–4/1/74); Financial Vice President and Treasurer (2/1/67–2/11/74).
7. Robert A. Luckett	Corporate Services Vice President, Controller, Director.
8. Richard Scarlata	Controller (3/1/75–4/2/76).
9. Robert J. Kelly	Vice President, General Counsel, Secretary and Treasurer from 10/22/74. Secretary and General Counsel (1/1/71–10/22/74).
10. Richard H. Rosenblum	Assistant General Attorney from August 1975.
11. Joseph Hinsey	Became Director in August, 1971; (also attorney and partner at White & Cased).
12. Earl Robert Kinney	Director.
13. Charles F. Phillips	Consultant (1971–1974).

II. *Documents examined by Trustee*

In relation to the examinations taken pursuant to Bankruptcy Rule 205, the Trustee has examined hundreds of thousands of documents as described below:

A. The following banks have produced a total of more than 120,000 pages of documents:

1. Morgan Guaranty
2. Citibank, N.A.
3. Chase
4. Manufacturers Hanover Trust Company
5. Chemical Bank
6. Marine Midland Bank—New York
7. Marine Midland Bank—Western
8. The Bank of New York
9. The Sanwa Bank, Ltd (excluding Japanese language documents)
10. Continental Illinois
11. Bank of America
12. Bankers Trust Company
13. Irving Trust Company
14. First National Bank of Toms River, N.J.

B. The following consultants or advisors have been subpoenaed and have produced a total of more than 30,650 pages of documents:

1. Morgan Stanley & Co.
2. Touche Ross & Co.
3. Ernst & Ernst
4. Booz, Allen & Hamilton, Inc.
5. Goldman, Sachs & Co.

C. Documents, totalling approximately 100,000 pages, remaining at the office of the bankrupt estate and which appear to be from the following officers or employees of Grant have been examined:

Name	Position
1. Robert Anderson	(see Ic (1) above)
2. James Kendrick	(see Ic (2) above)
3. Richard W. Mayer	(see Ic (3) above)
4. John Sundman	(see Ic (5) above)
5. Robert A. Luckett	(see Ic (7) above)
6. Richard Scarlata	(see Ic (8) above)
7. Joseph W. Chinn, Jr.	(see Ib (2) above)
8. Zang T. Chang	General Auditor of Grant (3/17/75–1/31/76)
9. Robert J. Kelly (Including Corporate Minute Books)	(see Ic (9) above)
10. John G. Curtin	(see Ic (6) above)

Appendix 3
Sample Interview Questionnaire
for W. T. Grant Company

The following is a sample interview questionnaire used for the case study of W. T. Grant Company. I used similar questionnaires for the other case studies.

4 April 1979

I would like to tape this interview, if that's all right with you, for several reasons: I know you have a good deal of very important and interesting things to say, and I would prefer to pay attention to you rather than be occupied taking notes. Also, I want to be as fair as possible in representing your position: I would like very much to avoid misrepresenting or misinterpreting your analysis. I can send you a transcript of the interview if you wish, and if there are any inaccuracies you can correct them. However, if there are things that you would rather say off the record, I can turn the tape recorder off and take notes, which I promise to keep in strict confidence; I will not quote you or assign attribution.

1. Why don't you begin by telling me what was unusual about this case that set it apart from others that are ostensibly similar?

Let's focus on bankruptcy a little.

2. Chapter XI of the bankruptcy law is usually reserved for companies whose problems are solvable. Why was Grant allowed to file under Chapter XI?

3. Why do you think Grant was then suddenly liquidated only five months later, without a thorough study of its financial condition?

4. One accountant was quoted as saying that Grant's should have been a Chapter X proceeding from the beginning. Do you agree? Why?

5. This same accountant was also quoted as saying, "In an XI everyone is supposed to be unsecured and equal, but that's not the way it was on this creditors' committee. There were too many vested interests." What do you think were these vested interests?

6. Some people view bankruptcy proceedings as a way of escaping employee obligations, such as pension payments and severance pay. Would you consider this a possible interpretation of such proceedings?

7. Some people say Grant's collapse was the result of mismanagement; others point to fraud as the cause of bankruptcy. What would you say caused the company's ultimate collapse?

8. Business and financial publications that covered this case indicated that you found allegations of corporate kickbacks. What was the nature of these kickbacks?

9. Are any of these practices standard operating procedure among retailers?

Business and financial publications suggested that management and the Grant Foundation both played important roles in this case. Why don't we talk about this point a little.

10. What was the official function of the Grant Foundation?

11. The published accounts of this case indicate that Grant had eight million authorized but unissued shares available for distribution to Grant's employees in the share purchase program. If this allegation is true, what was the justification for the purchase agreements between the foundation and Grant?

12. These same accounts of the case also indicate that Mr. Staley and Grant management rejected the initial proposal that the foundation buy Grant stock. Why did they reject it?

13. Why did they later change their minds?

14. Staley testified that he was concerned that the stock would fall into "unfriendly hands," resulting in a takeover of Grant. In your opinion, was that a real possibility at the time?

15. Do you think there was someone actually threatening such a takeover?

16. Who might that have been?

17. Morgan Guaranty was reported as saying that it "would have been delighted" by such a takeover. Why do you think Morgan would have been delighted?

18. Do you think Morgan itself may have been interested in taking over Grant?

19. Why couldn't the banks exercise power to *force* a takeover if they would have been delighted to see one happen?

20. Business and financial publications indicated that in 1973 400,000 shares of Grant's common stock remained in the foundation and that Edward Staley was trying to sell these. Apparently Staley was warned by the company's top financial officer that if the sale went through, a lot of "unfortunate questions would be asked." What do you think was meant by "unfortunate questions"?

21. Unfortunate for whom?

22. Staley was also quoted as saying that "unfortunate questions" referred to the idea that such a sale would indicate "that the performance of the company was bad, and that the selling of Grant stock by the Grant Foundation would be interpreted as a loss of confidence in the Grant company." Do you agree?

23. Staley was further quoted as saying that the sale had nothing to do with an actual loss of confidence in the company, that "it was a definite plan of the foundation liquidating their holdings of Grant stock." Do you agree? Why was that a definite plan in the first place?

24. If Staley was telling the truth, why didn't the sale go through?

25. John Curtin reputedly sent Staley a memo concerning the sale, stating that such a sale would be interpreted not only as a loss of confidence of the trustees of the foundation, but also as a loss "of information they might be receiving from both you and Mr. Fogler." What kind of information do you think that might be?

26. Do you consider it unreasonable to think such information might be made accessible to the foundation by Staley's and Fogler's presence on both Grant's board and the foundation's board of trustees?

27. Some observers would call the sale of such a large chunk of stock a practice known as "stock dumping." Would you say Staley and the foundation were trying to dump Grant's stock?

28. The published accounts of this case indicate that Staley gave Richard Mayer a "gift" of 6,000 shares of Grant common stock

shortly after Mayer's selection as Grant's new president. Louis Lustenberger and Raymond Fogler were reportedly "strongly opposed to the gift." Why would they oppose it?

29. Fogler was reported to have been "nagged" by the question of why such a gift was made. Why, indeed?

30. Is the giving of such a gift standard operating procedure in the industry when appointing a new officer?

31. Some people believe that this gift was intended to buy Mayer's loyalty to Staley. How would you account for such a gift?

32. Fogler was reported to have insisted that Staley exercised a "tremendous amount of influence" over Mayer. How would you describe their relationship? What was the nature of such "influence"?

33. Can you think of any instance that exemplifies Staley's influence over Mayer? Mayer's independence from Staley?

I'd like to focus on the role of the banks for a few minutes.

34. Mr. Rodman's suit against Morgan Guaranty and twenty-six other banks charged that these banks engaged in actions detrimental to Grant, its creditors, and its shareholders. What do you think those detrimental actions could have been?

35. In this same complaint, Rodman also pointed out the presence of DeWitt Peterkin, Jr., vice chairman of Morgan Guaranty, on Grant's board and on its executive and audit committees as evidence of Morgan's "dominance and controlling influence" over Grant's. How do you think Morgan exercised this dominance and control?

36. Is this standard operating procedure in relations between financial and nonfinancial corporations?

37. In a later suit, Rodman charged that these banks dominated Grant and concealed its real financial condition to serve their own interests. How were they able to do this? Why?

38. What do you think were the banks' own interests?

39. How did they differ from Grant's interests?

40. One reporter said that the banks were caught sleeping. Do you think that is what actually happened?

41. Some people argue that banks have a vested interest in making sure that industrials and retailers remain healthy profit-producing centers and therefore will do everything they can to help troubled nonfinancial corporations recover from financial crises. If so, why

do you think Morgan Guaranty and the other banks in the consortium apparently did everything in their power to have Grant declared bankrupt?

42. Why do you think the banks continued to pour money into Grant long past the point of prudence?

43. Is this standard operating procedure for banks?

44. Why do you think the banks gave first lien on Grant's money to the suppliers?

I have a few more questions.

45. Some people claim that banks were premature in pulling the plug on Grant. Do you agree or disagree? Why?

46. Do you think Grant's board fulfilled its responsibilities?

47. Why or why not? In what ways?

48. Why were the protests of the two directors who did spot trouble in 1971 (Fogler and Lustenberger) ignored?

49. Why did Mayer, Staley, and Curtin resign?

50. One reporter expressed surprise that only civil suits were filed and wondered why no *criminal* suits were ever filed. Why, indeed?

51. If you could point to one most important or fundamental cause of Grant's ultimate collapse, what would you say that was, and why?

Thank you. You've been most helpful. May I speak to you again if any further questions arise?

References

Aron, Raymond
 1950   "Social Structure of the Ruling Class." *British Journal of Sociology* 1 (March–June): 1–17, 126–144.
Bachrach, P., and M. Baratz
 1962   "Two Faces of Power." *American Political Science Review* 54 (4): 949–952.
Barkin, David
 1986   "Mexico's Albatross: The U.S. Economy." In *Modern Mexico: State, Economy and Social Conflict,* ed. Nora Hamilton and Timothy F. Harding, 106–127. Beverly Hills: Sage.
Barkin, David, and Gustavo Esteva
 1986   "Social Conflict and Inflation in Mexico." In *Modern Mexico: State, Economy and Social Conflict,* ed. Nora Hamilton and Timothy F. Harding, 128–147. Beverly Hills: Sage.
Barron's
 1973–1978
Bartimole, Roldo
 1977   "U.S. Ruling Puts CEI in Jeopardy of Losing $325 Million in Anti-Trust Suit to MUNY Light." *Point of View* 9 (14): 1–4.
Baum, Daniel J., and Ned B. Stiles
 1965   *The Silent Partners: Institutional Investors and Corporate Control.* Syracuse: Syracuse University Press.
Bearden, James
 1982   "The Board of Directors in Large U.S. Corporations." Ph.D. diss., State University of New York at Stony Brook.
Bearden, James, William Atwood, Peter Freitag, Carol Hendricks, Beth Mintz, and Michael Schwartz

1975   "The Nature and Extent of Bank Centrality in Corporate
            Networks." Paper presented at the meetings of the Ameri-
            can Sociological Association, San Francisco, August.

Beck, John H.
1982   "Is Cleveland Another New York?" *Urban Affairs Quar-
            terly* 18 (2): 207–216.

Berger, Peter L., and Thomas Luckmann
1967   *The Social Construction of Reality: A Treatise in the Soci-
            ology of Knowledge.* Garden City, N.Y.: Doubleday.

Berkman, Ronald, and Todd Swanstrom
1979   "Koch vs. Kucinich: A Tale of Two Cities." *Nation,* 24
            Mar., 297–299.

Blain, Robert R.
1985   "The U.S. Debt Problem." Paper presented at the Mid-
            western Sociological Association Annual Meetings, St.
            Louis, April.

Block, Fred
1977   "The Ruling Class Does Not Rule: Notes on the Marxist
            Theory of the State." *Socialist Revolution* 33: 6–28.

Bluestone, B., and B. Harrison
1980   *Capital and Communities: The Causes and Consequences
            of Private Disinvestment.* Washington, D.C.: Government
            Printing Office.

Bolles, Lynn
1983   "Kitchens Hit by Priorities: Employed Working-Class
            Women Confront the IMF." In *Women, Men and the Inter-
            national Division of Labor,* ed. June Nash and Maria
            Patricia Fernandez-Kelly, 138–160. Albany: State Univer-
            sity of New York Press.

Bonbright, James
1972   *Public Utilities and the National Power Policies.* New
            York: DaCapo Press.

Bonbright, James, and Gardiner Means
1969   *The Holding Company.* New York: August Kelley.

Born, Roscoe C.
1980   "Pension Power: Organized Labor Seeks to Wield It More
            Aggressively." *Barron's,* 1 Dec., 4–5, 28–29.

Branfman, Fred
1979   "The Cleveland Story: How the Banks Foreclosed Dennis
            Kucinich." *Nation,* 20 Jan., 43–46.

Breckenfeld, G.
1977   "Refilling the Metropolitan Doughnut." In *The Rise of the*

> *Sunbelt Cities,* ed. David C. Perry and Alfred J. Watkins, 231–258. Beverly Hills: Sage.

Brooke, James
1987   "'Financial Famine' in Africa Seen at Nigerian Parley." *New York Times,* 21 June, Y11.

Brooks, John
1973   "Annals of Finance: The Go-Go Years, III." *New Yorker,* Aug. 13, 34–63.
1980   *The Games Players: Tales of Men and Money.* New York: Times Books.

Bunting, David
1976–1977 "Corporate Interlocking." *Directors and Boards: The Journal of Corporate Action* 1. "Part I: The Money Trust" (Spring 1976): 6–15. "Part II: The Modern Money Trust" (Summer 1976): 27–37. "Part III: Interlocks and Return on Investment" (Fall 1976): 4–11. "Part IV: A New Look at Interlocks and Legislation" (Winter 1977): 39–47.

Bunting, David, and Jeffrey Barbour
1971   "Interlocking Directorates in Large American Corporations, 1896–1964." *Business History Review* 45 (3): 317–335.

Burch, Philip H., Jr.
1972   *The Managerial Revolution Reassessed.* Lexington, Mass.: D. C. Heath.

Business Week
1969–1986

Chandler, A. D., Jr.
1977   *The Visible Hand: The Rise of Managerial Capitalism in the U.S.* Cambridge, Mass.: Harvard University Press.

Chevalier, J. M.
1969   "The Problem of Control in Large American Corporations." *Anti-Trust Bulletin* (Spring): 163–180.
1970   *La Structure financière de l'industrie americaine.* Paris: Editions Cujas.

Chicago Tribune
1987

Clavel, Pierre
1986   *The Progressive City.* New Brunswick, N.J.: Rutgers University Press.

Cockcroft, James D.
1983   *Mexico: Class Formation, Capital Accumulation and the State.* New York: Monthy Review Press.

Cook, Earl
    1971   "The Flow of Energy in an Industrial Society." *Scientific American* 225 (3): 135–143.
Corm, Georges
    1982   "The Indebtedness of the Developing Countries: Origins and Mechanisms." In *Debt and Development*, ed. J. C. Sanchez Arnau, 15–110. New York: Praeger.
Dahl, Robert A.
    1961   *Who Governs? Democracy and Power in an American City.* New Haven: Yale University Press.
Daily News Record
    1973–1976
Dale, Richard S., and Richard P. Mattione
    1983   *Managing Global Debt.* Washington, D.C.: Brookings Institution.
Davis, Diane
    1986   "Macro-economic Development Strategies and the Dialectics of State Autonomy: Lessons from Mexico's Debt Crisis." Paper presented at the annual meetings of the American Sociological Association, New York, August.
Debt Crisis Network
    1985   *From Debt to Development.* Washington, D.C.: Institute for Policy Studies.
Delacroix, Jacques, and Charles C. Ragin
    1981   "Structural Blockage: A Cross-National Study of Economic Dependency, State Efficacy, and Underdevelopment." *American Journal of Sociology* 86 (6): 1311–1347.
Detroit Socialist Collective
    1980   "Behind Chrysler's Crisis: Dumb Management or Dumb System?" Detroit: Detroit Socialist Collective.
DeWitt, R. Peter, and James F. Petras
    1979   "Political Economy of International Debt: The Dynamics of Financial Capital." In *Debt and the Less Developed Countries*, ed. Jonathan David Aronson, 191–215. Boulder, Colo.: Westview Press.
Dhonte, Pierre
    1979   *Clockwork Debt.* Lexington, Mass.: Lexington Books.
Domhoff, G. W.
    1967   *Who Rules America?* Englewood Cliffs, N.J.: Prentice-Hall.
    1970   *The Higher Circles.* New York: Random House.
    1978   *The Powers That Be: Processes of Ruling Class Domination in America.* New York: Random House, Vintage Books.

1983   *Who Rules America Now? A View for the Eighties*. Engle-
            wood Cliffs, N.J.: Prentice-Hall.
Donnelly, John T.
1973   "External Financing and Short-Term Consequences of Ex-
            ternal Debt Servicing for Brazilian Economic Develop-
            ment." *Journal of Developing Areas.*
Dooley, Peter C.
1969   "The Interlocking Directorate." *American Economic Re-
            view* 59: 314–323.
Dun's Review
1970
Emerson, Robert M.
1981   "On Last Resorts." *American Journal of Sociology* 87 (1):
            1–22.
Erb, Guy F.
1982   "Bailing Out Mexico." *New York Times,* 20 November, 23.
Fine, B.
1975   *Marx's Capital*. London: Macmillan.
Fitch, Robert
1972   "Sweezy and Corporate Fetishism." *Socialist Review* 3 (6):
            93–127.
Fitch, Robert, and Mary Oppenheimer
1970   "Who Rules the Corporations?" Parts 1–3 *Socialist Re-
            view* 1 (4): 73–108; 1 (5): 61–114; 1 (6): 33–94.
Forbes
1969–1983
Girvan, Norman
1980   "Swallowing the IMF Medicine in the Seventies." In *The
            Political Economy of Development and Underdevelop-
            ment,* ed. Charles K. Wilbur, 169–181. 3d ed. New York:
            Random House.
Glaeser, Martin
1957   *Public Utilities in American Capitalism*. New York:
            Macmillan.
Glasberg, Davita Silfen
1987   "Bank Hegemony and the Relative Autonomy of the State:
            Mexico's Foreign Debt Crisis." *Research in Political Econ-
            omy* 10: 83–108.
Glasberg, Davita Silfen, and Michael Schwartz
1983   "Ownership and Control of Corporations." *Annual Re-
            view of Sociology* 9: 311–332.
Glasberg, Davita Silfen, and Kathryn B. Ward
1985   "Third World Development and Foreign Debt Depen-

dency." Paper presented at the annual meetings of the Midwestern Sociological Society, St. Louis, April.

Gogel, Robert M.
1977   "Interlocking Directorships in the American Corporate Network." Ph.D. diss., University of California at Santa Barbara.

Gogel, Robert, and Thomas Koenig
1981   "Commercial Banks, Interlocking Directorates and Economic Power: An Analysis of the Primary Metals Industry." *Social Problems* 29 (2): 117–128.

Gonzalez, Heliodoro
1985   "The Latin American Debt Crisis: The Bailout of the Banks." *Inter-American Economic Affairs* 39 (3): 55–70.

Gramsci, Antonio
1971   *Selections from the Prison Notebooks.* New York: International Publishers.

Haberler, G.
1958   *Prosperity and Depression.* Cambridge, Mass.: Harvard University Press.

Habermas, Jurgen
1975   *Legitimation Crisis.* Trans. Thomas McCarthy. Boston: Beacon Press.

Hamilton, Nora
1986a   "Mexico: The Limits of State Autonomy." In *Modern Mexico: State, Economy and Social Conflict,* ed. Nora Hamilton and Timothy F. Harding, 67–103. Beverly Hills: Sage.
1986b   "State-class Alliances and Conflicts: Issues and Actors in the Mexican Economic Crisis." In *Modern Mexico: State, Economy and Social Conflict,* ed. Nora Hamilton and Timothy F. Harding, 148–174. Beverly Hills: Sage.

Herman, Edward S.
1973   "Do Bankers Control Corporations?" *Monthly Review* 25 (June): 12–29.
1975   *Conflicts of Interest: Commercial Bank Trust Departments.* New York: Twentieth Century Fund.
1981   *Corporate Control, Corporate Power.* Cambridge: Cambridge University Press.

Hertsgaard, Mark
1983   *Nuclear, Inc.* New York: Pantheon Books.

Hilferding, Rudolf
1910   *Das Finanzkapital.* Paris: Minoit.
1986   *Finance Capital.* Translated by Tom Bottomore. Boston: Routledge & Kegan Paul.

Hobsbawm, Eric
1976   "The Crisis of Capitalism in Historical Perspective." *Socialist Review* 30 (October–December).
Hobson, J. A.
1905   *Imperialism: A Study*. Rev. ed. First published in 1902. Reprint, 1971. Ann Arbor: University of Michigan Press.
Iacocca, Lee
1984   *Iacocca: An Autobiography*. New York: Bantam Books.
James, David, and Michael Soref
1981   "Profit Constraints on Managerial Autonomy: Managerial Theory and the Unmaking of the Corporation President." *American Sociological Review* 46 (1): 1–18.
Jessop, Bob
1982   *The Capitalist State: Theories and Methods*. New York: New York University Press.
Kaysen, Carl
1957   "The Social Significance of the Modern Corporation." *American Economic Review* 47 (May): 311–319.
Knowles, John
1972   "The Rockefeller Financial Group." *Warner Modular Publications* 343: 1–59.
Koenig, Thomas
1979   "Social Networks and the Political Role of Big Business." Ph.D. diss., University of California at Santa Barbara.
Koenig, Thomas, Robert Gogel, and John Sonquist
1979   "Interlocking Directorates as a Social Network." *American Journal of Economy and Society* 38: 173–183.
Kolko, Gabriel
1976   *Main Currents in Modern American History*. New York: Harper & Row.
Kondratieff, N. D.
1979   "The Long Waves of Economic Life." *Review* 2 (4): 519–562.
Kotz, David M.
1978   *Bank Control of Large Corporations in the United States*. Berkeley and Los Angeles: University of California Press.
Kraft, Joseph
1984   *The Mexican Rescue*. New York: Group of Thirty.
Larner, Robert J.
1970   *Management Control and the Large Corporations*. New York: International Publishers.

Latham, Earl
    1952   "The Group Basis of Politics: Notes for a Theory." *American Political Science Review* 46 (June): 376–397.

Lenin, V. I.
    1917   *Imperialism: The Highest Stage of Capitalism.* First published in 1917. New York, 1979: International Publishers.

Levine, Joel H.
    1972   "The Sphere of Influence." *American Sociological Review* 37 (February): 14–27.

Lichten, Eric
    1980   "The Development of Austerity: Fiscal Crisis in New York City." In *Power Structure Research*, ed. William Domhoff, 139–172. Beverly Hills: Sage.
    1986   *Class, Power and Austerity: The New York City Fiscal Crisis.* South Hadley, Mass.: Bergin & Garvey.

Lichtensztejn, Samuel, and José Manuel Quijano
    1982   "The External Indebtedness of the Developing Countries to International Private Banks." In *Debt and Development*, ed. J. C. Sanchez Arnau, 185–265. New York: Praeger.

Lintner, John
    1966   "The Financing of Corporations." In *The Corporation in Modern Society*, ed. E. S. Mason, 166–201. Cambridge, Mass.: Harvard University Press.

Lipset, Seymour Martin
    1960   *Political Man: The Social Bases of Politics.* Garden City, N.Y.: Doubleday.

Lipson, Charles
    1979   "The IMF, Commercial Banks, and Third World Debts." In *Debt and the Less Developed Countries*, ed. Jonathan David Aronson, 317–333. Boulder, Colo.: Westview Press.

McGuire, Patrick
    1986   "The Control of Power: The Political Economy of Electric Utility Development in the U.S., 1870–1930." Ph.D. diss., State University of New York at Stony Brook.

Makler, Harry
    1985   "Financial Conglomerates in Brazil and Mexico: A Case of the Sorcerer's Apprentice?" Paper presented at the annual meetings of the American Sociological Association, Washington, D.C., August.

Mandel, Ernest
    1978   *Late Capitalism.* London: Verso.

Mariolis, Peter
1975   "Interlocking Directorates and Control of Corporations:
        The Theory of Bank Control." *Social Science Quarterly*
        56: 425–439.
1978   "Bank and Financial Control Among Large U.S. Corpora-
        tions." Ph.D. diss., State University of New York at Stony
        Brook.

Marschall, Dan, ed.
1979   *The Battle of Cleveland: Public Interest Challenges Corpo-
        rate Power.* Washington, D.C.: Conference on Alternative
        State and Local Policies.

Marsden, Keith, and Alan Roe
1984   "The Political Economy of Foreign Aid: A World Bank Per-
        spective." In *Foreign Aid and Third World Development,*
        ed. Pradip K. Ghosh, 133–144. Westport, Conn.: Green-
        wood Press.

Menshikov, S.
1969   *Millionaires and Managers: Structure of the U.S. Financial
        Oligarchy.* Moscow: Progress Publishers.

Merton, Robert K.
1968   *Social Theory and Social Structure.* Enlarged ed. New
        York: Free Press.

Metcalf, Lee, and Vic Reinemer
1967   *Overcharge.* New York: David McKay.

Miliband, Ralph
1969   *The State in Capitalist Society.* New York: Basic Books.

Mills, C. Wright
1956   *The Power Elite.* New York: Oxford University Press.

Mintz, Beth
1978   *Who Controls the Corporation? A Study of Interlocking
        Directorates.* Ph.D. diss., State University of New York at
        Stony Brook.

Mintz, Beth, and Michael Schwartz
1978a   "The Role of Financial Institutions in Interlock Networks."
        Paper presented to the European Consortium for Political
        Research, New Direction in Structural Analysis Confer-
        ence, Toronto, March.
1978b   "The Structure of Power in American Business." Paper pre-
        sented to the American Political Science Association, Wash-
        ington, D.C., September.
1981a   "Interlocking Directorates and Interest Group Formation."
        American Sociological Review 46 (6): 851–869.

1981b   "The Structure of Intercorporate Unity in American Busi-
         ness." *Social Problems* 29 (2): 87–103.
1983   "Financial Interest Groups in American Business." *Social
         Science History* 7 (February): 183–204.
1985   *The Power Structure of the American Business Commu-
         nity.* Chicago: University of Chicago Press.
Mizruchi, Mark S.
1982   *The American Corporate Network, 1904–1974.* Beverly
         Hills: Sage.
Moffitt, Michael
1983   *The World's Money: International Banking from Bretton
         Woods to the Brink of Insolvency.* New York: Simon &
         Schuster.
Mokken, R. J., and F. N. Stokman
1978   "Power and Influence as Political Phenomena." In *Power
         and Political Theory: Some European Perspectives,* ed.
         Brian Barry, 33–54. New York: Wiley.
Mollenkopf, John
1977   "The Crisis of the Public Sector in America's Cities." In
         The Fiscal Crisis of American Cities, ed. Roger E. Alcaly
         and David Mermelstein, 113–140. New York: Vintage
         Books.
Molotch, Harvey
1976   "The City as a Growth Machine." *American Journal of So-
         ciology* 8 (2): 309–332.
Monkkonen, Eric H.
1984   "The Politics of Municipal Indebtedness and Default,
         1850–1936." In *The Politics of Urban Fiscal Policy,* ed.
         Terrence J. McDonald and Sally K. Ward, 125–159. Bev-
         erly Hills: Sage.
Moody's Bank and Finance Manual
1982   New York: Moody's Investors Service.
Moody's Industrial Manual
1974–1984   New York: Moody's Investors Service.
Moody's Municipal and Government Manual
1979   New York: Moody's Investors Service.
*Morgan Guaranty Trust Company of New York v. Charles G. Rodman,
as Trustee of the Estate of W. T. Grant Company*
1975   Bankruptcy no. 75 B 1735. Southern District United States
         Court at Foley Square, New York.
Moritz, Michael, and Barrett Seaman
1981   *Going for Broke: The Chrysler Story.* Garden City, N.Y.:
         Doubleday.

Munson, Richard
1979   "The Price Is Too High." In *America's Future,* ed. Robert Engler, 349–354. New York: Pantheon Books.
Nelson, Philip B.
1981   *Corporations in Crisis: Behavioral Observations for Bankruptcy Policy.* New York: Praeger.
Neustadt, Richard
1976   *Presidential Power: The Politics of Leadership with Reflections on Johnson and Nixon.* New York: Wiley.
Newsweek
1969–1984
New York Times
1969–1986
O'Connor, James
1973   *The Fiscal Crisis of the State.* New York: St. Martin's Press.
1981   "The Meaning of Crisis." *International Journal of Urban and Regional Research* 5 (3): 301–329.
1987   *The Meaning of Crisis: A Theoretical Introduction.* New York: Basil Blackwell.
O'Donnell, Guillermo
1973   *Modernization and Bureaucratic-Authoritarianism: Studies in South American Politics.* Berkeley: University of California, Institute of International Studies.
OECD (Organization for Economic Cooperation and Development)
1984a   *External Debt of Developing Countries: 1983 Survey.* Paris: OECD.
1984b   "Pattern of External Financing of Developing Countries' Payments of Balances." In *Foreign Aid and Third World Development,* ed. Pradip K. Ghosh, 95–106. Westport, Conn.: Greenwood Press.
Offe, Claus
1972a   "Advanced Capitalism and the Welfare State." *Politics and Society* 2: 479–488.
1972b   "Political Authority and Class Structure: An Analysis of Late Capitalist Societies." *International Journal of Sociology* 2: 73–108.
1974   "Structural Problems of the Capitalist State. Class Rule and the Political System. On the Selectiveness of Political Institutions." *German Political Studies* 1: 31–57.
Olson, McKinley
1976   *Unacceptable Risk: The Nuclear Power Conspiracy.* New York: Bantam Books.

Pahl, R. E., and J. T. Winkler
1974 "The Economic Elite: Theory and Practice." In *Elites and Power in British Society,* ed. Philip Stanworth and Anthony Giddens, 102–122. Cambridge: Cambridge University Press.

Palmer, Donald
1983 "Broken Ties: Interlocking Directorates and Intercorporate Coordination." *Administrative Science Quarterly* 28: 40–55.

Patman, Wright
1970 "Interim Report on the Bankruptcy of Penn Central." *Congressional Record.* 91st Cong., 2d sess., 2 July. Vol. 116, pt. 17, 22632–22638.

Patman Committee
1963 *Chain Banking, Stockholder and Loan Links of the 200 Largest Member Banks.* Washington, D.C.: Government Printing Office.

Patterson, Tim
1975 "Notes on the Historical Application of Marxist Cultural Theory." *Science and Society* 39 (3): 247–291.

Payer, Cheryl
1974 *The Debt Trap: The IMF and the Third World.* New York: Monthly Review Press.

Pelton, Richard
1970 "Who Really Rules America?" Somerville, Mass.: New England Free Press.

Pennings, Johannes M.
1980 *Interlocking Directorates: Origins and Consequences of Connections Among Organizations' Boards of Directors.* San Francisco: Jossey-Bass.

Perlo, Victor
1957 *The Empire of High Finance.* New York: International Publishers.
1958 "'The People's Capitalism' and Stock Ownership." *American Economic Review* 48 (3): 333–347.

Perrucci, Robert, and Marc Pilisuk
1970 "Leaders and Ruling Elites: The Interorganizational Bases of Community Power." *American Sociological Review* 35 (December): 1040–1057.

Pfeffer, Jeffrey, and Gerald R. Salancik
1978 *External Control of Organizations: A Resource Dependence Perspective.* New York: Harper & Row.

Pivan, Frances Fox, and Richard A. Cloward
1978   *Poor People's Movements: How They Succeed and Why They Fail.* New Orleans: Pantheon Books.
Plain Dealer
1978–1979
Poulantzas, Nicos
1968   "The Problem of the Capitalist State." In *Ideology in Social Science,* ed. Robin Blackburn, 238–253. New York: Pantheon Books.
1973   *Political Power and Social Classes.* Translated by Timothy O'Hagen. London: New Left Books.
1975   *Classes in Contemporary Capitalism.* Translated by David Fernbach. London: Verso.
1978   *State, Power, Socialism.* London: New Left Books.
Presthus, Robert
1964   *Men at the Top.* New York: Oxford University Press.
Proxmire, William
1979   "The Case Against Bailing Out Chrysler." *New York Times,* 21 Oct., 30, 94–100.
Ratcliff, Richard E.
1980a   "Banks and Corporate Lending: An Analysis of the Impact of the Internal Structure of the Capitalist Class on the Lending Behavior of Banks." *American Sociological Review* 45 (Aug.): 553–570.
1980b   "Banks and the Command of Capital Flows: An Analysis of Capitalist Class Structure and Mortgage Disinvestment in a Metropolitan Area." In *Classes, Conflict and the State,* ed. Maurice Zeitlin, 107–132. Cambridge, Mass.: Winthrop.
1980c   "Capitalist Class Structure and the Decline of Older Industrial Cities." *Insurgent Sociologist* 9 (2–3): 60–74.
Ratcliff, Richard E., Mary E. Gallagher, and K. S. Ratcliff
1979   "The Civic Involvement of Business Leaders: An Analysis of the Influence of Economic Power and Social Prominence in the Command of Civil Policy Positions." *Social Problems* 26 (3): 298–313.
Reinener, Vic
1982   "Public Power's Roots," *Public Power* 40(5): 22–26.
Reynolds, Clark
1978   "Why Mexico's 'Stabilizing Development' Was Actually Destabilizing (with Some Implications for the Future)." *World Development* 6: 1005–1018.
Rifkin, Jeremy, and Randy Barber
1978   *The North Will Rise Again: Pensions, Politics, and Power*

in the 1980s. Washington, D.C.: People's Business Commission.

Rochester, Anna
  1936   *Rulers of America: A Study of Finance Capital.* New York: International Publishers.

Rogers-Millar, L. Edna, and Frank E. Millar III
  1979   "Domineeringness and Dominance: A Transactional View." *Human Communications Research* 5 (3): 238–246.

Rose, Arnold
  1967   "Confidence and the Corporation." *American Journal of Economics and Sociology* 26 (3): 231–236.

Ross, Joel E., and Michael E. Kami
  1973   *Corporate Management in Crisis: Why the Mighty Fall.* Englewood Cliffs, N.J.: Prentice-Hall.

Rubinson, Richard
  1977   "The World Economy and the Distribution of Income Within States: A Cross-National Study." *American Sociological Review* 41 (4): 638–659.

Rudolph, Richard, and Scott Ridley
  1986   *Power Struggle.* New York: Harper & Row.

Sallach, David
  1974   "Class Domination and Ideological Hegemony." *Sociological Quarterly* 15 (Winter): 38–50.

Sanchez Arnau, J. C.
  1982   "Debt and Development." In *Debt and Development,* ed. J. C. Sanchez Arnau, 1–14. New York: Praeger.

Schmitt, John
  1986   "Debt: South of the Border, Going South." *In These Times,* 15–21 October, 11.

Schultze, Charles L., E. R. Fried, A. M. Rinlin, N. H. Teeters, and R. D. Reischauer
  1977   "Fiscal Problems of Cities." In *The Fiscal Crisis of American Cities,* ed. Roger E. Alcaly and David Mermelstein, 189–212. New York: Vintage Books.

Schwartz, Michael, and Glenn Yago
  1981   "What's Good for Chrysler Is Bad for Us." *Nation,* 12 September, 200–203.

Scott, John
  1978   "The Intercorporate Configuration: Substructure and Superstructure." Paper prepared for the planning session on "Interorganizational Networks Between Large Corporations and Governments." European Consortium for Political Research, Grenoble, April.

1979   *Corporations, Classes and Capitalism.* London: Hutchinson.

Seiber, Marilyn J.
1982   *International Borrowing by Developing Countries.* New York: Pergamon Press.

Sherman, H.
1979   "Inflation, Unemployment, and the Contemporary Business Cycle." *Socialist Review* 44 (March–April): 75–102.

Sid-Ahmed, Abdelkader
1982   "The Conditionality of Drawings on International Monetary Fund." In *Debt and Development,* ed. J. C. Sanchez Arnau, 111–184. New York: Praeger.

Skocpol, Theda
1985   "Bringing the State Back In: Strategies of Analysis in Current Research." In *Bringing the State Back In,* ed. Peter B. Evans, Dietrich Rueschemeyer, and Theda Skocpol, 3–43. Cambridge: Cambridge University Press.

Smith, Adam
1776   *An Inquiry into the Nature and Causes of the Wealth of Nations.* Reprint, 1976. Oxford: Clarendon Press.

Sonquist, John, and Thomas Koenig
1975   "Interlocking Directorates in the Top U.S. Corporations: A Graph Theory Approach." *Insurgent Sociologist* 5 (3): 196–229.

Stallings, Barbara
1979   "Peru and the U.S. Banks: The Privatization of Financial Relations." In *Capitalism and the State in U.S.–Latin American Relations,* ed. Richard Fagen, 217–253. Stanford, Calif.: Stanford University Press.
1982   "Euromarkets, Third World Countries, and the International Political Economy." In *The New International Economy,* ed. Harry Makler, Alberto Martinelli, and Neil Smelser, 193–230. Beverly Hills: Sage.

Standard and Poor's Register of Corporations, Directors and Executives.
1969   New York: Standard and Poor's.

Stearns, Linda Brewster
1982   *Corporate Dependency and the Structure of the Capital Market.* Ph.D. diss., State University of New York at Stony Brook.

Stearns, Linda Brewster, and Mark Mizruchi
1986   "Broken-Tie Reconstitution and the Functions of Interorganizational Interlocks: A Reexamination." *Administrative Science Quarterly* 31: 522–538.

Swanstrom, Todd
  1985   *The Crisis of Growth Politics.* Philadelphia: Temple University Press.
  1986   "Urban Populism, Fiscal Crisis and the New Political Economy." In *Cities in Stress: A New Look at the Urban Crisis,* ed. M. Gottdiener, 81–110. Beverly Hills: Sage.
Sweezy, Paul M.
  1970   *The Theory of Capitalist Development.* New York: Monthly Review Press.
Sweezy, Paul M., and Harry Magdoff
  1975   "Banks: Skating on Thin Ice." *Monthly Review* 26 (9): 1–21.
Tabb, William K.
  1982   *The Long Default: New York City and the Urban Fiscal Crisis.* New York: Monthly Review Press.
Taylor, Lance
  1984   "Mexico's Adjustment in the 1980s: Look Back Before Leaping Ahead." In *Adjustment Crisis in the Third World,* ed. Richard E. Feinberg and Valeriana Kallab, 147–158. New Brunswick, N.J.: Transaction Books.
Thomas, William I.
  1928   *The Child in America.* New York: Knopf.
Tinnin, David B.
  1973   *Just About Everybody vs. Howard Hughes.* Garden City, N.Y.: Doubleday.
Truman, David B.
  1951   *The Governmental Process.* New York: Random House.
U.S. Congress, House of Representatives
  1968   Committee on Bank and Currency. Subcommittee on Domestic Finance. *Commercial Banks and Their Trust Activities: Emerging Influences on the American Economy.* 90th Cong., 2d sess. Washington, D.C.: Government Printing Office.
  1969   Committee on the Judiciary. *Investigation of Conglomerate Corporations: Leasco Data Processing Equipment Corp.* 91st Cong., 2d sess. Serial 23, pt. 2. Washington, D.C.: Government Printing Office.
  1979a   Committee on Banking, Finance, and Urban Affairs. Subcommittee on Economic Stabilization. *The Chrysler Corporation Financial Situation.* 96th Cong., 1st sess. Washington, D.C.: Government Printing Office.

1979b   Committee on Banking, Finance, and Urban Affairs. Sub-committee on Financial Institutions Supervision, Regulation, and Insurance. *The Role of Commercial Banks in the Finances of the City of Cleveland.* 96th Cong., 1st sess. Washington, D.C.: Government Printing Office.

1979c   Committee on Banking, Finance, and Urban Affairs. Sub-committee on Financial Institutions Supervision, Regulation, and Insurance. *Role of Commercial Banks in the Financing of the Debt of the City of Cleveland.* 96th Cong., 1st sess. Washington, D.C.: Government Printing Office.

1982   Committee on Banking, Finance, and Urban Affairs. *International Financial Markets and Related Matters.* 97th Cong., 2d sess. Washington, D.C.: Government Printing Office.

1983a   Committee on Banking, Finance, and Urban Affairs. *International Financial Markets and Related Problems.* 98th Cong., 1st sess. Washington, D.C.: Government Printing Office.

1983b   Committee on Banking, Finance, and Urban Affairs. Sub-committee on International Trade, Investment, and Monetary Policy. *Export-Import Bank Facilities for Brazil and Mexico.* 98th Cong., 1st sess. Washington, D.C.: Government Printing Office.

1983c   Committee on Banking, Finance, and Urban Affairs. Sub-committee on International Trade, Investment, and Monetary Policy. *To Increase the U.S. Quota in the International Monetary Fund and Related Matters.* 98th Cong., 1st sess. Washington, D.C.: Government Printing Office.

U.S. Congress, Joint Session

1984   Joint Economic Committee. Subcommittee on Economic Goals and Intergovernmental Policy. *International Debt.* 98th Cong., 2d sess. Washington, D.C.: Government Printing Office.

U.S. Congress, Senate

1975   Committee on Banking, Housing, and Urban Affairs. *Home Mortgage Disclosure Act of 1975.* 94th Cong., 1st sess. Washington, D.C.: Government Printing Office.

1980   Committee on Banking, Housing, and Urban Affairs. *Home Mortgage Disclosure Amendments of 1980.* 96th Cong., 2d sess. Washington, D.C.: Government Printing Office.

1982   Committee on Foreign Relations. Subcommittee on International Economic Policy. *World Debt Situation.* 97th Cong., 2d sess. Washington, D.C.: Government Printing Office.

1983a   Committee on Banking, Housing, and Urban Affairs. Subcommittee on International Finance and Monetary Policy. *Export-Import Bank Proposal of Credit to Brazil and Mexico.* 98th Cong., 1st sess. Washington, D.C.: Government Printing Office.

1983b   Committee on Banking, Housing, and Urban Affairs. Subcommittee on International Finance and Monetary Policy. *International Debt.* 98th Cong., 1st sess. Washington, D.C.: Government Printing Office.

U.S. Dept. of Commerce, Bureau of the Census
1988   *Statistical Abstracts of the United States, 1988.* Washington, D.C.: U.S. Government Printing Office.

U.S. Department of Labor
1982   Bureau of Labor Statistics. *Employment and Earnings.* June supplement. Washington, D.C.: Government Printing Office.

Useem, Michael
1979   "The Social Organization of the American Business Elite and Participation of Corporate Directors in the Governance of American Institutions." *American Sociological Review* 44 (4): 553–572.

1984   *The Inner Circle: Large Corporations and the Rise of Business Political Activity in the U.S. and U.K.* New York: Oxford University Press.

U.S. News and World Report
1978

Villarejo, Don
1961   "Stock Ownership and the Control of Corporations." Somerville, Mass.: New England Free Press.

Wall Street Journal
1969–1985

Wasserman, Harvey
1979   *Energy Wars: Reports from the Front.* Westport, Conn.: Lawrence Hill.

Weber, Max
1947   *The Theory of Social and Economic Organization.* Translated by A. Henderson and T. Parsons. Glencoe, Ill.: Free Press.

Weiner, Benjamin
  1983   "Mexico's Biggest Need." *New York Times,* 1 July, A23.
  1984   "Mexico's Miracle of Mirrors." *New York Times,* 15 January, F3.
Weinstein, James
  1968   *The Corporate Ideal in the Liberal State, 1900–1918.* Boston: Beacon Press.
Welles, Chris
  1975   *The Last Days of the Club.* New York: E. P. Dutton.
Whelan, Edward P.
  1975   "Mayor Ralph J. Perk and the Politics of Decay." *Cleveland Magazine,* September. Reprinted in *The Battle of Cleveland,* ed. Dan Marschall, 70–74. Washington, D.C.: Conference on Alternative State and Local Policies, 1979.
Whitt, J. Allen
  1979   "Toward a Class-Dialectical Model of Power." *American Sociological Review* 44 (1): 81–99.
  1980   "Can Capitalists Organize Themselves?" In *Power Structure Research,* ed. G. William Domhoff, 97–114. Beverly Hills: Sage.
  1982   *The Dialectics of Power: Urban Elites and Mass Transportation.* Princeton, N.J.: Princeton University Press.
Williams, G. A.
  1960   "Gramsci's Concept of Egemonia." *Journal of the History of Ideas* 21 (4): 586–599.
Women's Wear Daily
  1975–1978
Wood, Robert E.
  1986   *From Marshall Plan to Debt Crisis: Foreign Aid and Development Choices in the World Economy.* Berkeley and Los Angeles: University of California Press.
Young, Louise
  1973   *Power Over People.* New York: Oxford University Press.
Zeitlin, Maurice
  1974   "Corporate Ownership and Control: The Large Corporation and the Capitalist Class." *American Journal of Sociology* 79 (5): 1073–1119.
Zucker, Lynn
  1987   "Institutional Theories of Organization." *Annual Review of Sociology* 13: 443–464.

Index

Abatements
  tax in Cleveland, 126, 133
Accounts receivable, 30, 31, 36–37,
  39, 52
Acquisitions, 7, 103–5, 110, 112, 114,
  116
AFL-CIO, 10, 87
Africa, 149
Aid, official, 144–45, 147
Aid regime
  restrictions, 147, 170
Allen, Julius, 3
Allied Supermarkets, 100
American Federation of State, County and
  Municipal Employees, 142
American Motors, 65
American Public Power Association, 128
Anderson, Robert A., 43–44, 49, 50, 52
Andres, Willard D., 160–61
Anti-trust and Leasco, 114–15
Argentina, 149, 163
Aron, Raymond, 13
Austerity
  IMF programs, 168–71, 172, 174–78,
    190–91, 193
  Mexico, 159–60, 162
Autonomy
  relative, 2, 15–16, 99–100, 138, 147,
    149, 171–72, 174–75, 177–80,
    181–82, 184–91

Bachrach, Elinor, 63
Bailout(s), 23
  bank(s), 73–74, 166–72, 178–79
  federal, 60–61, 73–74, 90–91, 93–
    94, 97, 163, 181–82, 184–86,
    191

Bank for International Settlements, 158,
  161
Bank of America, 23
Bank of Boston, 23
Bankers' Trust, 9
Bankruptcy
  Chapter X, 48–50, 56
  Chapter XI, 25–26, 34, 44, 48–50,
    53, 55, 57
  Chrysler, 71, 74, 79, 84, 86, 97, 99–
    100
  and crisis, 21, 24
  involuntary, 181–82
  as last resort, 101
  and power, 6
Banks
  and capitalist transformation, 3
  and the state, 13–17
  as capital flow hubs, 181
  commercial, 4, 6
  in the world economy, 167
Barber, Randy, 5, 9–10, 82, 194
Barbour, Jeffrey, 11n
Barkin, David, 150, 153, 155
Bartimole, Roldo, 127, 128
Baum, Daniel J., 5
Bearden, James, 11n, 26
Beck, John F., 156
Beck, John H., 138
Becton Dickinson, 160
Berger, Peter, 18n
Berkman, Ronald, 142
Besse, Ralph, 131
Blain, Robert, 15
Blair, Claude MacClary, 133
Blanchard, James J., 83–84
Block, Fred, 139

Bluestone, B., 17
Blumenthal, Michael, 69
Board(s). *See also* Directorates, inter-
   locking
   and bank representation, 6, 26–27, 35,
      45, 59, 187
   CEI and bank representation, 129, 131,
      187
   constraints, 187–88
   interlocking, 112–13
   labor representation, 81–82, 87–
      88, 97
   W. T. Grant, 29, 46
Bonbright, James, 132
Bondrating
   Cleveland, 126
Bonds
   Cleveland, 136
   and power, 6
   and private utilities, 132–33
Born, Roscoe, 9
Branfman, Fred, 120, 128
Brazil, 149, 163, 168–69, 172
Breckenfeld, G., 21
Brooke, James, 149
Brooks, John, 104–11, 113–15
Bunting, David, 11n
Business
   and community, 12
Byrd, Robert C., 81

Capital
   and finance, 4, 5
   industrial, 4, 5
   redundant, 104
Capital flows
   and power, 185
   as a resource, 181
Capitalism
   finance, 3
   industrial, 3
   transformation, 3
Capital market
   structural transformation, 144–48,
      154
Carter administration, 82–83, 126–27,
   189
Centrality
   banks, 11
   and power, 3
Central National Bank, 122, 129n, 131
Chandler, A. D., Jr., 58
Chase Manhattan, 23, 36, 37, 43, 45, 57,
   110, 115, 167
Chemical Bank, 23, 46, 102–16, 158,
   182, 184, 188

Chevalier, J. M., 5, 9, 11
Chinn, Joseph W., 45, 53, 58
Chrysler, 23–24, 117, 143, 166, 178–
   80, 184–89, 191, 193–94
   board of directors, 10
   history, 60–69
Circulation
   of the power elite, 14
Citibank, 23, 36–38, 45, 47, 50, 57, 163
Clavel, Pierre, 126, 128, 142
Clayton Act, 115
Cleveland, 24, 182–84, 186–90, 193
   antitrust suit, 122, 128, 131, 138–39
   construction and debt, 125
   history, 120–21, 125–26, 141–42
Cleveland Electric Illuminating Company,
   122, 127–35, 138–42, 182, 183,
   187–88
   history vs. MUNY, 127–32
Cleveland Electric Lighting Company,
   141
Cleveland Planning Commission, 142
Cleveland Trust Company, 120, 122, 124,
   126, 131, 133
Cloward, Richard, 15
Cockcroft, James D., 150, 152–53, 156–
   58, 160
Competition
   and banks, 2, 4–5, 7, 22
   banks and industrials, 4–5
   and interlocks, 12
Concentration
   of capital, 3–4, 171
   commodity, 146
   of finance capital, 4–5
   of international capital, 149
   of lending organizations, 148
   of Mexican banks, 155
   of recipient countries, 148
Concessions
   banks to Chrysler, 75–77, 89
   banks to Mexico, 162–63
   Chrysler to labor, 87
   Chrysler to state, 74–75
   dealers and suppliers to Chrysler, 76,
      88–89
   labor to Chrysler, 80–88, 89, 96–97
   Mexico to IMF and banks, 174–75
   Mexico to the banks, 162–63
   Mexico to the IMF, 162
   state to Chrysler, 76–77, 88–89
Connecticut Bank and Trust, 32, 33
Consortia
   lending, 2, 6, 16–17, 36–42, 56–59,
      78, 117, 149, 179, 181–84, 187,
      189, 192

lending, as power, 148–49
lending, Chrysler, 70, 75, 77–78, 98
lending, Cleveland, 122–23, 129–31,
  133, 140
lending, state debt, 148–49
lending, W. T. Grant, 34–44, 56
and risk, 6
Constraint(s)
  banks', 55
  state, 171–72, 174–75, 178
  managerial, 19–20, 34, 59, 68, 74, 98
  state's, 60, 171–72, 174, 178
Continental Illinois Bank, 41, 109–11, 188
Control
  allocative, 75, 117
  of lending capital, 6
  operational, 75, 117
Corroon, Richard A., 110–11
Corm, Georges, 145n
Costa Rica, 163
Cravath, Swaine and Moore, 115
Credit
  CEI, 129–31
Crisis
  bankruptcy, 52, 56–57, 59
  of capitalism, 17
  corporate, 19–21, 102–3, 116–17,
    182, 184
  corporate and bailouts, 72, 85, 94–95,
    98–99
  defining and power, 5
  definition of the situation, 98–99
  fiscal, 184
  impending, 60–61
  in healthy firms, 102–3, 116–18
  international, 144–45
  international debt, 172
  international, as social construction,
    174
  as last resort, 174–75
  legitimacy, 21, 189–91
  municipal, 182
  objective, 17–19
  political, 17–18
  power to define, 2
  as sanction, 116
  as a social construction, 17–21, 181–
    82, 184–87
  and the state, 2
  state, 21, 182–83
  state, as a social construction, 188–91
  W. T. Grant, 25
Curtin, James G., 29

Dahl, Robert, 13, 188n
Dale, Richard S., 145n, 148n

D'Amours, Norman E., 73
Davis, Diane, 150–51
Debt
  Cleveland, 125–26, 137
  developed countries, 144–45
  developing countries, 144–48
  Municipal, causes, 119–20
Debt Crisis Network, 145n, 162
Debt servicing, 145–46, 149, 169–70,
  193
  developing countries, 170, 173–74
  Mexico, 160, 173–74
Decisions
  managerial, 26–34, 61–69, 95, 98,
    100
Default
  Cleveland, 125–26, 129, 136–38,
    141–43, 183
  Cleveland, preconditions, 134
  as last resort, 142
  municipal, 186–87, 188, 192
  social construction, 129, 133–34, 138,
    140–43
Delacroix, Jacques, 170
De la Madrid, Miguel Hurtado, 159–62,
  172, 174, 177, 190
De Larosiere, Jacques, 159, 161, 166
Dependence
  debt, 146–47
  trade, 146, 150, 170
Deregulation
  bank, 76, 80, 96, 194
Development
  dependent, 146–47, 170
Development Assistant Committee, 145
Dhonte, Pierre, 145, 148
Dialectic, class, 14–16
Diamond Shamrock Corporation, 136
Directorates. *See also* Board(s)
  boards of, 111–13
  interlocking, 111, 117
Discretion
  managerial, 19, 24, 26, 32, 35, 51, 75,
    98, 184
  state, 184
Disinvestment, 21
  in Cleveland, 131–32
Dividends
  Chrysler, 66
  and external investment, 7
  MUNY vs. CEI, 132
  W. T. Grant, 34
Domhoff, G. William, 12, 14, 16, 188n,
  189
Dooley, Peter C., 11n
Draper, William H., 169–70

Dudley King, 114
Dumping
  stock, 10–11, 21, 104, 107–11,
    116–18
Echeverria, Luis, 151–52, 176
Election recall, 121–25, 131, 133
Emergency Financial Control Board, 142
Emerson, Robert, 21, 186
Empires, industrial, 5
Erb, Guy, 157
Esteva, Gustavo, 150, 153, 155
Expansion, corporate, 2
Expenditures
  social welfare, 15
Export-Import Bank, 166, 168–70, 171,
    172, 179, 186

Federal Reserve, 115, 158, 161, 163–65·
Finance capital
  as a relationship, 183, 191–92
Financial institutions
  and intercorporate relations, 2
Financing
  external, 7
Fine, Ben, 17
First Boston, 23
First National Bank of Jersey City, 105–
    6, 111
First National City Bank, 9
Fitch, Robert, 1, 5, 6, 59, 188n
Fogler, Raymond H., 31
Forbes, George, 125, 126
Ford, 65–68, 83, 87, 90, 92–95
Fraser, Douglas A., 10, 80–85, 87
Fuel disruptions, 146
Fund(s). *See also* Pensions and Trusts
  Illinois State Teachers', 54, 56, 193
  Michigan Teachers', 54, 56, 193
  pension, 113, 114, 128
  pension, CEI, 129–31
  trust, 38

Galgay, Judge John, 51–52, 53–54
General Electric, 141
General Motors, 63, 65–68, 83, 87, 90,
    93–95, 157–58
Georgeson, 114
Girvan, Norman, 162, 192
Glasberg, Davita Silfen, 145n, 184, 192
Gogel, Robert, 7, 11n, 12, 34
Goldman Sachs, 23
Gonzalez, Heliodoro, 148, 167
Gramsci, Antonio, 22, 188n
Grant, W. T., 24, 25–59, 75, 77, 79, 117,

    181, 182–85, 187, 193
  W. T., history, 25–26
Grant Foundation, 32–34
Greater Cleveland Growth Association,
    121–22, 128, 134, 140, 187
  ties to banks and CEI, 134
Green revolution, 153, 176
Greenwald, Gerald, 72
Gross national product, 146
Grupa Alfa, 156
Guarantee(s)
  federal, 242, 249
  loan, 60–61, 69–89, 92–93, 95–97,
    100, 143
Gurria, Angel, 163

Haberler, G., 17
Habermas, Jurgen, 15, 17–18, 21, 188n
Hahn, Loeser, Freedheim, Dean and Well-
    man, 122
Hamilton, Nora, 153, 155–58, 160–61,
    172–73
Harrison, B., 17
Hegemony
  bank, 12, 21–24, 38, 55–59, 139, 143,
    171, 179, 181–86, 187, 192–93
  bank formation, 40–42, 43, 57, 58,
    77–79, 98–99, 164–66, 178, 180
  bank, international, 149, 161–62
  vs. control, 55–56
Herding effect, 11, 20, 102
Herman, Edward S., 10, 12, 57, 58
Hertsgaard, Mark, 133
Hilferding, Rudolf, 1, 3, 4, 7
Hobsbawn, Eric, 17
Hobson, J. A., 1, 3
Hubs
  in interlocks, 12

Iacocca, Lee, 60–63, 65, 67–68, 80, 85,
    87, 90, 93, 95, 98, 100
Inflation
  and external capital, 8
Influence
  banks in municipal policy, 131
  banks' over political process, 125, 138
  banks, W. T. Grant, 36–38
  on corporations, 2
  of municipal policy, 139
  on the state, 2
Ingraham, John, 51
Insolvency
  W. T. Grant, 46–47
Instrumentalism, 189
Instrumentalists, 14–15

Insurance, 4, 6, 22, 103–4
  and interlocks, 12
Interdependence
  corporations and banks, 5
  state and banks, 5
Interests
  banks' vs. Chrysler, 74, 89–90, 96–
    97, 99
  banks' vs. Cleveland, 138–39
  banks' vs. corporations, 142–43, 182
  banks' vs. labor, 96–97, 177–78
  banks' vs. labor, Cleveland, 140–41
  banks' vs. Penn Central, 59
  banks vs. the poor, 177–78
  banks' vs. state, 70–73, 76–77, 99,
    172, 176, 178, 179
  banks' vs. W. T. Grant, 47, 49–52, 56,
    57, 58–59
  common, 182–83, 187–88
  common, CEI and banks, 138–39,
    140–42
  competing, 181, 188
  IMF vs. Mexico, 172
  major banks vs. smaller banks, 164–
    65, 183
  state vs. labor, 177
  state vs. the poor, 177
  U.S. banks vs. foreign banks, 164–66
Interlock(s). *See also* Board(s); Directo-
    rates
  as access to capital, 35
  and banks, W. T. Grant, 34, 53
  banks and nonfinancials, 131
  board and banks, 32
  boards, 117
  capitalists and the state, 16
  CEI and banks, 129, 183
  directorates, 2, 5, 6, 11–13, 16, 19,
    22, 117, 181, 187–88
  directorates, Cleveland, 122, 139
  informational, 45–46, 53, 57–58, 106,
    188
  and local mortgages, 131–32
  and power, 12
  and their role, 181
International Bank for Reconstruction
    and Development, 145, 147
International Monetary Fund, 73, 145,
    147, 152, 158–62, 166–70, 172,
    174–76, 178–79, 186, 190–91, 193
  quotas, 166–68, 172, 179
Intervention
  banks, in W. T. Grant, 39–40
Investment
  joint, 12

Investment companies, 4
Invisible hand, 19, 21, 58, 183
Irving Trust, 46

Jacobs, Marvin, 52, 56
James, David, 19
Jessop, Bob, 14–15
Johnson, Tom, 141
Jones, Day, Reavis and Pogue, 122, 131
Justice
  Department of, 115

Kahn, Alfred E., 83
Kami, Michael, 19
Kaysen, Carl, 58
Kelly, Richard, 64, 80–81
Kendrick, James G., 27, 31, 37–38, 43–
    44, 48–49
Killefer, Tom, 72
Kingon, Alfred H., 171
Kirkland, Lane, 10, 87–88
Knapp, David W., 78–79
Knowles, John, 5
Koch, Ed, 142–43
Koenig, Thomas, 11n, 12
Kolko, Gabriel, 14
Kondratieff, N. D., 170
Kotz, David, 1, 5, 7, 9, 23, 187
Kraft, Joseph, 150, 152–55, 158–66,
    171
Kucinich, Dennis, 120–22, 125, 126, 129,
    132–43, 184, 186–87, 189–90

Last resort, 186–87
Latham, Earl, 13
Lazard-Freres, 137
Leasco, 24, 102–18, 143, 182–84,
    186–88
Lehman Bros., 113–14
Lehman-Goldman, 23
Leland, Marc E., 169
Lending
  and bank power, 2, 6–8
  and the state, 16
Lenin, V. I., 1, 3–6
Levine, Joel, 5, 11n
Lichten, Eric, 21, 142, 192
Lichtensztejn, Samuel, 145, 148–49
Lintner, John, 7
Lipp, Robert, 114
Lipset, S. M., 13, 188n
Lipson, Charles, 145n
Loan(s), 181, 185
  CEI, 129
  Chrysler, 66

Loan(s) (*continued*)
 Cleveland, 120
 Eurodollar, 155
 Euromarket, 147
 Mexico, 154
 and power, 1–2
 private, 147–48
 short-term, 6
 and the state, 2, 5, 13
 stipulation, 7
 and stocks, 10
 W. T. Grant, 34–44
Loan Extension Agreement
 W. T. Grant, 42–43
Lockheed, 26
London, Bank of, 112
Long, Russel, 81
Losses
 banks, Chrysler, 95–96
 labor, Chrysler, 96–97
Luckett, Robert A., 39
Luckmann, Thomas, 18 n
Lustenberger, Louis C., 31

MacArthur, Edward S., 110–11
McCall, Howard, 113
McDonough, William J., 99
McFadden, J. A., 106, 107
McGillicuddy, John F., 70–72, 99
McGuire, Patrick, 133
McKinney, Stewart B., 64, 75, 167
Magdoff, Harry, 7
Mancera, Miguel, 160
Mandel, Ernest, 14–15, 17, 188n, 191
Manufacturers Hanover, 57, 70, 99, 159
Mariolis, Peter, 11 n
Marschall, Dan, 125, 126, 132
Marsden, Keith, 145 n, 148
Mattione, Richard P., 145 n, 148 n
Mayer, Richard W., 29, 33, 37–38, 45
Means, Gardiner C., 132
Mellon National Bank, 9, 23
Menshikov, S., 1, 5–11, 22
Mergers, 2, 7, 8, 108–9
Merton, Robert, 20
Metcalf, Lee, 132–33
Metropolitan Life Insurance, 23
Mexico, 24, 147, 182–84, 186–87, 188, 193
 history, 150–56
Miliband, Ralph, 14, 99, 188n, 189
Millar, Frank E., 69n
Miller, G. William, 69, 79
Mills, C. Wright, 14, 188n, 189
Mintz, Beth, 3, 5, 11n, 12, 22, 184, 187

Mitsubishi, 90, 97
Mizruchi, Mark, 5, 11n, 12
Moffitt, Michael, 145n, 146, 148
Mokken, R. J., 12n, 184, 187
Mollenkopf, John, 21
Monkkonen, Eric H., 139
Monopolies
 capitalist, 4–5
Morgan, J. P., 141
Morgan, Stanley, 23
Morgan Guaranty, 9, 23, 32, 35–38, 41–42, 45–48, 57–58, 168
Moritz, Michael, 63, 65, 70, 89–90, 92
Municipal Lighting Corporation, 126–29, 131–32, 134–36, 138–42, 182, 186, 190
 history, 127–28
Munoz, David Ibarra, 155
Munson, Richard, 133

National Association of Exporters and Importers, 156
National City Bank, 122, 126, 131, 133
Nelson, Philip B., 56
Networks. *See also* Board(s); Directorates; Interlocks
 information, 106–7
 interlocking, 112–13
Neustadt, Richard, 13
New York City, 142–43, 192
Nuclear
 power in Cleveland, 132–33
Nuclear Regulatory Commission, 128

O'Connor, James, 15, 17–18, 21, 132, 140, 188n
O'Donnell, Guillermo, 14
OECD, 145–46, 148
Offe, Claus, 15, 188n
Offer
 tender, 104, 106–7, 111, 113
Ogden, William S., 167
Ohio Edison, 122
Ohio Public Interest Campaign, 142
Oligarchy, 4
Olmer, Lionel H., 169
OPEC, 146
Oppenheimer, Mary, 1, 5, 6, 59
Organization. *See also* Consortia; Hegemony
 of banks, 5
 and power, 2

Pahl, R. E., 98, 117
Palmer, Donald, 12

Pardo, Joseph, 55
Partido Revolucionario Institucional, 152, 159, 160
Patman, Wright, 11
Patterson, Tim, 22
Paul, Ron, 73
Payer, Cheryl, 147
Pelton, Richard, 5
Pemex, 153–54
Pennings, Johannes, 12n
Penn Central, 24, 25, 59
Pension(s), 181, 183, 185, 194. *See also* Funds
  and bank customers, 10
  and bank power, 10–11
  and banks, 8
  funds, 2, 3, 5, 8–10, 22, 112, 116–17
  funds, concentration, 9
  Illinois Teachers', 54, 56
  investment return, 10
  Michigan Teachers', 54, 56
  and stock dumping, 10–11
Perk, Ralph, 125–26, 128
Perlo, Victor, 5, 8–9
Perucci, Robert, 12
Peru, 147, 149
Peterkin, DeWitt, Jr., 27, 29, 31, 33, 35, 37–38, 43, 45–46, 49–50, 53, 57–58
Petrodollars, 146
Peugeot, 90, 97
Pfeffer, Jeffrey, 12
Pierson, Harry, 39
Pilisuk, Mark, 12
Piven, Frances Fox, 15
Pluralism, 13–14, 179–80, 188–89
Poland, 192
Populism
  in Cleveland, 120, 138, 140–42, 182
Portillo, Jose Lopez, 152, 154, 156, 158–60, 177, 190
Poulantzas, Nicos, 14–15, 58, 188n, 189, 190–91
Power. *See also* Constraints; Discretion; Hegemony
  allocative, 75, 177, 190
  and constraint, 190
  and control of capital flows, 5
  discretionary, 117
  operational, 75, 98, 117
  as organization, 181
  preemptive, 53
  reputational, 184
  and social construction of reality, 181–82

traces in interlocks, 187–88
transnational, 190–91
vs. influence, 183–84
Power elite, 14
Presthus, Robert, 13
Proxmire, William, 63, 70, 99–100, 169
Prudential Life, 23

Quijano, Jose Manuel, 145, 148–49

Ragin, Charles C., 170
Raid, bear, 107, 109
Ratcliff, Kathryn Strother, 131
Ratcliff, Richard, 16, 21, 131, 192
Reagan administration, 164
Recession
  and external capital, 8
Recovery
  Chrysler, 92–93
  Chrysler and labor, 92, 93, 94
  Chrysler and the banks, 93
  Chrysler and the state, 93–94
  Mexico, 172–74
Redlining, 21
  in Cleveland, 131–32
Referendum, Cleveland, 134–35
Regulations, federal, 61–65, 96
Reinemer, Vic, 132–33
Reliance Insurance Company, 103–4, 105, 110, 117–18
Relocation, corporate, 2
Remedies
  last resort, 21, 186–87
Renchard, William S., 105–7, 109, 111, 113
Research and development, 2
Resources, finance capital, 3, 5
Reynolds, Clark, 147, 150, 151
Rhodes, James A., 137
Riccardo, John J., 61, 63, 67, 90
Ridley, Scott, 141
Rifkin, Jeremy, 5, 8–11, 82, 194
Rochester, Anna, 5, 6
Rockefeller, Nelson, 115
Rodman, Charles G., 32, 37–39, 45, 53–55
Roe, Alan, 145n, 148
Rogers-Millar, L. Edna, 69n
Rohrbaugh, Rodney E., 79
Rose, Arnold, 13, 58, 188n
Ross, Joel, 19
Rubinson, Richard, 188
Rudolph, Richard, 141
Ryan, Judge Edward J., 55

St. Germain, Fernand J., 167
St. Louis, 192
Salancik, Gerald, 12
Sallach, David, 22
Sanchez Arnau, J. C., 145 n, 148
Savings and loan, 4, 22
Schmitt, 175, 176
Schumer, Charles, 168
Scott, John, 5, 188
Schroeder, John P., 36–37, 39, 41, 43,
    46–50, 59
Schwartz, Michael, 5, 11 n, 12, 22, 86,
    97, 100, 184, 187
Seaman, Barrett, 63, 65, 70, 89–90, 92
Seiber, Marilyn, 145, 146
Serrano, Jorge Diaz, 153
Shareholders, 116
Shearson Hammill, 112
Sherman, H., 17
Shumway, Norman D., 73
Silva, Jesus Herzog, 155–56, 159–60
Simmons, Richard, 114–15
Skocpol, Theda, 14
Smith, Adam, 19
Smith Barney, 23
Smyth vs. Ames, 132
Sonquist, John, 11 n, 12
Soref, Michael, 19
Sparkman, John J., 115
Squire, Sanders and Dempsey, 122, 131
Staley, Edward, 33–34
Stallings, Barbara, 145, 146, 147, 148
Stanton, Thomas B., 106
Stearns, Linda Brewster, 8, 12
Steinberg, Saul, 102–4, 106–7, 109, 111,
    114, 116–18, 143, 188
Stewart, Donald W., 81
Stiles, Ned B., 5
Stock(s), 5, 107, 181–82, 185
    banks', 10–11
    CEI, 129–31, 183
    Chrysler, 76–77, 79, 85, 89, 93, 99,
        100
    dumping, 182, 185, 186
    employee ownership, 81–82, 86
    and lending, 6
    ownership, 5
    and power, 2
    voting, 10
    W. T. Grant, 32–34, 38, 43
Stockholding, institutional, 2, 5, 8–11,
    187
Stokes, Carl, 125
Stokman, F. N., 12 n, 184, 187
Strategic withholding, 147
Structural distortion, 146

Structuralists, 14–16
Sundman, John, 40, 45, 49–50, 56
Swanstrom, Todd, 120, 139, 142–43
Sweezy, Paul, 7, 17
Symons, Howard J., 68

Tabb, William K., 142
Takeover(s), 2, 23, 103, 105–12, 114–16
    and external capital, 7
Taxes, 5
Taylor, Lance, 153, 159, 172–73
Tello, Carlos, 159
Theorists, critical, 15–16
Thomas, W. I., 20
Toledo Edison, 131
Toms River Bank, 40–41, 46
Townsend, Lynn A., 66–67, 90
Toys R Us, 100
Truman, David, 13
Trust(s), 181, 183, 185. *See also* Funds
    funds, 2, 5, 22, 116–18
    funds, concentration, 8–9

Unemployment
    after Chrysler bailout, 90–92, 96–97
    Mexico, 157, 173, 175
Unification
    and competition, 2
    structural, 3
United Auto Workers, 69, 76, 80–88,
    94–97, 100, 142, 184, 194
Unity, structural, 181
Up-front fees, 168, 172, 175, 187
    Mexico, 163
Useem, Michael, 12, 14, 16

Velasquez, Fidel, 159
Vento, Bruce F., 72
Ventures
    joint, 181
    new, 7
Villarejo, Don, 9
Voinovich, George V., 136–37, 140,
    143 n, 193
Volcker, Paul, 158–59, 161, 163–64,
    166–68

Wall Street, 11, 102–3, 115–16, 118
Ward, Kathryn B., 145 n
Wasserman, Harvey, 133
Weber, Max, 13
Weiner, Benjamin, 172, 173
Weinstein, James, 14, 188 n, 189
Weir, Brock, 124, 126, 129, 133
Whelan, Edward P., 125
White Consolidated Industries, 122

White Weld, 113–14
Whitt, J. Allen, 14, 16, 139
Williams, G. A., 22
Winkler, J. T., 98, 117
Wood, Robert, 145 n, 146–47, 154, 160, 186
World Bank, 145

Yago, Glenn, 86, 97, 100

Zeller's LTD, 31, 37, 39, 50, 52
Zucker, Lynn, 185

Compositor: G & S Typesetters
Text: 11/13 Sabon
Display: Sabon